i

Warriors who Win

Gene N. Landrum, PhD

"You can't strengthen the weak
By weakening the strong"

Abraham Lincoln

ISBN-13:
978-1456599546

ISBN-10:
1456599542

Cover Design by:
Chelsi Roberts

Editing and Interior Layout by:
Jody Ortiz
jo@jodyortiz.com

Book Distributed by:
Genie-Vision
% of Gene N. Landrum, PhD
7897 Cocobay Drive
Naples, FL 34108

Table of Contents – Wizard Warriors

Tables on Warrior Wizards that Win

Dedication

For my warrior daughter Sherry
&
Rockne Skybyrg who gave me the inspiration
and feedback to create this work on the
inner magic that makes iconic warriors tick

"And whoever wants to be a creator in
good and evil, must first be an
annihilator and break values. Thus the
highest evil belongs to the greatest
goodness: but this is being creative." -
Frederick Nietzsche, Thus Spake
Zarathustra

The Wizardly Ways of Warrior Wunderkinds

"Conquering the world is easy, governing it is hard" – Genghis Kahn

Warrior Wunderkinds are enlightened zealots on a mission to reach the Pinnacle of Power. They show up armed with an aura that inspires disciples and frightens adversaries since they are fearless visionaries.

"Invincibility is in oneself, vulnerability is in the opponent" – Sun Tzu

Wizardly Warriors Live in a Shangri La of the Mind

Warrior Wizards dare what mere mortals only dream and it enables them to go where mere mortals fear. This daunting attitude is why those that alter the world are special and why Alexander the Great, Catherine the Great, Napoleon, and Geronimo, were able to alter history in many ways. It led American aviators in World War II to call out the name "Geronimo!" when they first jumped behind enemy lines. Great warriors leave a lasting legacy for wannabe followers. Sun Tsu, in his The Art of War, kindled fires in the likes of Mao Zedong, Ulysses Grant, Gandhi, and Norman Schwarzkopf. Ironically, half of the warriors featured in this work were left-handed. Their deeds and exploits often came from the aphorisms of those before them such as Ram Dass in Here & Now who said, "As soon as you give up power you can have it all; as long as you want power, you can't have it. The minute you don't want power you'll have more than you ever dreamed possible." Such words of wisdom leave a resonance of power in the minds and souls of later warriors:

"Soft countries breed soft men. It is not the property of any one soil to produce fine fruits and good soldiers too." **– Cyrus the Great**

"There is nothing impossible to him who will try." **– Alexander the Great**

"Where I have passed, the grass will not grow again" – Attila the Hun

"Power is my mistress" **- Napoleon**

"I will return" – General Douglas MacArthur

"Power grows out of the barrel of a gun" – Mao Zedung

"Dear Ike, today I spat in the Seine" – General George Patton

"Burn the boats men, there is no turning back." **– *Conquistador Cortes***

"Transcendence from mediocrity to eminence occurs at a point just beyond the apparent limit of one's ability" Hawkins *Power v Force*

Preface

"The more corrupt the state, the more numerous the laws." - Tacitus

"Decreased latent inhibition is associated with increased creative achievement in high-functioning individuals."
- J. Pers, Social Psychologist Sept, 2003

Why a book on Warrior Wizards who win? The above aphorisms tell it all. The bottom line is, when in charge, take charge. Mitigating strategy or tactics was not the way of an Alexander the Great, Napoleon, or General George Patton. They went for the jugular and analyzed their move later. Warriors are not just those in the military or doing battle. Many warriors can be found in the world of sports, business and the art world. Mohammed Ali was a warrior as was Babe Didrikson Zaharias – two athletes you had better not mess with. Sam Walton was a warrior as was Ted Turner. In the professional world Picasso and Ayn Rand were warriors that most people feared with a passion. But in this work it was Alexander the Great, Joan of Arc and Napoleon who exemplify the ardor from within that attracts disciples and casts fear in one's adversaries. The legacies of these warriors are discussed at the very end of this work, but many were unusual such as Alexander mimicking the behavior of his mythical hero, Achilles. For Joan of Arc, it was turning into an androgynous woman, dressing and riding her mount like a man. With Hernándo Cortés, it was sending a psychological message to his men by burning his eleven boats and letting them know there was no going back. In the case of Chairman Mao Zedung, it was staying power by being tenacious. Patton offered sage advice on his role as a warrior saying, *"Lead me, follow me, or get out of my way."* Moshe Dayan validates his role, *"If you want to make peace, you don't talk to your friends. You talk to your enemies."* Touché!

Selecting which warriors to use for this study was not an easy task. All of the ones chosen were those that had in some way altered the world. Each had opted for a different path to the top and was willing to follow some inner catharsis. And, every one of them did things that the herd never does, and they did them with panache, style, and a fearless verve. They took power that was not theirs and never looked back. Their calculated actions and lack of remorse is why they became the most revered and feared warriors of their times.

When the young Aztec Indian, Goyathlay, lost his mother, wife, and three children to Mexican banditos, it would leave an indelible imprint on his psyche that would never leave. From that moment, he had become inflamed with the need for revenge. He would become the most fearless warrior in the Far West. The Mexicans would rue the day they had messed with this man and when they heard that he was on his way, they would scream, *Cuidado! Watch out! Geronimo!"* The name stuck, and, half a century later when the first World War II paratroopers were being asked to jump behind enemy lines, they would scream *"Geronimo!"* to show they were like this warrior from the frontier. Aubrey Eberhardt was the first to use the Indian's name when he headed the first United States' parachute platoon in 1940. On the night before their very first jump, they went to see the movie, *Geronimo.* Eberhardt was eager to prove his toughness and he wanted to show everyone he wasn't afraid to jump. So, upon jumping that first time, he screamed, **"Geronimo!"** as promised and the shout quickly caught on with his fellow paratroopers.

Some time later in WWII, General George Patton would prove his mettle to the point that his troops would call him **"Old Blood & Guts."** Such labels have evolved from those earlier chants, such as the Roman warriors who called Attila the *"Scourge of God."* It would be a few centuries later that a little man with a passion for becoming a messianic leader would be born Napoleon Bonaparte. Napoleon conquered most of Europe and would be called *"an enlightened despot"* by his friends and enemies. The Little Corsican knew what was behind his power. He wrote of it in his memoirs, saying, *"I reign only through the fear I inspire."* Such intransigent power and energy was a product of his bi-polar illness that led him to *think faster, ride faster, work faster, and win faster* than virtually any warrior before him. In his memoirs, he would write, *"I will lose a man but never a moment."* Napoleon once killed five horses in five days in a mad dash across Europe. His valet, Constant, would tell the media, *"He is perpetual motion. I never comprehended how his body could endure such fatigue; he never even stopped to change clothes."* (Landrum 1996. P. 129) One Napoleon biographer wrote, *"The very mania that gave him such advantages in battle doomed him to waste the victories and destroy his empire."* His mortal enemy was the British warrior, the Duke of Westminster. Testimony to Napoleon's charismatic power came from this man who wrote, *"The Corsican's presence on the field of battle was equivalent to 40,000 men."* These are the kinds of qualities and personality traits that will be pursued to find the underlying causes – psycho-biographical insights if you will – for those wannabe warriors looking to reach the very pinnacle of power in any world, in any era.

In each case, there were many life events and cultural nuances that made a difference. Most experienced an epiphany that transformed the individuals from potential to life's possibilities. Some of the factors and epiphanies from within that contributed to each warrior becoming a wunderkind are summarized in the following table:

Table 1

Epiphany = Metamorphosis = Power

Genghis Kahn – Father killed by rival tribe; he was taken prisoner where he learned early the means of survival. Temujin escaped to become the most powerful man in the world in 1206.

Cyrus the Great – At age ten, kidnapped and escaped but would grow into the man who consolidated the Ottoman Empire.

Alexander the Great – At twenty travelled to see the Oracle at Delphi who told him, "You are invincible my son," and he took the prediction to heart and within eight years had conquered the known world.

Attila the Hun – He killed his brother to take power and for 19 years ruled Europe with an iron hand between the Ural River to Germany and from the Danube to the Baltic Sea and would be called the Scourge of God by the Romans.

Joan of Arc – A mystical vision at twelve led her to believe she was God's messenger for running the Brits out of France. Dauphin Charles gave her an army at seventeen, and she donned a male uniform and won the Battle of Orleans.

Catherine the Great – At thirty-three knew it was poison or power – she chose power and donned a Captain's uniform and led troops to fight an imbecile husband Peter, won and crowned herself Empress of Russia.

Hernán Cortés – In 1521, Cortez landed in Mexico, establishing Veracruz and burned his ships to send a message to his men, Win or die in Mexico!

Napoleon Bonaparte – At twenty-four, in the Battle of Lodi, was outmanned by 2:1 but used guile and guts to win and walked back to his tent and wrote, "I am a superior being." In four years, he was crowned Emperor of France.

Geronimo (Goyathlay) – In 1858, Mexican soldiers attacked Geronimo's camp and murdered his mom, wife, and three children. They would rue the day, screaming, "Geronimo!" for help from God.

Mao Zedong – At 42 led the Long March and took power from nemesis Chiang Kai-shek who fled to Taiwan. At fifty became Chairman of Communist Party.

Mahatma Gandhi – At twenty-four was thrown from a train in Marizburg, SA. He emerged as a "David" fighting political "Goliaths" using **Satyagraha** = Non-Violent opposition as "my moral principle."

George Patton – Finished fifth in a1912 Pentathlon and collapsed at finish line unconscious. A competitive zeal molded a warrior icon on a mission to power.

Moshe Dayan – Israeli Hero - At fourteen joined the newly formed Jewish militia, Haganah, and was soon born a warrior. He lost an eye at 26 and it would become his mark of a warrior on a mission for Jewish autonomy.

Norman Schwarzkopf –Attended schools in Iran, Switzerland, Germany, and Italy – fluent in French and German, and groomed to be a warrior at West Point.

For this study into the psyche of the great warriors, many subjects were considered. However, the limits of space and analysis left many qualified warriors out of this tome. Warriors such as Roman—Julius Caesar, Charlemagne, Ivan the Terrible, Peter the Great, Frederick the Great, Simon Bolivar, Joseph Stalin, Adolph Hitler, Douglas MacArthur, Colin Powell, and Generals Grant and Lee from the American Civil War were not used. Both Ulysses S. Grant and Winston Churchill were included until the final draft. But, their quotes will be used to make important points. Those finally chosen were fairly normal individuals who started with very little and ended with a lot. Much of their power came from an indomitable will that dominated their lives and successes.

During the American Civil War, President Abraham Lincoln spoke of the power of Ulysses S. Grant, saying, "*He's the quietest little fellow you ever saw. He makes the least fuss of any man you ever knew.*" William Sherman would write, "*It will be 1,000 years before Grant's character is fully appreciated. Grant is the greatest soldier of our time if not all time. He fixes in his mind what is the true objective and abandons all minor ones. He dismisses all possibility of defeat. He believes in himself and in victory. If his plans go wrong, he is never disconcerted, but promptly devises a new one and is sure to win in the end.*" A short time later, the Indian warrior, Geronimo, would offer this insight from within: "*I was born on the prairies where the wind blew free and there was nothing to break the light of the sun. I was born where there were no enclosures.*" In World War II, Mao Zedong offered his means of having taken power in Communist China saying in his Little Red Book, "*For me there is only 200 days in a year,*" meaning that he slept sparingly and stopped bathing in order to do more in less and less time. That is the classic model of a bipolar, power-hungry zealot on a mission. He led the Long March in China to save the nation via retreat. This 6,000 mile trek to keep from being captured by superior capitalistic forces was led by a 42-year old man with no formal education. His reign would end with his creation of the *Cultural Revolution* in July 1966. Few realized that Mao actually killed more people than Hitler and Stalin put together. Also, like Hugh Hefner, Mao spent most of his time in bed with 2,000 concubines to salve his sex drive. Once he was in power, he would go whole days without dressing or leaving his bed.

Warriors Who Win

The men under George Patton excelled due to his own blatant bravery and willingness to walk with them prepared to die for his mission. Winston Churchill had the same fortitude as Patton. He was one of Britain's leaders in a time of peril. He would tell his constituency, *"A pessimist sees the difficulty in every opportunity; an optimist sees the opportunity in every difficulty."* Such insight is the underpinning of power. Winston would offer this advice during the dark days of World War II when German bombs were falling around him in London, *"If the British Empire and its Commonwealth last for a thousand years, men will still say, this was their finest hour."* And on the continent, leading allied forces was General Patton who never carried a white flag, but screamed at his men, *"We're gonna keep fighting. Is that CLEAR? We're gonna attack all night, we're gonna attack tomorrow morning. If we are not VICTORIOUS, let no man come back alive! There's only one proper way for a professional soldier to die: the last bullet of the last battle of the last war."* He was fighting against a man who was bipolar and had taken over a nation of which he was not a citizen – Adolph Hitler. The fuehrer was a man to be reckoned with since he was only interested in winning or dying for his cause of building a 1,000-year Reich. One of his biographers would write, *"When Hitler spoke men groaned and hissed, women sobbed caught up in the spell of powerful emotions – four women killed themselves over this power maven."*

Charismatic power was a universal force in each of these warrior zealots who were willing to die for their cause. Their mesmerizing words only added to their personal valor. It is interesting to note that when Hitler was on stage mesmerizing crowds with his rhetoric, he would become so excited that he would come to orgasm at the very peak of his talk. Embarrassed, the Fuehrer asked his physician for medications to stop this from happening. The physicians explained that passion and zeal were inextricably tied to his ability to communicate, and the drugs to inhibit arousal would stifle his charisma. Biographer, George Stein said, *"Hitler had the magnetism of a hypnotist."* Most people are unaware that the wives of German industrialists were the ones who financed the Nazi party. Women were mesmerized by him—this man who had never had a legitimate job and was a user of whomever he touched. They could not resist the power of his charm. They gave him millions of deutschmarks to fund his blaze to the very top of a nation of which he was not even a citizen. When Russian and American troops were approaching his bunker, he would kill himself and his mistress, Eva Braun. One very bright disciple,

Winifred Wagner, daughter of no other than composer Richard Wagner killed herself and her six children in memory of her hero. The age at which these warrior wunderkinds made it to the pinnacle of power is interesting, as shown in the following table, as they were in their twenties to forties when fate offered the opportunity to lead and conquer:

Table 2

Age at which Warriors Ascended to Power

<u>Cyrus the Great</u> – In his twenties, he rose to lead the Macedonians to world-wide power.

<u>Genghis Kahn</u> – At forty-four, he took over from his father as leader of Mongolian dynasty. By 1219, he ruled from China to Afghan border and Siberia to the border of Tibet.

<u>Alexander the Great</u> – Defeated the Persian Empire in his early twenties and never lost a battle.

<u>Attila the Hun</u> – Took power of Huns at twenty-eight; murdered his brother, Bleda, at thirty-eight for total power.

<u>Joan of Arc</u> – Eighteen when she fulfilled her mission from God, but dead by nineteen.

<u>Catherine the Great</u> - Thirty-three when she took power from Peter and became Russian Empress.

<u>Hernando Cortez</u> – Captured Montezuma in 1521 at age thirty-six ending the Aztec reign.

<u>Napoleon Bonaparte</u> – An upstart smart-ass who became General at twenty-four at Lodi - Emperor by thirty.

<u>Geronimo</u> (Goyathlay) – At age twenty-nine, he became a raging beast against Mexican bandits.

<u>Mao Zedong</u> – Co-founder of Communist party in China at age twenty-eight and the Chairman at fifty.

<u>Mahatma Gandhi</u> – In 1915, he returned to India as Mahatma; was forty-six when christened Mahatma.

<u>General George Patton</u> – In his thirties, he made Captain; General at fifty during WW-II.

<u>Moshe Dayan</u> – At age fifty-two, Moshe became Minister of Defense for Israel in 1967.

<u>General Norman Schwarzkopf</u> – Promoted to Major General (1983) at age forty-nine.

A prescient example of the power of the will to motivate a warrior to live and refuse to die in the face of awesome odds was told no better than in what happened to an American football hero, Mario Tonelli. Young Mario was not expected to live due to a genetic bone disease, but he did, and rose to fame at Notre Dame as a football All-American in 1937. His father nursed him back to health despite the prognosis of top medical men in Chicago who said he would never walk again. Did he walk? Yes! In fact, he would run so fast he was virtually unstoppable as a running back at the University of Notre Dame. His team earned a trip to the Rose Bowl in Pasadena, California in 1937 where he was a one-man torpedo destroying the formidable opponent the University of Southern California. Providence was there that day as a Japanese exchange student at USC was at the game and watching this superstar regale the fans.

A few years later, World War II began and Mario enlisted. He ended up in the famous *Bataan Death March* after General Douglas MacArthur left the Philippines for Australia. Mario was one of the men in that infamous Death March in which 10,000 American GI's perished due to unbelievable conditions. One day when Mario, who had dropped from 200 to 125 pounds was suffering from Malaria, a Japanese soldier that expected him to die, walked up to him and took his Notre Dame ring. The soldier was bragging about his prize in his quarters when the commanding officer, the same man who had been a USC student watching that Rose Bowl back in 1937 saw the ring and recognized it. He took it away from the soldier and found Mario and put it back on Mario's finger. It not only made him cry with emotion, but many years later he would tell the media, *"It gave me hope to finish the march. I saw it as a symbol that God wanted me to keep on going."*

Upon MacArthur's return to the Philippines, Tonelli and the other surviving prisoners of war were shipped back to Japan to the Nagoya prison. By this time, the one-time All-American had shriveled away to only 100 pounds; his will to live had gone since life as a POW was tough. When the guards at Nagoya prison issued Mario his prison garb, he looked down and there was a number, and lo and behold it was 58—the same number he had worn in that USC game for Notre Dame in the Rose Bowl. In 2005, Mario was still alive, and he told the media, *"A surge of energy surged through me that day and I knew I was going to make it."* He had had two memorable events come into his life with such a

Warriors Who Win

powerful message that he should not die like a man who had been defeated.

Chapter One

Warriors Who Win Leave a Long Legacy

Sun Tsu – Cyrus the Great – Attila the Hun - Genghis Kahn

"If you do not know others and do not know yourself, you will be imperiled in every single battle." – Sun Tzu

"Soft countries breed soft men. It is not the property of any one soil to produce fine fruits and good soldiers too." – Cyrus the Great

"Continual learning is the key to success for a Hun." – Attila the Hun

"The greatest joy for a man is to defeat his enemies, drive them before him and take from them all they possess, to see those they love in tears, to ride their horses and to hold their wives and daughters in his arms." – Genghis Kahn

Warrior success is far more mental than physical—mind not guns. Even millenniums ago, this was true. As Alexander was reading from Achilles prior to going into battle, he saw himself in a surreal sense. Excess and Empowerment defined everyone from Attila the Hun to Geronimo to George Patton. All were maniacs on a mission with Genghis known as "Son of the Sky," Attila the "Scourge of God," and Cyrus "The Great" saying, *"Conquering the world is easy, governing it is hard."* Many were willing to kill and maim, yet they would then treat their adversaries as friends by taking care of them. Warriors are maniacs on a mission to realize some inner dream of conquest and eminence – all zealots who left a lot of devastation in their wake. Eminent warriors were on a mission to some mythical Shangri La of their imagination. They were willing to bet all for attaining that mystical place in their hearts.

The warriors in this chapter set the tone for those that followed them. These men were warriors who saw themselves as already dead. Consequently, they were without fear. They chased their dreams without wincing in the winds of adversity. Once these individuals sense the end, the top is easier to obtain since they are driven beyond the pale of the ordinary. An example is when Genghis Kahn's father was murdered and he was taken prisoner at age nine. The same happened to Alexander, but he was twenty and he took power. Cyrus was kidnapped at age ten, but he escaped and would rise to power with that early problem lingering in his mind. For Attila, his mind-modeling took place from being reared in a Hun world where "kill or be killed" was the mantra for maintaining. When Hernando Cortes landed on Mexico's coast, he had his ships burned, and he told his men, "There is no retreat. We win or we die." When Catherine the Great was told her husband, Peter, the newly crowned emperor of Russia was on his way to imprison her or put her in a nunnery, she jumped on a white stallion in a captain's uniform and took charge. Napoleon, Mao Zedung, and Gandhi all considered suicide in their teens, but rose out of that gutter of the mind to reach the pinnacle of power. Interesting personality factors are that half were left-handed and one-third bipolar. Ultimately, Mao would kill more people than both Adolph Hitler and Joseph Stalin combined. Let's now look at the early role models that influenced the warrior wizards who won big.

Sun Tsu – The Art of War – Chinese General in 512BC

"Invincibility is in oneself, vulnerability is in the opponent."

Few documents ever put the process of the warrior into elegant words of wisdom more than Sun Tsu, the Chinese maven who in the sixth century B.C. wrote a testimony to the art of the warrior. One of his aphorisms was, *"Regard your soldiers as your children, and they will follow you into the deepest valleys. Look on them as your beloved sons and they will stand by you even unto death!"*

One of the most profound psychological insights into the motivations of man came from this sage 2,600 years ago:

"So it is said that if you know others and know yourself, you will not be imperiled in a hundred battles; if you do not know others but know yourself, you win one and lose one; if you do not know others and do not know yourself, you will be imperiled in every single battle."

Only in the past fifty years has the west come to grips with what this warrior wizard said some 2500 years ago. His words are akin to what was written on that wall at the Oracle read by Alexander the Great - *Know Thyself*. To excel, it is important to look within. Most people have not learned this valuable lesson and should go look in the mirror when they find their lives are in a state of chaos. It is crucial to spot the weaknesses within before attacking another's weakness. In other words, when shit happens, find the source and deal with it. This was the philosophic rhetoric from Tsu so many millenniums ago. Tsu had a great grasp on the art of winning warriors. Strategy and tactics to meet goals was his forte. He knew that it was man himself that was in charge and must take charge. The art of inner delusion ranked high with Tsu who told us, *"Even though you are competent, appear to be incompetent. Though effective, appear to be ineffective."*

Early Years and Warrior Games

The legend of Sun Tzu began in a place that is today's Shandong—a part of China just north of Shanghai. It was the homeland of this philosophical warrior, as well as Confucius and the really tasty Shandong Chicken. His name, Sun Tsu, is an honorific name for his birth name Sun Wu – meaning Martial, Military, or sometimes related to Martial Arts. For a time in which few were educated, Sun was highly educated. Like Machiavelli, he wrote a military treatise in order to get noticed and then gain employment with royalty. However, unlike Machiavelli, it worked! Sun would be given military positions. Sun Wu would then expand his thirteen chapter—*Art of War*—into eighty-two chapters. He would then train the army under his aphorisms of what it takes to be a winning warrior. Eventually, he broke the peace by invading the southern state of Yue. In many of his battles, the strategic insights would work, despite his men being outnumbered. This would prove to work for Napoleon who found fame in the battle of Lodi where he was outnumbered by 2:1. Napoleon had been a fan of Sun's, and had read the *Art of War* while young. In Sun's most memorable win, his troops were outnumbered 30,000 to 200,000. Yet, he was victorious.

One legend of Sun Tzu's life was that the King of Wu tested his skills by having this young maestro participate in a warrior game. The king commanded him to transform a harem of 180 concubines into soldiers. Sun divided the ladies into two companies, appointing two of the king's favorite concubines as company commanders. Then, Sun ordered the concubines to face right. They giggled. Sun Tzu blamed himself for not knowing the girls misunderstood the order, and he reiterated the command. But, once again the concubines giggled. Sun Tzu then ordered the execution of the king's two favored concubines, despite protests from the king. He told his head man that if a soldier misunderstood commands and did not obey, it was the fault of the officers in command. Conversely, when they understood and still refused, then they were at fault and must be punished. Sun preached to those under his command that they must carry out their mission, even if their boss, in this case, the king, would protest the act. After both concubines were killed, new officers were chosen to replace them. The message was clear: follow orders or die. Ultimately, both companies performed their maneuvers flawlessly. They had learned that when in charge, take charge.

Later, Alexander the Great, Frederick the Great, Genghis Kahn, and Napoleon would be motivated by the words of Sun Tsu. During the Persian Gulf War in the 1990's, both General Norman Schwarzkopf, Jr. and General Colin Powell practiced Sun Tzu's principles of strategic deception, speed, and attacks on the enemy's weakness. Mark McNeilly writes in *Sun Tzu and the Art of Modern Warfare* that a modern interpretation of Sun and his importance throughout Chinese history is critical in understanding China's push to becoming a superpower. Modern Chinese scholars explicitly rely on the strategic lessons found in *The Art of War*. His work is used in developing theories and tactics needed in the modern struggles they are facing. There are many values to be learned from his sage words of advice for warriors trying to alter local thinking and make it to the very top with more global thinking. Sun Tzu's teachings are used regularly in developing the strategies around the world. Some of the aphorisms he gave us are:

All warfare is based on deception. There is no place where espionage is not used, so offer the enemy bait to lure him into your lair.

- Appraise war in terms of the fundamental factors. The first of these factors is moral influence.
- Nothing is more difficult than the art of maneuvering for advantageous positions.
- Keep your friends close, and your enemies closer.
- Be extremely subtle, even to the point of formlessness. Be extremely mysterious, even to the point of soundlessness. Thereby you can be the director of the opponent's fate.
- The best victory is when the opponent surrenders of its own accord before there are any actual hostilities...It is best to win without fighting.

- A military operation involves deception. Even though you are competent, appear to be incompetent. Though effective, appear to be ineffective.
- Victorious warriors win first and then go to war, while defeated warriors go to war first and then seek to win.

Sun Tsu's sage words on warfare and the actions of warriors are profound in their philosophical nature and simplicity of context. Here are some his concepts that have been used by later warriors who win:

"Those skilled at the unorthodox are infinite as heaven and earth ... There are only two kinds of charge in battle; the unorthodox surprise attack, and the orthodox direct attack."

"When opponents are at ease, it is possible to tire them. When they are well fed, it is possible to starve them. When they are at rest, it is possible to move them."

"The consummation of forming an army is to arrive at formlessness. When you have no form, undercover espionage cannot find out anything, intelligence cannot form a strategy."

"Military formation is like water – the form of water is to avoid the high and go to the low... So a military formation has no constant formation, water has no constant shape; the ability to gain victory by changing and adapting according to the opponent is called genius."

"Act after having made assessments. The one who first knows the measures of far and near wins – that is the rule of armed struggle."

"Once people are unified, the brave cannot proceed alone, the timid cannot retreat alone – this is the rule for employing a group."

Regard your soldiers as your children, and they will follow you into the deepest valleys. Look on them as your own beloved sons, and they will stand by you even unto death!"

Legacy of a Warrior Word Wizard

Sun's words left their mark on many warriors from vastly different cultures. No doubt his words had much to do with Chinese Taoism, but it didn't stop there, as Japanese military leaders admitted to being highly influenced by the *Art of War*. During the Viet Nam War, General Vo Nguyen Giap, would credit Tsu with his mastermind victories over both American and French armies. The *Art of War* would become honored by the famous samurai warriors, and was crucial for three warrior wizards in this work. French warrior maven, Napoleon, was a voracious reader on military might. Historians speak extensively on how Napoleon turned to the strategies and tactics of successful attacks on weaknesses. Later, Mao Zedong credited Tsu with his victory of Chiang Kai-shek in the Long March in 1949. The book would also influence Mao's own writings in his *Little Red Book* on the strategy to implement in guerilla warfare. In America, *The Art of War* is used in training at General Staff College, and it is found in every library on military bases. During the Persian Gulf War, General Norman Schwarzkopf practiced its principles such as Deception, Speed, and the art of attacking an adversary's weakness as key elements to victory over Iraq. Today, modern Chinese scholars rely heavily on the strategic lessons to be learned in achieving worldwide eminence.

Chapter One – Warriors Who Win Leave a Long Legacy

Cyrus the Great – Ottoman Empire Maven 550-530BC

"Soft countries breed soft men."

The rise of Persia under Cyrus's rule would become the seat of an expansive Ottoman Empire that historians attribute to Cyrus more than any other warrior. The Persian Empire was the largest empire, geographically and it was Cyrus that put it all together – a span of three continents: Asia, Africa, and Europe. At its height, the empire included the modern nations of Iran, Afghanistan, Pakistan, Central Asia and Asia Minor, Thrace and Macedonia, much of the Black Sea coastal regions, Iraq, northern Saudi Arabia, Jordan, Israel, Lebanon, Syria, and all significant population centers of ancient Egypt as far west as Libya. Is that a power of the sword for a leader in the sixth century BC?

The Ottoman Empire would institute a centralized system of control, not unlike modern day's bureaucratic administrations. When Cyrus conquered a nation, he would permit them to continue their cultural heritage. Cyrus had a large professional army and civil service, inspiring similar developments in later empires like those of Alexander. One of his prophetic quotes was, *"Give out rewards that are not in the rules, give out directives that are not in the code."* This iconoclast would invade much of what Cyrus had created. Testimony to the reason for Cyrus leaving a legacy of peace came from his magnanimous words on what a winning warrior should do when in power.

> **"I have given leave to as many of the Jews that dwell in my country as please to return to their own country, and to rebuild their city, and to build the temple of God at Jerusalem on the same place where it was before. I have also sent my treasurer Mithridates and Zorobabel, the governor of the Jews, that they may lay the foundations of the temple, and may build it sixty cubits high, and of the same latitude, making three edifices of polished stones, and one of the wood of the country, and the same order extends to the altar whereon they offer sacrifices to God."**

Cyrus was a man before his time. One reason for his eminence as a warrior comes from one of his aphorisms, *"All men have their frailties; and whoever looks for a friend without imperfections, will never find what he seeks."* His dynamic empire would have a profound impact on the course of world history due to his savvy military magic. One of his innovative ideas was creating an organized army labeled "The Immortals" consisting of 10,000 soldiers trained in the art of winning at any cost. They were fierce! They would be comparable to America's Special Forces such as the Green Beret's in Nam or the Navy Seals.

Cyrus would also form a very innovative postal system throughout the empire with strategically located relay stations. A woman writing on Cyrus won a Nobel Prize for Peace in 2003. In her acceptance speech, Shirin Ebadi, said of Cyrus: *"This emperor proclaimed at the pinnacle of power 2,500 years ago that he would not reign over the people if they did not wish it."* One of Cyrus' contributions was his open-mindedness on dogmas, especially religious tolerance. Like Alexander who followed him, he would conquer a territory and permit those defeated to maintain their cultural lifestyles and to practice their faith as they wished. He was innovative in guaranteeing freedom for all in his reign. The life and ideas of Cyrus should be studied in the history of human rights. As a result of Cyrus' policies and progressive religious tolerance, the Jews honored him as a dignified and righteous king. He is the only Gentile to be designated as "Messiah," a divinely appointed leader.

Cyrus would reign for thirty years, during which time he built the Ottoman Empire by fighting and conquering first the Median Empire, then the Lydian Empire and the Neo-Babylonian Empire. He would integrate these diverse cultures into one congenial whole. In many ways, this was similar to the Hegelian Dialectic where a thesis (friend) and its antithesis (foe) results in a superior synthesis of togetherness.

Cyrus led an expedition into central Asia prior to Alexander a couple centuries later. This resulted in major campaigns that subjugated every nation in which he entered without exception. Cyrus did not reach Egypt, as he would die in a battle with the Massagetae tribes in Central Asia. He perished along the Syr Darya in December 530 BC at the age of fifty.

Early Years & Warrior Games

Cyrus succeeded his father, Cambyses I, as King of the Persians. He was born around 580 BC in a family of warriors, but was kidnapped and sent off to a farm where he was discovered by those that saw he was too noble to be a herdsman. The title "Cyrus the Great" would not come until after his many great victories and magnetic leadership. Herodotus claims that when Cyrus was ten years old, it was obvious that the young boy was not a farm boy and that he could have big potential as an adult. Astyages was the head of the clan at the time and was enamored that the boy resembled him. He allowed the boy to return to his biological parents. When Cyrus was in his twenties, he took power in his Persian city, and then recruited others to follow him on his conquest of the known world. In 539 BC, Babylon surrendered to Cyrus without going to battle. The Babylonian Empire included Syria and Palestine. Cyrus was seen as a very humane ruler. In 537, after Cyrus conquered Babylonia, he allowed the Jews to return to Palestine. It would be a legacy of a warrior with compassion for his fellow men, even if they were once an adversary. It was due to this that the Jews came to regard him as *The anointed of the Lord.*"

Cyrus issued a decree citing his policies and aims, which became known as the Charter of the Rights of Nations. This charter was the first declaration of Human Rights, and is now displayed at the British Museum. A replica of the charter is on display at the United Nations. In portions of the charter, Cyrus wrote:

> "When my soldiers in great numbers peacefully entered Babylon...I did not allow anyone to terrorize the people...I kept in view the needs of people and all its sanctuaries to promote their well-being. Freed all the slaves, I put an end to their misfortune and slavery."

By 540 BC, when Cyrus was about forty, he captured Elam, and its capital, Susa. Historians have said that prior to that battle, his adversary, Nabonidus, had ordered cult statues from outlying Babylonian cities to be brought into the capital to help in holding off the Persian onslaught. Iranian philosophy, literature, and religion would all play a strong role in world events from that period forward. Despite the Islamic conquest of Persia, the work and legacy of Cyrus would leave its mark on the Middle East during the Islamic Golden Age. His many conquests would be instrumental in the growth and expansion of Islam as it exists today.

When the Russian born Ayn Rand was quite young, she would be highly influenced by the power of Cyrus, having been inspired by his many conquests and then permitting them to remain autonomous. This influenced her writings, as did the Communists taking power while she was in college. They took her dad's business and forced everyone to alter their beliefs and lives. Her protagonist, John Galt, would be endowed with many of the characteristics of Cyrus the Great with Objectivism part of the puzzle of warrior leadership.

As for his personal life, Cyrus had a wife named Cassandane as well as four children: Cambyses II, Bardiya, Atossa, and a daughter. Cyrus was highly enamored of Cassandane. When she died, every nation in Cyrus's empire observed a great mourning, in particular, the capital of Babylonia. The public mourning lasted for six days – from 21–26 March 538 BC. Her tomb is at Cyrus's capital, Pasargadae. Later, Cyrus would meet and marry the daughter of the Median King, Astyages. In that era, amorous wanderings were not only acceptable, but considered very good in that it would be a way to spread the seed of such a powerful warrior as Cyrus. Consequently, he would be with many women. Historians have anointed this warrior as one of the most remarkable that ever led men into battle. He was the founder of the modern Persian Empire, and the most successful military leader in history. Many of those he had beaten would speak of him in glowing terms, and speak of his legacy as a warrior among warriors. Aside from being a ferocious combatant, he was merciful and wise. In the Bible, he was credited with the return of the Jews to Jerusalem from their captivity in Babylon. Religious freedom was his greatest legacy.

When questioned as to why he did not invade foreign lands, Cyrus replied, *"Soft countries breed soft men. It is not the property of any one soil to produce fine fruits and good soldiers too."* Historians have stated that few other men could have created such a vast empire and still be endowed with a nickname as he did as *"The Father"* from the people he had conquered. The reason for such adulation by the vanquished comes from his immortal words on not permitting his soldiers to plunder or rape. Further testimony to the heritage of Cyrus can be found in Australia where the Iranian faction has erected a bas-relief of Cyrus the Great located in Sydney's Bicentennial Park.

Attila the Hun – The Scourge of God

"The quality of unyielding drive to accomplish assignments is a desirable and essential quality of leadership. The weak persist only when things go their way. The strong persist and pursue through discouragement, deception and even personal abandonment."

Attila was a ruthless demigod who said, "Where I have passed, the grass will not grow again." That is from a man who knew what he was doing and would be known as one of the greatest barbarians of all time. This leader of the Huns ruled over the Mongoloid, people and had the temerity to attack the mighty Roman Empire. Attila justified his invasions by saying, "When you're right, you are right!" Sure! Attila was so furious in his attacks he was named *"THE SCOURGE OF GOD!"* Attila ruled the Huns from 434 until his death in 453. His mighty sword ruled the area form the Danube River in the West to the Baltic Sea in the East. Attila marched 1,000 miles between Romania and France and controlled the Danube River area north for most of his life. It was his lightning quick raids in which he annihilated all cities in his path that would be his legacy. The cities he took had withstood the charges of the mighty Roman Empire, but fell before this Hun. He Led the nomadic Huns and taught them to be faster than their adversaries. How? By removing the baggage as he had each man carried his own provisions on sturdy horses making them faster by using stronger horses. And he would lead 100,000 men into a battle and savagely destroy all in his path.

One innovation of this warrior was being viewed as a wrathful Hun and then asked for money to not attack. Peace for pay was his mission and it worked well. Before Attila, the power brokers took the cities and then had to manage them to maintain their power. After he assassinated his brother, Breda, for power, he would then head for the city of Naissus on the Danube – the birthplace of Roman Emperor Constantine – and with that would send a message loud and clear that the Huns were a force to be reckoned with. When a giant earthquake shook Constantinople, it crushed buildings along with fifty-seven towers of defense. Attila offered peace for money. Theodosius II paid Attila to take his Huns to the West. Despite the fact that Attila had no formal education, he celebrated learning and would say, *"Continual learning is the key to success for a Hun."* He was a true warrior with a mantra of, *"Kill or be killed,"* and it led him to enormous power throughout Europe.

Both Persians and the Roman Empire feared this warrior with vengeance in his soul. His armies marched through Gaul (modern France), and made it as far as Orleans (home of Joan of Arc), and into Italy. He absolutely dominated Germany. The Huns were descended from Eurasian nomads who had emerged from the Volga and migrated into Europe. The brothers ruled for ten years. They had accumulated much wealth, but that wasn't enough for Attila. The younger brother wanted total power. They had both become wealthy with their pay for peace strategy. The Romans had paid them 700 Roman pounds annually to stay north of the Danube River. The money permitted Attila to come up with new weapons like battering rams and rolling siege towers. With success, they returned to challenge the mighty Roman Empire again and ask for more homage. This time the ante for peace had grown to 6,000 Roman pounds, and they would pay yearly to keep from being attacked by the Huns. In 445, the Huns withdrew from Byzantium. It was then that the wily Attila had his older brother, Bleda, killed in a hunting accident.

Early Life and Success Imprints

Attila was born in the plains of Scythiea in 406 in a modern day part of Russia and Kazakhstan. The name—Attila—meant *"Little Father"* in Gothic. This strong-willed son was left-handed and driven from a heritage of war. The Huns belonged to a group of Mongolian and Turkish nomadic tribes from the East. Attila's tribe was one of most advanced in the production and deployment of an array of innovative weaponry. Like most Huns, Attila was trained in the art of riding, archery, and as a swordsman; he learned to play the game of war. He was also fond of art, magic, and poetry.

Attila was a Prince, and when his uncle passed in 434, he and his brother, Bleda, took power. The Huns were originally from a tribe of Mongolians from Central Asia. When Attila was born, they were in what today is Hungary. Attila's name has become a byword for cruelty and barbarism since he would sack at least one-hundred cities, murdering the monks and raping the women in the process. He was leading the way for future warriors like Genghis Khan and Tamerlane, but was setting a bad example since he was cruel, clever, and blood-thirsty. The character of Attila was quite complex. He spoke Gothic had been trained in Latin and Greek in order to negotiate in Rome and Constantinople. He and his brother, Bleda, took power when he was only twenty-eight in 434. The Huns were nomads by nature, and would start their scourge. Their main military techniques were mounted archery and javelin throwing. In their first major triumph in 434, they had Emperor Theodosius II offering Attila 660 pounds of gold to be paid annually in hopes of securing peace forever. It was not to be, as they wanted more gold and more power.

In 441, Attila's Huns would attack the Eastern Roman Empire. That empowered Attila. His empire then stretched from Central Europe to the Black Sea. Attila's army sacked numerous cities and razed Aquileia completely, leaving no trace of it when he left. Roman emperor, Valentinian, fled from Ravenna to Rome. It was Aetius who remained in the field, but lacked the strength to offer battle against Attila. They would meet with Pope Leo I, and then turned his army back. Fate had intervened as there were pandemic and famine back home. He was weakened by disease. He saw the Roman legions forming from the new Byzantine Emperor, Marcian. Some historians have proposed that the Pope was aided spiritually by Saint Peter and Saint Paul convincing him to turn away from the city. Whatever his reasons, Attila left Italy and returned to his palace across the Danube. From there, he planned to strike at Constantinople again and reclaim the tribute that Marcian had cut off. Attila invaded the Eastern Roman Empire, seizing the Balkans and threatening earthquake-ravaged Constantinople in 447. As barbarian, the

Huns would grow and become so great that more than a hundred cities were captured. Constantinople came into danger, and most citizens fled. There were so many murders and blood-lettings that the dead could not be numbered. Roman Emperor Valentinian III was trying to make an alliance with Attila. Valentinian's sister, Honoria, was offered as a peace payment to an older Roman, but she was not interested. She sent an appeal to Attila for help. Along with her message was an engagement ring. It sent the wrong message, as he assumed she wanted him. But, she was only trying to avoid marrying the Roman. Attila responded as only a warrior would with a required dowry of half the Roman Western Empire – most of Gaul. Valentinian's mother convinced her son to leave the country or to kill his sister Honoria. Attila was upset, and he returned in 452 to claim his marriage to Honoria, anew, invading and ravaging Italy along the way. The city of Venice was founded as a result of these attacks when the residents fled to small islands in the Venetian Lagoon. The central base of Attila's kingdom was north of the Danube in the region known during medieval times as Hungary. Attila ruled the Balkans with little or no opposition. Once, his Huns surrounded Constantinople, but failed to take the city. In 450, a new emperor came to power who decided to take a hard line with the barbarians. He cut off the tributes to the Huns and this led Attila to turn his attention to the west, which was far weaker than the east. It was at this point that he allied himself also with several German tribes and crossed the Rhine. Many Gallic towns were sacked during his attacks and it was then that he would be given the name "The Scourge of God" for his predatory acts. On Attila's return from Italy, he married a teenaged girl named "Ildiko." The marriage took place in 453 and was celebrated with a grand feast and copiousness amounts of alcohol. After dinner, the married couple went into their wedding chamber to celebrate passionately. Attila did not show up the next morning. Nervous servants opened the chamber door and found their leader dead on the floor covered with blood. His new bride was huddled in a corner in a state of shock. The weakened Roman Empire looked at the loss of Attila as the Hun leader as a sign. They celebrated the death of the "Scourge of God." Testimony to his death, he was buried in three caskets; one gold, one silver, and one iron. They were valuable for the time. The nature of the Huns in such matters was that the men who buried their king were all killed to ensure they would never tell anyone where Attila was interred.

Temujin - *Genghis Kahn* – Mongolian Power Maven

"Conquering the world on horseback is easy; it is dismounting and governing that is hard."

Genghis Kahn was a consolidator of tribes and ruled by unmitigated slaughter of all those defying his rule. He employed Chinese engineers to help him develop new siege warfare to make him superior to those not so progressive. He actually employed foreign engineers and craftsmen as part of his Mongol armies. It worked and he had the soldiers trained to be cruel and to kill anyone not bowing to their rule. Look into those eyes of this warrior and the others in this work to find the power behind the gusto. Tumujin endured many trials and tribulations prior to becoming one of the world's great warriors. He assumed command when in his thirties and by the time he was forty he had united many of the nomadic tribes of northeast Asia from Turkey to the Pacific Ocean. After consolidating the Mongol Empire at age thirty-six, he was in a position to dominate the Asian world through the power of the sword.

Tumujin was nine when his father was killed by the Tatars. He was born on the banks of the river Onon, in the northeast corner of present-day Mongolia. But, he and his mother had to flee from the Tatars who never wanted this kid to assume his family heritage as a leader of the Mongols. By the time he was nineteen, he would marry, but his young wife was kidnapped. Talk about early breakdowns that lead to breakthroughs due to empowering resilience! At this time, he became the protégé of Toghril who ruled a Christian tribe in central Mongolia. It was with the aid of Toghril and a young Mongol chieftain called "Jamuka" that Temüjin was able to rescue his newly married wife who had been carried off by the Merkits. Temüjin and Jamuka remained friends. Their long alliance would come to an abrupt end when Tumujin was elevated to power by his tribe and he was given the Mongol name "Genghis Kahn" – *Universal Monarch*. Kahn was thirty when he was given power, but he was in his early forties when he was finally in charge of Mongolia in 1203.

Genghis was quite the thinking warrior, saying things like, "Conquering the world is easy, governing it is hard." This warrior of warriors started the Mongol invasions that resulted in the conquest of most of Eurasia – from China and the Great Wall all the way through Persia. These included invasions across the Middle East and into India, and all the way East to the Pacific Ocean. These campaigns were often accompanied by wholesale carnage of civilian populations where he purportedly massacred thousands. By the end of his life, the Mongol Empire occupied a substantial portion of Central Asia and China. What were the primal attributes that led to such awesome power? Genghis put absolute trust in his generals and regarded them as close advisors. And, he was famous for extending his disciples the same privileges and trust normally reserved for close family members. His men were permitted to make decisions on their own when far from the Mongol Empire capital of Karakorum. Successful warriors expected unwavering loyalty in return. Genghis granted them a great deal of autonomy in making command decisions. The Mongol military was also successful in siege warfare, cutting off resources for cities and towns by diverting certain rivers, taking enemy prisoners, and marching them in front of his men. He would adopt innovative new ideas and would implement novel techniques and tools that he would find in the places he had conquered. He was especially adept at employing Muslim and Chinese siege engines and engineers to aid the Mongol cavalry in capturing cities. Another standard tactic was the commonly practiced feigned retreat to break enemy formations. Once they had taken a different tack, he would race back and ambush or counterattack. Genghis was also creative in developing new communications and supply routes aimed at speeding up the gathering of military intelligence. This sensitive warrior established a winter-only hunting season to preserve game for the hardest times. He is also credited with bringing the Silk Road to fruition due to his efficient system of communications and a cohesive political environment. In essence, he had integrated and systematized the trade routes between the West, Middle East, and Asia. In essence, Genghis instituted an incredible amount of meritocracy in his rule, religious tolerance beyond the norm, and he communicated with his soldiers on a first-name basis, as did Alexander and Napoleon. That is how to build unwavering allegiance.

Early Life and Success Imprints

Temujin was the second son of Yesukhie, born in North Central Mongolia in 1162. Mongol legend says that the baby was born with a blood-clot in his fist, a sign that he would be a great warrior. When the destined warrior was nine, his father took him to a neighboring tribe to work for several years to earn a bride who would was a girl named "Borje." On the way home from this event, Yesukhei was poisoned by rivals and he died. Upon learning this, Temüjin returned home to claim his father's position as chief of the tribe, but rivals refused to be led by a boy so young and Temujin returned home to be with his mother. The clan then exiled the whole family in hopes they would die. The family survived in the wilderness by eating roots, rodents, and fish. Young Temujin and his brother, Khasar, grew to resent their eldest half-brother, Begter, and they killed him, shades of Attila the Hun who had killed an older brother to get power. As punishment for the crime, Temujin was sent off to be a slave. His term would last for five years. On his way up the success ladder, he learned to cope with adversity. He had his cousin and best friend, Jamuka, strangled to death. Not unlike Joan of Arc a couple hundred years later, during his time alone as a slave, he claimed to have had a divine revelation that inspired him to conquer the world. He would call himself the "Sun of the Sky." On his climb to fame and fortune, he would have to fight rival clans and then would form a Mongol confederacy after the powers that be had made him Genghis Khan. It would take time as the most memorable conquests would take place in the last sixteen years of his life. He would gain a reputation as an intransigent warrior, infamous for slaughtering entire populations and destroying fields and irrigation systems. Yet, he was revered for his many contributions. He was in many cases like an ancient Robin Hood. Kahn would tell friends, "*In the space of seven years I have succeeded in accomplishing a great work and uniting the whole world in one Empire."* It would be *Diplomacy, Ruthlessness, and Military Prowess* that empowered him.

Genghis was mad for power, but very divine in the management of his conquests. He decreed the adoption of the Uyghur script as the Mongol Empire's writing system. He promoted religious tolerance in the Mongol Empire. Then he would create a unified empire of nomadic tribes. Present-day Mongolians regard him highly as the founding father of Mongolia. When he was twenty-seven, Temujin held a referendum among the Mongols who elected him to head them in their quest for power. The Mongols were only a sub-clan and they played off one another. The inner drive that took him to great victories as a warrior was due to his vision stated as:

> **The greatest joy for a man is to defeat his enemies, to drive them before him, to take from them all they possess, to see those they love in tears, to ride their horses, and to hold their wives and daughters in his arms.**

In 1209, Kahn would be on a roll to the pinnacle of power. He penetrated the Great Wall of China and conquered his neighbors to the south, taking Peking in 1214. Mongol expansion followed the tribal unification. He would divide China into three states: the China Empire in the north, I-Hsia in the northwest, and the Sung Empire in the south. By 1219, he had expanded his rule from China to the Afghan borders and from Siberia to the Tibet border in the South. In 1219 – The Year of the Hare – he left for the west and didn't return for seven years. His travels took him into India where he annihilated all in his path. Early in 1221, Genghis crossed the Oxus to destroy the ancient city of Balkh, and then part of the Persian province of Khurasan. He sent his youngest son, Tolu, to complete the subjugation of that province. He subjected it to such devastation that it would not recover for hundreds of years. Genghis advanced southward through Afghanistan to attack the Sultan Jalal al-Din, the son of Muhammad. Then he met and fought Jalal al-Din on the banks of the Indus and soundly defeated him. American General, Douglas MacArthur would eulogize Genghis in his tormented battles during World War II saying that he learned more from Genghis than anyone else. Genghis was able to mobilize an unusually high proportion of the adult male population. He married human and technical resources to win. Historians would write that Genghis would establish an empire that would last more than one-hundred and fifty years. Over time, his empire was divided and weakened. Most of his conquests were lost, but he had made it all happen.

Legacy Left for Warriors

Genghis Khan has been lauded for putting absolute trust in his generals, regarding them as friends. He would extend them the same privileges and trust normally reserved for close family members. He allowed them to make decisions on their own when far from the Mongol Empire, and he granted them autonomy to do what was necessary to maintain control. The Mongol military was very skilled in siege warfare. Like Attila, they hit the enemy hard before they knew what had hit them. Another tactic was the commonly practiced feigned retreat to confuse the enemy.

Among Khan's advancements, he revolutionized the social structure and reformed traditional law in Mongolia. His would build a very egalitarian culture where the best rules were what was best for all. War booty was divided evenly among all warriors, regardless of social status. Unlike most rulers of the time, Genghis trusted loyal followers implicitly. Khan forbade the kidnapping of women, probably due in part to his wife's experience, but also because it led to warfare among different Mongol groups. He outlawed livestock rustling and established winter-only hunting. This was an enlightened ruler who had been a very barbaric and ruthless murderer; quite a paradox. He protected the rights of Buddhists, Muslims, Christians, and Hindus, despite his own propensity for worshipping the sky. Kahn forbade the killing of priests, monks, nuns, mullahs, and other holy people. When he became ill, he would say, "*My life was too short to achieve the conquest of the whole world*," and he would leave that task to his sons.

Chapter Two

Warriors Leave a Legacy for Future Leaders

"Anyone who becomes master of a city accustomed to freedom and does not destroy it, may expect to be destroyed by it." - Nicolo Machiavelli, *The Prince*

Warriors are whirlwinds on a trek to nirvana, at least in their minds and the minds of their disciples. Men like Geronimo were able to imprint strong sentiments in the minds of his tribal followers. When wounded, he would keep fighting, as the alternative was death in that arena. It would turn out that he would suffer gunshot and knife wounds repeatedly. Yet, miraculously, he survived. It would cast him as a special man among the Apaches who felt he was special. His people followed him of their own free will since he possessed many powers beyond the pale of ordinary Indians. They felt he was favored or protected by the Apache High God, Usen. For this accolade, Geronimo would paint the faces of his warrior disciples as a means of godly protection. This author advises that we must all paint our psyches with a warrior imprint like Geronimo, and we too can be of a warrior nature.

Cyrus the Great told us, *"Soft countries breed soft men,"* and Genghis Kahn offered advice saying, *"Conquering the world is easy, governing it is hard"* an insight that is still true in today's world is Attila the Hun's aphorism, *"Continual learning is the key to success for a Hun."* Those words are the fuel for the legacies of their disciples. Cyrus had a similar attitude in creating the Ottoman Empire with words like, "All men have their frailties; and whoever looks for a friend without imperfections, will never find what he seeks." Such is the thinking of powerful warriors.

How do Warrior Wizards become so Powerful?

Warriors who win big and make it to the very top seem to be uniquely different than their followers. Many have adopted a hero-mentor to model their own drive to the very top. Others have an ethereal vision to motivate them beyond the norm. It's that surreal sense of life and success that fuels them to glory. Often, these men and women are fueled by an inner messianic sagacity like those that alter paradigms or in visionaries like Leonardo da Vinci, Isaac Newton, and Nikola Tesla from other disciplines. Such people are never normal, but are zealots on an impossible mission. Most have discovered early how to use power to get power. Many were imprinted with a prescient sense of self early in life as was the case of Napoleon in writing a sequel to Goethe's *Young Werther*. Others like Hitler and Jim Jones had a penchant for getting weak people to follow them to salvation in their own deluded Promised Land. There are those like Attila the Hun who killed his older brother to put power in his hands. American General, George Patton had an early premonition of his destiny, writing as a teenager, *"I plan to be a hero."*

Many religious zealots had a similar beginning as these warrior wizards. Some made the people see them as a witch doctor with a direct line to salvation or food and surety. To keep the herd in line, they frightened the pack with hell and promised them salvation – the age-old strategy of gurus like Gurdjieff, Jim Jones, David Koresh, or Osama Bin Laden. These gurus promised deliverance to those who would follow them blindly into their own *Neverland* of the mind. Adolph Hitler gained power in Nazi, Germany through a similar, mesmerizing message of charismatic power that was based on employment, elimination of uncontrolled inflation, and deliverance from the beast from the east – Communism. Hitler is a superb example of how such power can be learned since Adolph was a pathologically shy man who was trained by a German intellectual named Dietrich Eckert to gain power over people. Eckert took the young Hitler under his wing and trained him in the art of personal persuasion. It worked, as Hitler learned to speak passionately in "mind control" and would mesmerize German audiences. On his death bed, Eckert said, "Follow Hitler, he will dance, but it will be to my tune." It was a fundamental power rule of those that find a way to lead others. Their mantra is usually, *"Follow me! I'll take you with me on my trek to Shangri La – just don't question or think rationally since I am messianic."* Such is the message conveyed by warrior wunderkinds.

Ruthless Brain Power Reigns Supreme

Alexander the Great was outnumbered by 3:1 when he went into Asia Minor with his armies and defeated the Persian King Darius III. He used his brains to do be faster with a more mobile army and armed his men with 14-foot sarissa's. Much later Napoleon, his protégé in using the mind to defeat the enemy went into Italy and at the battle of Lodi faced forces that were two and half times larger and came away with a decisive victory by personally leading a bayonet charge across a bridge earning himself the name the Little Corporal. When the Spanish Conquistador Cortes landed in Mexico he was too outnumbered by the Aztec forces under the command of Montezuma. He used a peace pitch to get support from the Mayans and the Aztecs and would take over a nation with far superior forces. What did all these warriors do? The used brain-power rather than military might or gunpowder to become great.

Esalen, located in California's Big Sur area, became a haven for such gurus during the middle of the twentieth century. It is where Gestalt psychology was born. Hanging in this sanctuary was a leader of the Gestalt movement, Fritz Perls, where he could be found reciting his eulogy in the form of the Gestalt Prayer – I do my Thing & You Do Your Thing. It was in this place underneath giant redwood trees where many grandiose ideas were born. One of the leaders in this arena would pioneer one of the most important factors found in the warrior wizards of yesteryear, getting into that place the Chinese label *"chi"* and Americans call *"The Zone"* or sometimes *"Flow."* An expert on the "zone" – those times when every single word you speak and each move you make is pure elegance - was Mike Murphy. He wrote a book titled *In the Zone* in which he stated, *"Step into the terra incognita by deed seems to trigger opening the terra incognita of meta-normal experiences."* The infamous guru, Jim Jones, of the *People's Temple* was one of the most nefarious of all those who seemed to know that path into a surreal arena. It was, although, a unique power found in the research on men like Cyrus the Great, Alexander the Great, Joan of Arc, Attila the Hun, Genghis Kahn, Mao Zedung, and the American General George Patton. Jim Jones convinced 900 passionate disciples to leave America to find their Promised Land in Jonestown, Guyana. It was a gigantic con game that would result in the deaths of 260 disciples on November 18, 1978 in a mass suicide by cyanide-laced Grape Koolaid. It is not coincidental that seventy percent of the victims were black, and two-thirds were female; all there to be helped in coping with life in the fast lane that turned out to be the bad lane. Not long after, it would happen again in Waco, Texas when a self-proclaimed messiah by the name of David Koresh concocted his own Promised Land labeled the *"Branch Davidian"* cult where eighty-six needy adults and their twenty-two children willingly died in this 1993 holocaust.

These means to power were not much different than those of warriors on a mission to greatness. Alexander was so bold as to say, *"If I were not Alexander, I would be Diogenes."* This young Grecian warrior, who conquered much of the known world by age twenty-eight, was comparing himself to the Greek mythological god who walked around Athens with a lamp to find just one honest man. Such are the ideas burning deep within most warriors. It is why Joan became a Saint and not her siblings. She went where they were far too traditional to go. How did a young German princess become the Empress of Russia? She believed she was special and made herself special. In Alexander's case, his mother was quite the sorceress, and she sent him to the Oracle at Delphi who told him, *"You are destined for greatness my son."*

It was similar deep inner zeal that would lead a one-hundred pound, near-naked Gandhi to topple the mighty British Empire. The Mahatma had been transformed at a very young age by heroic ideas from books. He used them to go where others feared. What led General George Patton to become a leader feared by the Nazi military, no matter his mission? It was not guns, tanks, or bullets. It was an inner zeal beyond the norm. Often, simple things imprint us when we are quite young. In the case of Patton, it would be a memory of his being baptized in a family picture with him sitting astride a military tank. It would be a fixture in the family living room as he grew into adulthood. Books and fantasy heroes modeled many of these warriors. They worshipped fantasy role-models and most fashioned their lives after these imaginary heroes. In the case of Alexander, he would take a book on his hero, Achilles, into every single battle and emulate his hero as he attacked an adversary. In China, a young kid who hated his father ran away from home as a teenager and would escape into the books of men like Marx, Lenin, and Darwin, although none would be as transformational psychologically for a Communist as Robin Hood – a fictional character in Britain who stole from the rich to give to the poor.

One strange anomaly was found as a fundamental factor in the success of each of the warriors in this work. Everyone had a near-death experience, or some other monumental crisis that pushed their heads and hearts to the very brink of disaster. Chaos was found in the lives of each of these warrior wizards – a kind of breakdown that one Nobel Prize winner would label a "bifurcation point." That is a place we all go when on the precipice and not sure if we will fall in or can escape and save ourselves. It has been called "facing a breakdown to find a new breakthrough." Each of these warriors came face-to-face with disaster and, because of having visited the very bottom, went to the very top.

Prior to Temujin becoming Genghis Kahn, he would be kidnapped at age nine after his leader father had been murdered by adversaries, and they took him away so he would not take power. He escaped and would return. Those early experiences were fundamental to his path to the top. Indian warrior, Goyathlay was similarly altered. One day his life would change dramatically. While off on a trek to find food, a Mexican band killed his mother, wife, and three children. He was still in his twenties. By age thirty, he would be called "Geronimo" by Mexicans who were calling on St. Jerome to save them from his wrath. It was an early life in a Palestinian kibbutz that would lead Moshe Dayan to learn the life of a warrior along with survival techniques. As a boy, not yet in high school, Norman Schwarzkopf would be with his military dad, seeing death and survival first-hand.

The following table will offer insight into the transmutation that took place within their minds and hearts:

Table 3

The Bottom as a Catalyst to the Very Top

Alexander the Great – Became *Achilles* when in battle due to early challenges with a horse that he tamed. His father hired Aristotle to train him.

Genghis Kahn **Tumujin**– Named *Genghis* when hit top after father murdered and kidnapped.

Joan of Arc –*Saint Joan* emerged out of the horrid 100-Year War against Britain.

Catherine the Great – A German princess forced to marry a Russian Prince who was an idiot that played toy soldiers. She read and became empowered.

Hernan Cortes – Became a *Conquistador;* demoted in Cuba, but still invaded Mexico with a band of men and defeated Montezuma to take power.

Napoleon – Death/Fighting in Corsican revolution fueled him to become a French military man. When the bipolar, insecure boy felt power, he took it.

Goyathlay – Named *Geronimo!* by frightened Mexicans after they killed his family. He talked to Indian god, Ushen, and this shaman became an untamed assassin.

Mao Zedong – Beaten by dad and ran away from home as teen. Escaped into books of heroic warriors and became modern Robin Hood for underprivileged in China.

Mahatma Gandhi – Attempted suicide at fifteen. Dad died when sixteen. Mother died when nineteen. When thrown from SA train as undesirable in twenties, became transformed warrior.

George Patton – Old Blood & Guts suffered many head injuries, collapsing at end of Pentathlon in 1912 Olympics. Bipolar affliction took him to pinnacle of power.

Moshe Dayan - Life in kibbutz, member of Hagannah as teen. Lost eye at twenty-six. Zionist hero.

Norman Schwarzkopf – *Stormin' Norman* evolved from early life in Kuwait with dad, learning to deal with death in Nam and Purple Heart for valor.

Often, a mentor or role model can propel one to go beyond where they might have gone without having had such a person they respect to mimic or impersonate as did Alexander with his hero, Achilles. The warrior wizards proved this far beyond what would be expected. Most read voraciously, as did Catherine before she became *Great*. Such philosophical insights led to Catherine becoming close with Voltaire and Diderot. Escaping into books gave them heroes to model their lives after, as was the case for Gandhi, George Patton, and Schwarzkopf. St. Joan and Geronimo were inspired by visionary spirits. Napoleon's early hero was Goethe's *Young Werther,* and it inspired him to go far. China's Mao Zedong became a voracious reader, inspired to chase his dreams by reading Marx, Lenin, and stories of Robin Hood.

The following table offers insights into the psychological mentoring to the top:

Role Models Can Fuel the Trek to the Very Top

Alexander the Great – Father Philip, King of Macedonia, and Oracle at Delphi told him he was destined to be great leader; Homer's Achilles was his role-model prior to each battle.

Attila the Hun – Born a Prince, but killed older brother, Bleda, to lead the Huns to conquest.

Joan of Arc – Preordained voices of empowerment at twelve from St. Michael and St. Catherine.

Catherine the Great – German-born as Princess Sophia; read voraciously about great heroes, and befriended Voltaire and Diderot when young. An empress was born.

Hernan Cortes – Quit the university in Spain at eighteen to chase his dreams in Cuba; became a renegade Conquistador with a mission to destroy the Montezuma and the Aztecs.

Napoleon Bonaparte – Alexander and Corsican Paoli were childhood heroes, and then books like Goethe's Young Werther empowered this manic hero-worshipper.

Geronimo (Goyathlay) – Father and grandfather leaders of Aztec tribe, but mom made him study and worship Indian god *Ushen* that imprinted divine majesty – Apache from Zuni word *enemy*.

Mao Zedong – Ran away from home at thirteen and escaped into books about Marx, Lenin, and Robin Hood. These heroic role models led him to the very top.

Mahatma Gandhi – Voracious reader; books were bibles. After Rushkin's *Unto This Last* he said was "transformational" and fueled his dreams of an optimum life.

General George Patton – Family of military leaders led him to declare he would be a hero and pursue a military career like role models; was baptized with photo riding a tank.

Moshe Dyan – In Israel, became an Invincible Demi-God after Six Day War victory.

General Norman Schwarzkopf – Father a Brigadier General and childhood as war-brat.

Charismatic Power – The Fuel to the Top

Most of those in this work had charisma to spare and they used it often to overcome problems. The textbook definition of charisma comes from the Greek meaning *"Gift of Divine Grace."* A Canadian writer on Charismatic Leadership said, *"Charismatic leaders are effective because they arouse power motivation in their followers. They always personify the forces of change, unconventionality, vision, and entrepreneurial spirit."*

Napoleon, in writing his memoirs as a prisoner at St. Helena wrote, *"I saw myself founding a religion."* Those are pretty strong words from a man who would admit to being an agnostic. A general in his Grande Army spoke of the mesmerizing effect Napoleon had on him saying, *"That devil of a man exercises a fascination on me that I cannot explain. When I am in his presence I am ready to tremble like a child. He could make me go through the eye of a needle and throw myself into the fire."* And Wellington, his mortal enemy on the field of battle would tell the media, *"The Corsican's presence on the field of battle was equivalent to 40,000 men."* It was similar to what a Hollywood columnist would write about meeting with the U.S. President, John F. Kennedy. Rowland Evans wrote, *"Jack was simply the most appealing human being I ever met*." Such was the effect that men like Alexander the Great had on both allies and enemies. It was also an effect that Catherine the Great had on the Russian people. A German hearing the Fuehrer speak in Berlin would say, *"When Hitler spoke, I felt I had come face to face with God. The intense will of the man flowed from him into me."* George Stein, a biographer of Hitler wrote, *"Hitler had the magnetism of a hypnotist."* For those readers interested, it has been found that charisma can be learned, and it was true of Hitler who was taught how to use powerful words that would pass energy between him and those listening. It was a kind of psychic energy that came through when he spoke, even on a podium.

These mesmerizing warriors got to the very top by daring, as well as the use of words to inspire others to follow them to their destiny. Hernan Cortes was such a man as was Golda Meir, the first female Prime Minister of Israel. Both had magnetism to burn and it helped them to rise above more skilled warriors. Golda's name as a young girl was the "Golden Girl" in reference to her way with words. Most people are not aware that when the state of Israel was trying to find peace with the Arabs, in the early days they faced an impending war with neighboring Jordan. Not one male soldier would travel across the Sinai desert to meet with the king of Jordan, as it was almost certain death. Who went? It was Golda who crawled across the Sinai Desert when no male dared to meet with King Abdullah to seek peace. This lady was fearless, and it showed when surrounded by millions of Arabs in the Yom Kippur War. Her soldiers were about to be annihilated. They needed tanks desperately or they would be blown away by the Arab armies. While it was morning, her time, she called Henry Kissinger. It was the middle of night in Washington. The woman who answered told Golda, "Please call back in the morning." Golda was not a woman to take no for an answer; anytime, or anywhere. She responded, "And I'm surrounded by four million Arabs and will be dead by morning and the Israeli State will be history. Wake up the asshole. I need tanks." She got her tanks, and when *The New York Times* asked this gal who grew up in Milwaukee prior to going to Israel, "How could a country with 250,000 beat one with four million?" Golda, in her charismatic simplicity answered, "No choice." Was that profound or what? She was saying that the Arabs could and should have won, but if they didn't, they would go back to their homes and live a long life. Had the Israeli's lost, they would have been history. The new Israeli state would have been gone forever. A few years later, when Margaret Thatcher was asked about her favoring the death penalty, the media was furious. She told them, *"If you take another's life, you just forfeited the right to yours."* Touché!

The teachers of the process of mesmerizing and attracting disciples are as follows:

Table 5

The Source of Charismatic Power

- ✗ EGOISTIC FERVOR: Believe, and people will follow you to a Promised Land - George Patton

- ✗ HAVE PURPOSE: Grab hold of a mystical vision to attract followers - Cyrus & Mao

- ✗ BE REAL & OPEN: Vulnerable people attract legions to their side; cite Hernando Cortez who burned his boats, Alexander, and Catherine the Great

- ✗ BE MYSTERIOUS: Enchantment comes from the unknown – Joan of Arc and Geronimo

- ✗ BE UNINHIBITED: Never compromise; go where mere mortals fear and take journeys with unbridled sexual energy - Napoleon and Moshe Dayan

- ✗ BE ELOQUENT: Use powerful words and concepts to impart your emotional message ala - Napoleon, Catherine, Gandhi, and Norman Schwarzkopf

- ✗ USE THEATRICS: To communicate with disciples by donning sartorial robes in order to appear larger-than life – Mao Zedung swimming rivers at 70 and George Patton

- ✗ BE ADVENTUROUS: Unconventionality is exciting and thrilling for those wallowing in mediocrity; brazen courage is magical - Cortez and Saint Joan

- ✗ MAGNETISM: Look into the eyes of the magic man - Genghis Kahn and Napoleon

Extrinsic Powers – Muscles, $, Mind & Position

When young, the kids with the biggest muscles are the ones that have the power. As they age, those with the most smarts or money emerge on top. But in those territories known as *Banana Republics* are the ones with the biggest guns or who control the army. For them, it is the power of physical force. Physical power is about bodily skills. Children playing on the street learn early that the biggest girl gets to pitch and the strongest guy gets to play quarterback. Later, those with a car or money date the blonde cheerleaders. Those with very high SAT scores get the scholarships to Harvard and Stanford. Money is the key to gaining financial power. This is often followed by what I have labeled "Titular" or "Position Power." Using the lower powers to get elected President or Pope gives one enormous power.

The *Hierarchy of Power* in the table below shows that Physical Power is at the very bottom. The next up the scale is money, followed by smarts. An example of this comes from Alexander the Great who at age ten jumped on a wild stallion and tamed him to the amazement of grown men. That was **Physical Power,** but his father, Philip, was so impressed he bought the horse for his amazing son, **Money Power**. Philip then saw potential in Alexander and hired Aristotle to be his teacher between age 13 and 16 – **Mind Power and** when Philip was assassinated, Alexander at age 20 was given **Position Power** – he was made king of Macedonia**.**

As a person moves up the Hierarchy of Power, the lower powers like force, money, and smarts become less powerful, and the inner powers become crucial to success. *Fortune* wrote an article on why talent alone is not power or the key to success, saying, *"Research now shows that the lack of natural talent is no longer irrelevant to great success. To be great takes mental models of work and insight."* This simple axiom is often lost on most people who believe icons like a Bill Gates and Tiger Woods are more endowed. Not true! David Hawkins in *Power & Force* (2002) told us, "Muscles strengthen and weaken from positive or negative stimuli." This was further validated by the *Wall Street Journal*, "A gene contributes zero percent of what you become since if you don't grow up in an environment that turns the gene on, the environment contributes nothing. (WSJ Jan 13, 2006 p. 1A) This is important information for wannabe warriors. An example is Alexander, who having fulfilled the Physical, Financial, and Knowledge aspect of growth, used his incredible

Charismatic Power that he was given by the Oracle at Delphi that told him, *"You are invincible my son."* It was then that the will of Alexander fueled him for a twelve year journey to conquer the world. That is the consummate *Will-to-Power* that emanates from deep within a seething psyche.

Will and Charisma

In 1893 at the Chicago World's Fair, Nikola Tesla had reached the breaking point with his lifelong nemesis Thomas Edison. The brilliant icon who had invented alternative energy took a wire in one hand, and with Edison's light bulb in the other, he pulled a switch and put two million volts through his body to light the bulb to screaming cheers from the audience. That takes guts, smarts, charisma, and an intransigent will-to-power. Such warriors show that we are all akin to an electric wire with similar properties of magnetic attractions. The higher the power of the current running through a wire, the greater is the magnetic field that it generates. Force does affect its magnetic field in physics and warriors. This is a metaphor that couch potatoes don't seem to fathom. Psychotherapist Carl Jung saw this and wrote, "*We carry our past with us and it is only with an enormous effort that we can detach ourselves from this burden.*"

Reaching the pinnacle of power as a warrior lies within the mind, and from a Buddhist's perspective, life is not a destination, but a programmed journey. Most men's frailties cause them to never become a warrior. How do we deal with that? We must alter the inner programs that limit us and replace them with those that lead to transcendence. Change is inextricably tied to rebirth, not of the physical being, but of the mind. Self-reflection and introspection are crucial for warriors like Alexander and Gandhi. Both were willing to go beyond the obvious and live in a *Neverland* to find *Nirvana*. For them, the force of will led them to an elevated state of enlightenment. It is obvious that the magic of will-power lies in the mind of those that believe and refuse to permit the demons to interfere with their journey.

Table 6

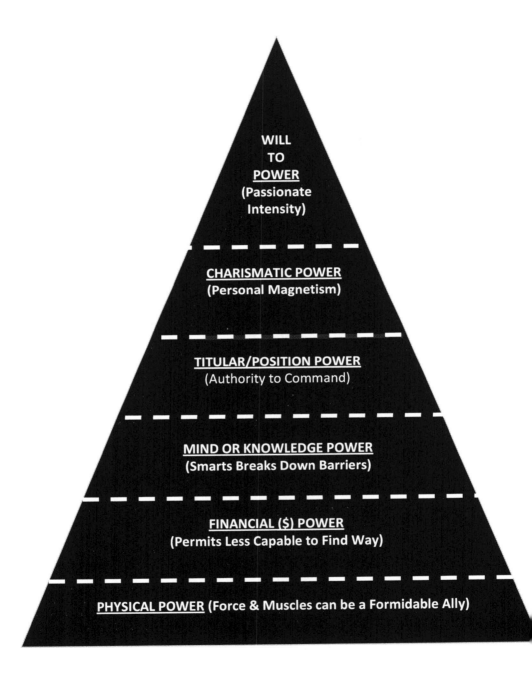

Behavioral Kinesiology's John Diamond wrote in *Life Energy*, "*All illness starts as a problem on the energy level. About 95% of the population tests low on Life Energy.*" Such power is what fueled leaders like Catherine, Napoleon, and Adolph Hitler. It was also a driving force in the successes of Cyrus the Great, Attila the Hun, Genghis Kahn, Mother Teresa, and today's Oprah Winfrey. And, such inner will-power is also what led Hitler, Jim Jones, and David Koresh to kill and pillage. The negation of inhibition is the source of power. Those with a strong will, get powerful. Diamond went on to say, "*The lowering of inhibition frees the powerful to shake up organizations, fearlessly challenge the status-quo, do the right thing regardless of unpopularity and follow a more daring vision.*" Carl Jung became a fan of free love, writing, "*Where love rules, there is no will to power; and where power predominates love is lacking. The one is the shadow of the other.*" This begs the most eloquent power philosophy from Lord Acton, who wrote, "*Power corrupts and absolute power corrupts absolutely.*"

In China, Mao tse Tung proclaimed, "Power comes out of the end of a gun." Russian writer, Aleksandra Solzhenitsyn offered further insight, "You can have power over people as long as you don't take everything away from them. But when you've robbed a man of everything he's no longer in your power." Power does come in a wide variety of forms. Think about the power under the hood of a NASCAR race car. The most powerful cars seldom win it all. The winners turn to some other element that supersedes the horsepower or thrust. Those with titular power have risen to the top of organizations. Those with the most money become real estate titans. With sufficient charisma, an individual can get elected to public office. A man with an audacious reputation can become Pope. It takes the right bloodline to become King or Queen of England. Speaking of bloodlines, let's look at Catherine the Great's rise to power in Russia. When her idiot husband was about to put her in a nunnery and his mistress on the throne of Russia, she audaciously put on a Captain's uniform and mounted her stallion like a male and told her guard to follow her into battle. Her Titular power would be as Empress of all the Russia's. This would not have happened had she not had the bucks to get married to the grandson of Peter the Great, nor the incredible mental powers from the myriad of books she read while learning to speak fluent French and English, as well as German. All of these powers enhanced her Charismatic power and led to an incredible Nietzschean Will-to-Power.

Napoleon would follow Catherine a few years later to take the power in France. The Little General began using guns during the French Revolution and the Reign of Terror when he shot and killed men who did not obey his orders. It got him promoted, and the money went along with his education from a French military school. Not much later, he would win a battle at Lodi, Italy that he was supposed to lose. Within four years, this upstart, who was not even French, would crown himself Emperor – the consummate Titular Power. Then, he imposed his Charisma to gain disciples to take charge. And, with that he was able to attain the ultimate crown as emperor of France – *Titular Power* - with the aristocracy groveling at his feet and the Pope kissing his ring while kneeling before him. That is the definitive *Will-to-Power*.

Further examples of a *Hierarchy of Power* come from the warrior wunderkinds in this work. Ironically, Joan of Arc actually began at the top, but she so frightened the British they would burn her at the stake. At the age twelve she heard voices – her **Will-to-Power** – and it empowered this peasant girl enough for her to tell King Charles to give her an army to fight the Brits in the One Hundred Year War. Think about an illiterate peasant girl convincing a king to give her authority – that is **Charismatic Power** – and when the king gave her an army to lead, it would be the ultimate **Titular Power.** When a warrior moves beyond the pale of the ordinary, those with the lesser powers of muscle, money, and smarts lose to those who have moved beyond those lesser powers. Joan's price was being charged with heresy and being burned at the stake at age nineteen. But, the traditional hierarchy was working with General George Patton. As a kid, he won wrestling matches and was a formidable foe – *Physical Power*. It got him the funding – *Financial Power* and then further education and into West Point where he was imprinted with *Mind Power*. These early powers got him to be a Colonel and later a General – *Titular Power*. And the chivalry and words of wisdom like "There's only one proper way for a professional soldier to die: the last bullet of the last battle of the last war." Soldiers in World War II were spellbound in his presence – *Charismatic Power*. These powers emboldened him and he would actually write, *"I've always felt that I was destined for some great achievement, what I don't know."* That is the essence of a kind of transcendent *Will-to-Power* that was off the charts. It got him eulogized and it almost cost him everything.

Zealots Have Powerful Drives

There is a paradox of success. What most people think is best and most prudent is often what will destroy them. And, what is wild and crazy can move mountains. Zealots on a mission to the impossible are those that move mountains because they are willing to go where traditionalists fear. This was true of the warriors who died early due to their wild lifestyle like Alexander the Great and Joan of Arc who were both dead at ages thirty-three and nineteen. The irony of their plight is that what made them would destroy them. Having paid the ultimate price, Alexander became a legendary icon, and Joan would become a saint. Living in life's fast lane has a big downside. But neither would have opted for playing in the so-called slow lane. Moderation is prudent, but the payoff is mediocrity. Proactive people are a small percentage of any given cohort, but they are the ones that alter paradigms. Such people make up about five percent of any given population. One such zealot was Frederick Nietzsche who wrote, "*The sedentary life is the very sin against the Holy Spirit.*"

Obsessive people not only don't have time for trouble, they seldom have time for sleep. Most sleep sparingly because they are so turned on by what they are doing, they have a need to do rather than sleep like normal people. Nikola Tesla, the father of the alternating current, slept but two hours a night for much of his long life. Edison refused to leave his lab for days at a time and would be found asleep on the floor. He often went without eating when totally immersed in a new idea. Mao Zedung went days without going to bed and would write in his *Little Red Book*, "*For me there is only 200 days in a year,*" implying that he never slept the other third of the time. Napoleon was of a similar nature. This manic-man once killed five horses in a mad dash across Europe in which he never stopped to sleep. As previously mentioned, his valet, Constant, said, "*He is perpetual motion. I never comprehended how his body could endure such fatigue. He never even stopped to change clothes in five days when five of his horses perished.*" (Landrum 1996. p. 129) One Napoleon biographer wrote of his perpetual motion, "*The very mania that gave him such advantages in battle doomed him to waste the victories and to destroy his empire.*" Was Napoleon aware of his maniacal lifestyle? Sure! But like most bipolar personalities, they come to believe that if they stop, they will perish. Napoleon wrote in his memoirs in St. Helena, "*I will lose a man but never a moment.*" Psychiatrist John Diamond has studied the power of energy and writes, *"All illness starts as a problem on the energy level."*

Power Accedes to Those Who Take It

Nietzsche in *Thus Spake Zarathustra* said, *"Power accedes to he who takes it."* Power is an anomaly since the power of penultimate performance is in conflict with those trying to get it. Try to get it and when you don't get it, you can be mocked by friends and foes. Power must ensue as the by-product of executing well. What this says for those wanting power is to chase a dream and pursue it with unmitigated passion and, if lucky, you will become powerful. Thus power is a by-product of doing - not chasing. Consider the enormous power wielded by a newborn baby. When it cries, hardened adults jump up in the middle of the night to soothe the child. Conversely, a bully only has the power given him by his victim. Bullies only pick on the weak that permit them to be bullied. Mahatma Gandhi had none of the traditional vestiges of power. But, this quiet man brought down the mighty British Empire through a system known as **"Satyagraha"** - passive resistance through positive non-violence. Gandhi's power was ethereal. Here was a pauper who could not be bribed by money, position, imprisonment, or physical harm. Even sexual persuasion was of no merit to a man who was empowered from a greater force within. This befuddled the Brits who had never encountered such a man. The enigma of Gandhi was his faith in a power beyond the pale of ordinary men. When imprisoned, he went on a hunger strike. Fearing he would die and become more of a threat as a martyr, the Brits capitulated. The power from within is a far greater force than material powers like weapons of destruction.

Men like Gandhi are fueled with a philosophic passion. Even a wild warrior like Napoleon saw himself as more philosopher and poet than military guru. Alexander was of a similar ilk, and much of that came from his teacher Aristotle. Catherine the Great grew powerful by modeling her life from protagonists out of books. That was also the case in the embattled General George Patton – "Old Blood & Guts" as he men called him. The warriors in this work had a very holistic view of life and their causes. They seldom confused their maps with the territory they were transgressing. All had a kind of mystical vision of their opportunities and refused to permit the little stuff to interfere with their dreams. One of these warriors had a Servant/Leader mentality. Mahatma Gandhi was a ninety pound acetic who was not susceptible to the things of ordinary men. The Indian warrior was the personification of a man who cannot be bought, enticed, bribed, or seduced. His power was that Nietzschean Will-to-Power that bewildered the British politicians who had never dealt with such a force. They attempted to control him with military might and force, but it failed. Gandhi's power came from a deep commitment to a cause larger than life. It brought the powerful British Empire to their knees. Gandhi's biographer, Louis Fischer, spoke to that ethereal power that transcended weaponry or rhetoric, *"He was diffident yet independent. Self-confidence filled him with exuberant energy and radiance which no follower could resist."*

At the very first university, The Academy, Plato would state, *"There will be no end to the trouble of states until philosophers become kings."* This was not a self-serving professional pitch, but words from a man who saw the power of reason and ideas. Macho warriors and superstars in all disciplines are similarly inclined. They have been men on a philosophic mission to some surreal target. They had a poetic mindset beyond the pale of ordinary men and women. Such warriors are big-picture oriented to a fault and seldom capitulate to the little stuff on the highway of life. Concrete-sequential types are all from Missouri – the Show me State – and must have proof of what is around the next pass or mountain before going there. They fear becoming lost, not something ever found in the lives and works of real warriors. The unknown is a new opportunity for visionaries and the Achilles Heal for the meek and who label the innovator warriors as crazy. Aristotle wrote of this saying, *"No great genius is without some mixture of insanity."* A close look at these warriors shows that the Greek philosopher to be more than a little correct. Napoleon, Chairman Mao, and General Patton were all driven by debilitating manic-depression. Catherine the Great had to deal with what she called *"uterine frenzies,"* that led to her spending the equivalent of $1.5 billion in current dollars on her paramours. Mediocre leaders seldom bare their weaknesses, but warrior wizards are not so inclined. When the Romans saw the weakness of Caesar for his mistress Cleopatra, they decided he wasn't strong enough to lead their nation. It is okay for a leader to dally. It is not okay for them to be weakened by the indulgence. There is always a limit to allowing the libido to weaken you, although, once in power, Mao Zedung purportedly slept with 2,000 concubines, in addition to four wives. Hernando Cortez and Geronimo had a similar propensity. These men made President Bill Clinton look like a slouch. It was no accident that women put Clinton in office, but once in power, like Catherine the Great, you can dally as you please.

Psychic Energy as a Power Source

It is a paradox that Catherine the Great was not Russian, Napoleon was not French, and Hitler was not German. But, that simple fact did not deter them from taking power. Catherine took over Mother Russia due to a threat by a child-like husband that she would describe as "poison, prison, or power." It would be a few years later that the intrepid warrior, Napoleon, took advantage of the tumultuous French Revolution to wrest power in France. The Little Corsican became emperor despite being of Italian heritage. Later, Adolph Hitler would use nationalism as a rallying call to take power in Germany under his National Socialist party. The mad Austrian was granted power by a nation buried in debt, inflation, and the fear of the Red Menace from the East. Fear leads people to take perilous paths as most evangelists have learned—*frighten them with hell and they'll follow you anywhere.* Warriors seem to learn early that mantra of frightening people to make them followers. Many of these power brokers had a mystical sense of transcendence, and had a love of books. Catherine funded the first encyclopedia by Diderot, was a patron saint of the Russian arts, and became an intimate of Voltaire. Napoleon loved poetry. Prior to a major battle, he would read poems, not unlike his hero Alexander who read of Achilles' exploits prior to engaging in combat. An example of how such philosophic ideas can motivate positively and negatively is when Napoleon attacked Egypt in the likeness of his hero Alexander. Napoleon would write, *"God gave me the will and the force to overcome all obstacles."* Hitler was even more messianic, telling his disciples, *"I am more godlike than human."* What was the genesis of such mystical energy? Perhaps from an inner sense of destiny manifested within a mind on a mission.

Many adopted a fantasy mentor from a book. Hitler carried copies of Schopenhauer's books to the front in World War I. During his adolescence, Hitler became so enthralled with Wagner's operas he would escape into a reverie of hope and bizarre enthrallment. Teen friend, August Kubizek, told the media of Hitler's wild escapes during the *Rienzi* opera: *"He entered a state of ecstasy and rapture with visionary powers [as] though a demon had possessed him."* In speaking of his youth, Hitler would admit that these emotional escapes were key to his success, saying that his powers came from a vision to *"lead Germany out of servitude and to heights of freedom,"* claiming, *"It was at that moment that it all began."*

Warriors Don't Get Lost in the Little Stuff

Great warriors realize quite early that the mind is the true master of their destiny. They never seem to get lost in the little stuff that stifles traditionalists who are what psycho-therapists call "concrete-sequential" – those who see the world as either black or white. Visionary warriors know the world is gray at best. Left-handers like Alexander the Great, Joan of Arc, Napoleon, Gandhi and Norman Schwarzkopf tend to be above the action on the battlefield. They are like chess-masters who play ahead of the action and tend to defeat traditionalists (right-handers) who are locked into what psychologists label concrete-sequential – A then B then C no matter the situation. Those that play above the action have an edge and is why Alexander and Napoleon defeated superior forces to the amazement of their adversaries and their allies. Research shows the right-hemisphere dominant warriors are more empathetic than traditionalists. And when a warrior senses what another is thinking or likely to do they are playing with a superior hand. They sense what the other might do and are ahead of them as they have long-since moved past that move. It made Napoleon somewhat invincible as it did Alexander before him and both were uncanny strategists who walked into battle with an edge – it was a head edge, not a military one.

Another left-hander and visionary was the physicist Albert Einstein, a numbers guy who never permitted the numbers to interfere with his moves or theories. His boat was named "Intuition" since that was what he considered the true path to eminence. When Hitler took over in Germany, this Jewish intellectual left for America and a new job at Princeton University. When he landed, a journalist stopped him and asked, *"Mr. Einstein, you as a world-renowned physicist must be able to tell our readers how many miles it is around this earth?"* Einstein looking a bit bewildered at such an inane question, answered, *"I have no idea."* The reporter said, *"Mr. Einstein, American high school seniors knows this answer."* Einstein looked at this man without an idea on the majesty of the mind and said, *"Look, my mind has a limited amount of space and I refuse to fill it with trivial data. If I need to know the answer to that question, I can easily find it, but I prefer to fill my head with more relevant information for my work."* Wow! Educators around the world should have listened as they still force children to memorize facts that will be forgotten within weeks. The left-handed visionary soon saw that many students and leaders in America were prone to become lost in the little stuff with number-crunching becoming a distraction in looking at other larger concepts that might alter paradigms. Thus, this world-renowned physicist, in teaching doctoral candidates at Princeton, would write on his blackboard an aphorism to help his students get real saying, *"Everything that can be counted doesn't count, and everything that counts, can't be counted."* Even more profound are the words of Alexander the Great who told us, "Greater is an army of sheep led by a lion, than an army of lions led by a sheep."

Chapter Three

Alexander the Great - Providential Power

"Were I not Alexander, I would be Diogenes."

Alexander became the King of Macedonia, leader of the Corinthian League, and the man who would beat the Persian King, Darius. Despite having killed more people than any other warrior in history, he has left a legend of compassionate ambition. Here was a man whose father saw in him the power early and told him, "My son, look out for a kingdom worthy of yourself, for Macedonia is too small." Wow! He internalized the words and went on to conquer most of the known world. And when he did take power he was magnanimous enough to let those conquered to keep their faith and religious autonomy. The new king would ever wear their garments and follow their traditions. Alexander was inspired by the Greek titans of the Iliad and when he landed in Asia Minor to fight against the mighty Persian Empire led by Darius III he would be outnumbered by thousands but went where they didn't expect and utilized methods they were not used to – the mind overcame the machines in this case.

This Macedonian integrated the Grecian world into his Macedonian tribe and then defeated Persia and all would become a heterogeneous arena for many centuries. Sparta was an adversary until he conquered them viciously and, with that creating a Hellenist empire larger than any others before him. This warrior king never lost a battle and would revolutionize the way in which wars would be waged. Why was he able to conquer the world at such a young age? He was steeped in Aristotelian logic and imprinted with a mystical sense of magical potential at a very young age, made to believe he was the son of the mythical gods Zeus and Dionysus, and thus not subject to the rules of mere mortals. With such a mind-imprint, he was able to go where mere mortals only dreamed and conquer the known world by age twenty-eight. Did he pay a price? Yes, and he would be dead by thirty-two.

All warriors pay a price for their ambition. Some feel the price is worth the cost. One of Alexander's many aphorisms offers insight into what drove him, especially when he said, "Were I not Alexander, I would be Diogenes." For those not steeped in Greek lore, Diogenes had carried a lamp around Athens looking for just one honest man. Another prophetic quote of this warrior wunderkind was, *"There is nothing impossible to him who will try."* Alexander was special after that day at age ten when he tamed a wild stallion that grown men feared. That got him the horse and tutoring by Aristotle, since his father saw this young man as someone with huge potential. That potential would reach a pinnacle of power when in Persia he was faced with solving the mystery of the Gordian Knot. Once he pulled his sword and cut it and entered Babylon, he was a man on an impossible mission. For his disciples, he would remain a visionary, but one with an ability to work with the average man saying, *"I would rather excel others in the knowledge of what is excellent than in the extent of my powers and dominion."* The message here is that he knew he had to attract a legion of followers to go with him on his quest to conquer the world. But, he had to know each and to never flaunt his station. Early in life he had discovered that no man is a mountain. He would need other men to take him to where he wanted to go.

Alexander's doting mother, Olympus, was a princess steeped in a mythological mindset. She would rear her talented son to believe he was unlike other boys. Her husband, Philip, was never home. He had taken many women into his life, and she became a fierce and overly possessive mother, filling her son with a deep resentment of his father. She told him that he had been fathered by titan gods and not by King Philip. She mapped out his life before he was able to carry a sword or any other weapon, planting seeds of his majesty and other brazen ideas of being abnormal, thus not having to behave normally. The words of Olympus were more surreal than real, but that is not known to a boy so young. She told him about the exploits of Achilles and Prometheus and actually told him that their sperm had fathered him. Her ideas would make the boy special from a very early age. When Philip passed, he was already steeped in the knowledge and feeling that it was now his time to show his mettle. The first thing his mother did was to send him to Delphi to hear the mystical words of the Oracle who would tell him, "You are invincible my son." The words resonated deep within his psyche and motivated the twenty-one-year-old to embark on a twelve-year journey to conquer the world, from which he never returned. Success for Alexander was always a bizarre trek to conquer the world. For him, it was okay to go beyond the realm of the possible where the improbable becomes possible. The words of the oracle would resonate in him for the rest of his short life. Nurtured by Aristotle and others, he would become the most celebrated member of the Aegean Dynasty, creating of one of the largest empires in ancient history. Normal was not in his lexicon and, being left-handed made him feel he was special just as his tutor Aristotle. The right-hemisphere dominance of the off-handed warrior also gave him an advantage in hand-to-hand combat with the ability of empathetic insight—one more edge. Believing he was a little god offered further advantages in the form of self-esteem that educators would later describe as a High Internal Locus of Control – more simply as the belief that any mission is possible. Those inner feelings of power permitted Alexander to go where mere mortals feared. He would become the messiah of legions of men who followed him on his perilous journeys.

The Path to Glory of a Philosopher King

Early in life Alexander was tutored by Acarnian Lysimahus who had him play a game where he would be Achilles, the mythical warrior protagonist out of Homer's book *The Iliad.* It would leave an impression of heroism that would last his whole life. As a background on such modeling behavior, the psychological concept of modeling to find success is known as NLP – Neuro-Linguistic Programming. It is basically about mimicking the behavior of a superstar to attain a similar ability. Such modeling has been found to work better than reading about a skill or even practicing it. It involves watching an expert, and then emulating their acts and deeds. Alexander saw the titan, Achilles, as a heroic being. He emulated his acts for the rest of his life. Those so inclined have been found to reach eminence faster than those taking a more traditional path.

When Alexander was ten, his father, Philip, purchased a beautiful wild stallion from a horse trader and tried to ride it. The horse refused to be mounted by Philip and his other macho men. The horse wanted to be free. Philip ordered it to be taken away. Alexander saw something and asked if he could solve the problem and mount the wild horse. With intuitive powers, he sensed that the horse's fear had come from a fear of his own shadow. So, he led the animal out of the sun and mounted it to the amazement of the men and his dad. Today, psychologists understand the interactions between men and animals. Teachers of Organizational Behavior have been known to have their students approach a horse in a field and find that those who approach the horse with a bad attitude or fear are unable to work with the horse. Those approaching the horse with a positive mindset will find the horse snuggling them and wanting to be stroked. The horse knows. When Philip saw his son mount and control this wild beast, he was overjoyed and interpreted it as great courage and ambition. He walked up to his wayward son and kissed him tearfully, declaring, *"My boy, you must find a kingdom big enough for your ambitions. Macedon is too small for you."* He purchased the horse for his son and then hired the great philosopher Aristotle to instruct him on the wiles of the world from age thirteen until he was sixteen.

In 336 BC, Alexander would follow his father on the throne of Macedon after Philip was assassinated by Pausanias, the captain of his bodyguard. As Pausanias tried to escape, he tripped over a vine and was killed by his pursuers; two of whom were Alexander's companions - Perdiccas and Leonnatus. Alexander was immediately proclaimed king by the Macedonian army. The new man in charge was only twenty, but old beyond his years - having been groomed for this role for many years. He immediately followed his father's path in attempting to merge the various city-states of mainland Greece. One of his battles would come against the Persian King, Darius III, at a mountain past northwestern Syria. In this battle, there were 30,000 Macedonians under Alexander's command, but it was a much smaller force that Darius had. And, the Persians were elite fighters and not accustomed to losing. Roman historian, Curtius, wrote of how Alexander raised the morale of the Macedonians through the power of words, despite their huge disadvantage. This would be repeated many centuries later by one of Alexander's patrons, Napoleon, and later again by General George Patton in World War II.

Darius's army greatly outnumbered the Macedonians in the *Battle of Issus,* and when Alexander won, tens of thousands of Persians, Greeks, and Asians were dead, but a new king was crowned. King Darius fled in panic before the Macedonian king, leaving his mother, wife, and children behind. The way Alexander dealt with them would become a lasting tribute to his being a conquering warrior. He treated the family of his enemy kindly and with respect for their royalty. Such moral dignity of a conquering hero would leave its mark on his adversaries who were used to being slaughtered when captured. When Alexander entered Babylon, the kingdom established millenniums before by Cyrus, the populace treated him with great majesty as a hero and their new ruler. They crowned this Macedonian intruder as King of Babylon and saw him as a divinity that had come to take care of them. His having cut the Gordian Knot played a part in his new role. Cutting the Knot was an impetuous act of a twenty-three-year-old that was now on a roll. When he entered Babylon, the prophecy he had broken would lead him to believe in his own mystical powers. It wouldn't be long before he attacked Egypt and founded the city of Alexandria after having marched through Gaza. The Egyptians hailed him as a god as this Macedonian had freed them from Persian rule. They anointed him as a Pharaoh, since once again he honored their cultural heritage and respected their temples of worship. Historians have cited this period (he was still just twenty-five-years-old) as a time he began to think that he was messianic and had been sent to save the world. That spawned his movement into Cyprus and then East to Afghanistan and India.

Early Years and Trek to Eminence

Alexander was born in Pella in 356 BC and in those glory days of Greek Philosophy Alexander would benefit as a boy with a higher calling and a mission as the Prince of Macedonia and taught from the master logician Aristotle how to marry mind and methodologies to a larger end. The three years with this great philosopher left its mark on the boy who was now groomed for great things than the little nation of Macedonia. Alexander had grown into a man with global insights. Aristotle had bestowed on his pupil a formalized system for reasoning, observing that the validity of any argument can be determined by its structure rather than its content. A classic example of an Aristotelian argument is his syllogism: *All men are mortal; Socrates is a man; therefore, Socrates is mortal.* It would be no accident that when such a man is your tutor that you too become very special. It would be in Plato's Academy where Alexander was groomed for greatness in the words and wisdom of men who would later be called the seat of Western civilization. Philip offered the job of training his son to Aristotle, and Philip gave them the Temple of the Nymphs as their classroom.

Alexander's first army had 25,000 Macedonians, 7,600 Greeks, and 7,000 Thracians. His chief officers were Macedonian, placed in charge in order to ensure the foreign troops under their command would remain faithful. Even the Grecians served under Macedonian chiefs and were given limited tasks. It was normal for a Greek to enter Alexander's service from an Aegean or Asian city through the practice of some special skill set or other advantage. If this soldier could read and write, keep figures, or sail, he would be accepted. Some Grecians from the mother country would also move into military service. It was a fact that the role of a Greek man in Alexander's service was not much different from what their role had been in their own culture. Once Alexander ascended to the Macedonian throne, he quickly killed all of his Athenian enemies by ordering their execution. Like a sage warrior, he could not afford to have enemies within his ranks. He wanted men following him to be friends and allies for the fight that would be far away from Macedonia. Philip's death had led to a series of rebellions among the conquered nations and the Illyrians and Thracians. This occurrence had many opting for a chance for independence. Knowing this, Alexander acted swiftly. His first move was to lead his army into Greece, despite the fact that the roads leading there were blocked by many adversaries. As soon as his Macedonian rule was certain in northern Greece, he marched south. His speed and audacity shocked the Greeks, and he took the nation by storm. They had no choice but to give him power and he was just twenty-one. Believing Greece would remain calm Alexander returned to Macedonia and led his armies east into Thrace. His march would proceed as far as the Danube River. In a series of battles, he drove the rebels beyond the river. He could have continued, but his mind was on the Persians who had been the menace of Macedonia for many centuries. After his victories, he marched back across Macedonia. In one week, he crushed the threatening Illyrians. Then Alexander led his men into Asia Minor where his first action was to free the Greek city of Ionia from Persian rule. From there, he marched into Syria, then into Phoenicia, and finally donned his warrior wizardry into Egypt.

Alexander's namesake would be born in the new city of Alexandria. It would become the bastion of Greek pedagogy and culture for the next 150 years. In his conquest against a Persian island, this boy king opted for a siege strategy, surrounding the island with ships and blasting the city walls with catapults. When the walls were finally breached, his Macedonian men poured their anger over the city defenders killing 7,000 people, selling another 30,000 as slaves. Alexander would enter their temple of Melcart and did a sacrifice. Success was beginning to beget more success and he was on his way to glory.

Charismatic Power Proves Prophetic

In *The Campaigns of Alexander*, Arrian would describe him as a young titan possessing great personal beauty, invincible power of endurance, and a keen intellect. He described him as being a very brave and adventurous warrior. Historians describe the boy wander as being temperate in the bodily pleasures, although his libidinal passions were insatiable as is the case of those with high testosterone that becomes the fuel driving their lives and loves.

Being a left-handed warrior would contribute to his role of being different. Here was a visionary who saw the big picture more than his adversaries; a warrior with a penchant for taking complex situations and simplifying them to his needs. No con-men or liar ever caught him off-guard, and his strength was that his word was his bond and he was always inviolable. Alexander would spend much of his time and energies in trying to do what was right in his burgeoning empire. One magnanimous move took place when he defeated his adversary, Porus, on the banks of Hydaspes. Here, he had taken over a massive new territory and could have destroyed his adversary, but he did not. He would permit his one-time enemy to rule his own Indian people, extending the borders of his original powers. During the siege of Miletus, the empathetic Alexander felt pity for the besieged people. He made a truce with them, but then found that they refused to be ruled and wanted to fight to the death. The new Achilles pardoned the starving soldiers who had stolen food during the march through the Gedrosian desert. It would be these attributes that would be his legacy, and it led to great dignity, admiration, and a magnetic attraction to both friend and foe.

Alexander was a mesmerizing magnate who was quite compassionate toward women, a by-product of his close relationship with his adoring mother. Consequently, those cities he conquered made him a hero and, in the long run, made him a charismatic maestro. After the torrid battle of Issus, he would show total compassion for his enemy's family. Upon his arrival in Babylon, the family of Darius was grieving in the belief that Darius had been killed in battle. Alexander explained to them that he was still alive, but he had fled for his life. In total acquiescence to their royalty, Alexander treated them all honorably. When Darius's soldiers came to rescue Darius's mother, she refused to leave since she felt very comfortable in the rule of Alexander. After Alexander died, she mourned his demise and fasted to her own death. That is charismatic power.

It was a fact that Alexander loathed the rape and abuse of women. This is quite remarkable for the era since those that won were supposed to feast on their enemy's money and women, and their children were to be taken as hostages. They were considered legitimate spoils of war that included the raping of the young women. On one noteworthy occasion, Alexander was offered one hundred armed girls by the viceroy of Media. But, he dismissed them from the army, fearing that they might get violated.

Shaman Fantasies as Motivational Mantras

Alexander was a precocious child of a princess and king, and he was tutored early in the majestic power of the Greek Titans of Homer. His shaman experience would be the heroic warrior, Achilles, who became a lifelong mythical mentor. That early training left an indelible imprint and he would try to emulate his hero for the rest of his life. *The Iliad* was his book of choice, and like most eldest born, he escaped into books and wild stories of past heroes. In the book, Achilles was merciless to those he conquered. He took the royal women to his bed to lie with once their leaders were beaten. Until the end, Alexander slept with his favorite book under his pillow as well as a sword. He could have had any of the women in the city, but he did not. He venerated Achilles in war and his hero in peace was Heracles – the Greek titan who labored for the good of mankind. Together, these two fantasy mentors would lead to a man who was vicious in battle, but benevolent once his foe had been vanquished and his life was almost arcane in a mystical way.

Alexander had been armed with a kind of Nietzschean will-to-power by his teacher Aristotle. His belief that he was a god-like man would program his mind with grandiose ideas that were more god-like than man-like. His mother's mystical influence left an indelible imprint in his mind and his heart. Historians have noted that danger was his pal and he flirted with disaster, as it seemed to turn him on like some elixir of life. Achilles was such an influence that he would read of his exploits just prior to each battle to see what his hero would do in such a situation. It would be the one trait that separated Alexander from the also-rans in history. Modern psychology has noted modeling behavior would make a man special and Alexander is a poster child for this axiom. Watch someone putt a golf ball and you will putt it much better than if you actually practice putting. That is true in sports, business, and battle. The visions in the mind are far more important than skill sets. An example of this in Alexander's time is when he once spared the city of Phthia since it was the city where his hero, Achilles, was born.

Transformational Epiphany of Warriors

The most dominant influence in Alexander's early life was having been asked by a tutor to emulate Achilles while learning about Homer's *The Iliad*. Those games would never leave this man who truly believed he was a warrior titan in the image of Achilles. When Alexander was ten, it was his temerity in taming the wild horse that proved to be transformational throughout his life. Such experiences are what remakes men and are often a metamorphosis of the mind. A few years later, another transformational experience occurred that would mold his mind and heart. He was a teenager enjoying honoring his father's new bride, Cleopatra, despite his still being betrothed to Alexander's mother, Olympus. One of Philip's generals, Attalus, would make a repulsive remark about Philip now being able to father a legitimate heir—implying that Alexander was illegitimate. Today, it would be equivalent to calling Alexander a bastard and that he was not of pure Macedonian blood since his mother was from a nation outside Macedonia. Alexander threw a cup of wine at this drunken general for implying that he was illegitimate. Philip was intoxicated, yet shocked that his son would throw wine in the face of his generals. He stood up and drew his sword. He charged at Alexander, but would trip and fall on his face in a drunken stupor. With that, Alexander, upset was ready to do battle with the world, including his father, the king. And, to assuage, his loving mother shouted, *"Here is the man who was making ready to cross from Europe to Asia and cannot even cross from one table to another without losing his balance."* Expecting the worst, Alexander fled with his mother to Epirus and would not return for a couple of years when the animosity had waned. But, his relationship with Philip would never again be the same. Alexander would remain isolated and somewhat insecure in the Macedonian court. In the spring of 336 BC, with Philip's Persian invasion already set in motion, Philip was assassinated by Pausanias, a young Macedonian noble, during a wedding ceremony in Aegae. Why Pausanias killed the king remains unanswered through history.

Eccentric Wizardry & Empowerment

This son of Zeus - his mother told him he was conceived by Zeus - had a mythical life from an early age. It would create a warrior who was always willing to follow his own causes and never bow to those of more traditional men. Being left-handed had given him a right-hemispheric sense of the world around him. It made him feel unique and empowered him to be diverse. Being left-handed gave Alexander an advantage in kid's games and later when engaging in hand-to-hand combat, he was prone to distinctive moves not expected by an adversary. Mary Renault wrote in her biography of his homosexual behavior and other eccentricities saying, *"The real loves of his life were friendships, including his sexual loves. Though he had the classic family pattern for homosexuality, it was probably the mere availability of men rather than women which directed his emotional life."* Olympus had told him when quite young that King Philip was not his father and that he was a supernatural being. Author Renault would add to this writing, *"That this man did not emerge a psychopath like Nero is one of history's miracles."* This author has found many anomalies and eccentricities in the psycho-biographies of the eminent. Most were of that ilk due to having received wayward *"success imprints"* early in life that made them renegades on an impossible mission. When an eight-year old is told, *"You are sure godlike,"* it leaves a surrealistic mind-imprint. Studies show that "super learning" occurs during youth since kids are in a "theta state" of mystical reverie, such as what happens for adults just prior to falling asleep or waking. Children walk around in this theta state and it is why they learn new languages quicker than adults and also adapt quicker. When a cousin looks at a ten-year-old and tells him, "You are going to make a great gang leader," there is a strong likelihood for the boy to grow up seeking such a destiny. But, in the case of Alexander who was told by a doting mother that he had god-like blood flowing through his veins, he felt empowered to go where mere mortals were not inclined to go.

Alexander had many *success imprints* programmed in his mind and being tutored by Aristotle would have a lasting impact on his personality and leadership acumen. These would lead inextricably to a long and amazing military career. In the spring of 327 BC, Alexander and his army marched into India, invading Punjab. One of his greatest battles would take place that day on the shores of the river Hydaspes. King Porus was one of the most powerful Indian rulers that he would defeat. It was in the summer of 326 BC when Alexander's army crossed the heavily defended river during a violent thunderstorm to engage Porus and defeat the Indian ruler in a fierce battle. During this battle, the Macedonian army would come face-to-face with an enemy riding elephants as their cavalry. The Macedonians had never seen such a combative force before, but they persevered and captured Porus. Respecting the cultural differences and rights of his captive, Alexander permitted him to continue to govern his people. In this battle, Alexander's horse, Bucephalus, was wounded and died. Alexander had ridden Bucephalus into every one of his battles in Europe and Asia, so when the stallion passed, he was grief-stricken and founded a city which he named "Buckephalia," in his horse's name.

World Wide Influence

General Norman Schwarzkopf told *PBS* that his role model was Alexander, saying, "When I was a young man, everything was shades of black and white and Alexander was one of my heroes, because he conquered the entire known world by the time he was twenty-eight." Earlier, the Little Corsican would admit the same and in his memoirs admitted that the reason he had led French forces into Egypt was because his hero-mentor had done so a couple millenniums earlier. For France in the early nineteenth century, it made absolutely no sense, but in the mind of Napoleon, it did. When he was victorious and put on a pedestal as a reigning monarch, it was pure joy. Many historians have spoken of Alexander as having Hellenized the modern world. His major influence was both strategic and tactical, for he was not a man of just weapons and guns, but a warrior on a trek to humanize the rest of the world. Alexander's authority would stretch from Eastern Europe into India. A shining example of his influence was the way he defeated an adversary and then set them up to rule under his authority. When he defeated the Persians, he appointed many Persians as provincial governors in his new empire. Then, to the amazement of his Macedonian warriors, he pushed the window of opportunity even further by adopting the Persian dress for ceremonies and enlisted Persian soldiers to serve in his armies. He even encouraged his Macedonian troops to marry Persian women. After conquering Persia and marching into India and winning battle after battle, he would make rash decisions. Once, he held a great victory celebration at Susa where he and eighty of his closest friends married Persian noblewomen. He would legitimize these marriages between his men and women of the occupied territories and gave them rich wedding gifts.

One of the legacies of Alexander was his willingness to place himself in harm's way when in the middle of a merciless battle. He would not ask any man to go where he would not. That fearless kind of move would become a similar action in the heroics of Napoleon and George Patton. Alexander would always ride up to the very front of a siege and then speak to his men and call each out by their first name. They responded in kind since they knew their leader was there for them and he too would fight to his death. They did likewise.

The Macedonians won every battle due to Alexander's personal courage. He was a master of motivation and innovation and was one of the first to offer his troops gold and other incentives if they succeeded in a battle to the death. Due to this, his armies would become the world's liberators and would subdue all races on Earth – from Europe to the Far East. In the early days of his leadership, he was interested in attaining a closer alliance with the Greeks against the hated Persians and had to defeat them to do so. The Persians had burned their temples and cities and raped their women, but Alexander turned to Aristotelian logic to win them over. He would leave a legacy of mindful ambition saying, *"I had rather excel others in the knowledge of what is excellent than in the extent of my power and dominion."* Here are words of a rebel with a purpose who was willing to lead his men into battle at the head of the cavalry. Often, he was stabbed or shot with arrows and sometimes clubbed, but he refused to be deterred by such wounds. During one desert March, hundreds of Alexander's men fell from exhaustion and dehydration. Yet, some of his men found some much-needed water. They offered water to their leader and Alexander dumped it on the ground choosing to share every discomfort of his soldiers. Such valor would make

Alexander an inspiration for later conquerors such as Hannibal, Pompey, Caesar, and Napoleon.

Toward the end of his reign, Alexander would win a battle with Opis. At the victory celebration, he allowed 10,000 Macedonian veterans to be sent home to their families and he gave Craterus orders to replace Antipater and have him send new reinforcements to him in Asia. But, the army mutinied. An enraged Alexander found the ring leaders and had them punished. Then he stood before them and gave a famous speech reminding the Macedonians that without him they would have still been living under the tutelage of Persia. Because of his deeds and decisions, they were now a powerful force in the world. This reconciled the men with their king and 10,000 of them set out for home leaving their children of Asian women with Alexander. At this time, another 30,000 Persian youth had been trained in the Macedonian ways of war and were recruited to be in his army. Alexander prayed for unity between Macedonians and Persians, and by breeding a new army of mixed blood, he hoped to create a new royal army, which would be under his tutelage.

However, Alexander would never see this magnanimous idea take place as he contracted a high fever after attending a private party for Medius of Larisa. It was due to malaria. As he drank from the cup, he shrieked aloud as if struck a violent blow as the fever in his body could not tolerate the alcohol. The fever grew worse and worse until he could no longer talk. The Macedonians would file past his bed one last time before he finally succumbed on June 7, 323 BC. This incredible warrior of warriors had drawn his last breath at age thirty-two. Alexander passed without appointing a successor to the Macedonian Empire. The Greeks and Persians mourned his passing as they knew this had been a great man who would very difficult to replace. The Wall Street Journal in 2011 wrote an editorial in which they called Alexander of Macedon "The greatest of them all, that even a pacifist age in which we live could not wither the incomparable mystique and terrifying glamour" of this warrior wizard.

Chapter Four

Joan of Arc – Pre-Ordained Power

"I am not afraid. I was born to do this."

How could an illiterate, teenaged, peasant girl convince a king to give her command of his army to attack the nation's mortal enemy, the British? Easy! Joan of Arc had a powerful and mesmerizing message delivered with guile to a weakened monarch who had no idea of how to beat the British who had occupied France for many years. This all took place at the end of the infamous 100 Years War between France and Britain and timing is everything for warriors who rise to the pinnacle of power.

Henry V had invaded France near Burgundy in 1415 when Joan was just three-years-old. Why? The British king had been asked to come to France's defense of their insane King, Charles I. The plan was for King Henry to marry Charles's daughter and thus inherit the throne of France on Charles's death. The Treaty of Troyes made all this possible as it had disinherited the insane king's son, the Dauphin, living in a kind of exile in Southern France. Charles II was without much power and was terrified that the British would invade southern France and remove any chance for him to ever take the throne of France. The key city in this wacky game was the city of Orleans. This bizarre scenario was taking place while Joan was growing up on a farm in the area. In 1429, Joan was sixteen and had been thinking about some visions from above while working on her father's ranch. She had been wondering how to use her new-found insights to keep France independent and not a vassal of Britain. It was at the time when it appeared Orleans was about to fall to the hated British, and it would push her to the limits. She would do something she would never have done had the future of France not been in the balance. If the British took Orleans, Charles II would never ascend to the throne.

When Orleans was near the end, both Henry V of Britain and Charles I died. One of the ironies in this Greek Tragedy is that Joan's birth town of Domremy was one of the few places in France still holding allegiance to Charles II, a very weak dauphin who had no idea how to deal with the tragedy about to take place. It had been three years since Joan had been visited in the fields near her farm by St. Michael, St. Catherine, and St. Margaret. They told this peasant girl the secrets of saving her homeland. Later, under questioning, she would retell, *"They told me of the pitiful state of France, and told me that I must go to succor the King of France."* She made a few feeble attempts to talk to the authorities in power, but to no avail. On her third try, the king, who was at his wit's end, agreed to see her. Charles was told not to listen to some peasant girl, as it was a waste of his time, at best. Charles soon discovered that this was a poor, uneducated peasant with no power. But he was distraught and knew of no other solutions to his great dilemma. A mystical man nurtured in a highly Roman Catholic nation, he was not quite sure if this teenaged girl might not just have a direct conduit to God. As is the case with many weak leaders, Charles the Dauphin, was cowering from the long One Hundred Years War with England and was lost in what to do. French visionary Marie d'Avignon would influence him since he had been preaching to all who would listen that the nation was being destroyed by inaction and could only come back to its once lofty place of power by an armed virgin from the marshes of Lorraine. How prophetic were these words that were in concert with this young teenager who came from nowhere to offer to save the nation and king.

It was almost too coincidental for Charles to ignore when Joan showed up as a messenger of God, offering to personally deliver the country back to self-rule. Amazingly, just as her voices had instructed, Joan would become the angel that would lead some troops and cause the Dauphin Charles to regain power and be coronated as the French King. As word of her achievements against the English occupying forces spread, there was talk that a "*saint*" was leading the French to victory with the help of God.

The simplicity of the message and deeds of the Maid of Orleans was her legacy, and this guileless girl would show up with a calm assurance and give the men the power to achieve success. This was highly unlikely for an autocratic country unused to giving power to the little people. Power was found only in those from the aristocracy, the landed gentry, or mother church. No woman was a part of these, as they were vassals in the hands of a paternalistic land and they were told to use their power in the kitchen. In February 1429, this teenaged warrior would be accompanied by six men carrying weapons who led her into the court to be scrutinized. Joan had set out on her perilous journey to the court of the dauphin at Chinon expecting to be given power to fight for the French against the hated British. Charles was reticent, but had no other answer. The popular opinion in his court interceded and he granted her an interview. In that session, Joan persuaded him to use her as a weapon against the hated British. Charles was still wary and had to test her acuity. He had shown up at the interview in a disguise in an attempt to confuse her in an effort to see if she had a true vision from God. To his amazement, Joan looked right at him in his disguise as a courtier. That would prove to be one of many convincing acts that would give Charles assurance that she was truly a power from above.

During her meeting, the girl with a surreal power from within would impress the dauphin with a secret prayer that he would tell his confidantes, and could only be known by God. During this initial meeting, Charles had Joan checked out by a commission of doctors as well as a council of matrons who reported that she was still a virgin and nothing evil was lurking in her soul. Charles gave permission for this girl with a fighting spirit to take on the Brits with an army of 5,000 men to retake Orleans. Joan came to her role donned in a coat of mail, armed with an ancient sword that was rumored to have been used by Charles Martel to vanquish the Saracens. In her possession was also a white standard of her own design embroidered with lilies with an image of God seated on the clouds and holding the world in his hand on one side. On the other side was a representation of the Roman Catholic Annunciation. Joan would enter the city of Orleans on the 29th of April 1429. With great pomposity, she led an army of men with unremitting sallies and an indomitable will that would not give up. The English gradually succumbed to her ceaseless barrages and would become discouraged. On May 8th, 1429, they gave up and retreated. In the next month, Joan would lead her charges to victory in both Jargeau and Beaugency. Those were soon followed by a big win at Patay where Talbot was taken prisoner and the hated English invaders were driven beyond the Loire. With some difficulty, the dauphin was then persuaded to set out toward Reims, which he entered with an army of 12,000 men on the 16th of July. On the following day, holding the sacred banner, Joan stood beside Charles at his coronation in the cathedral.

This teenage girl would become the catalyst that would bring a weak king to power. It is quite interesting how dissenters become allies when it appears the innovator is real and they could gain by backing that individual. Such transitory support occurs no matter the era or arena and in this case it was a weak French nation with an ever weaker sovereign who would give Joan the power to lead an army against the hated British. During the first days of her arrival the generals and other military leaders purposely tried to mislead the young Maid of Orleans and tried to have her believe they would be somewhere different than they would actually be stationed. When Joan discovered the duplicity, she immediately went to where they were, and exclaimed with great indignation, *"In God's name, the counsel of the Lord your God is wiser and safer than yours. You thought to deceive me and it is yourself above all whom you deceive, for I bring you better succor than has reached you from any soldier, in any city; it is succor from the King of Heaven!"* Such was the power within that would grant Joan many disciples during her short stint as the young girl who had created a kingdom.

The Path to Glory

One thesis of this work is that Promethean personalities – in psychology this is a person who sees the big picture and deals with what they see in a very structured manner – are the ones who alter paradigms and improve the world. They are change-masters and leaders in the likes of Abraham Lincoln, Albert Einstein, and Thomas Edison. Such wizardly warriors go where the pack fears and deal with what they see in a very rational manner. They are the world's change-masters who go where the meek fear, and are often in unknown venues, but are never lost. Traditionalists tend to avoid these types like the plague until some magical insight such as what happened with Joan brings them into the fold. This happened to Einstein, who, in his theory of relativity, was released. He was laughed at, cajoled, and unable to get a teaching position. He was employed at the Postal Service in Switzerland since no university would hire him. Only when his theory of relativity was accepted as truth was he able to get a job, and that was not for fifteen years. Finally, he was considered a genius and given a Nobel Prize. Mark Twain had his innovative novels *Huckleberry Finn* and *Tom Sawyer* banned in Boston. It would take him years to be accepted, and then he became the literary maven of an era. Such is the way of the world if you are pushing the limits of belief by traditionalists. One evaluation of a historian on Joan described her as:

> **"This maid has a virile bearing, speaks little, and shows an admirable prudence in all her words. She has a pretty, woman's voice, eats little, drinks very little wine, she enjoys riding a horse and takes pleasure in fine arms, greatly likes the company of noble fighting men, detests numerous assemblies and meetings and readily sheds copious tears and has a cheerful face."**

Wow! This description of a young woman on a trek to save her nation defines the quintessential change-maker labeled a "Promethean personality," not unlike that of later female icons such as Catherine the Great, Golda Meir, and Margaret Thatcher. Such women represent a very small percentage of any given cohort, but they have a larger vision and deal with it very adroitly. They have an indomitable spirit that will not be quenched by the establishment. In repeated psychological studies, they represent a very small percentage of any cohort. Joan was of similar ilk, although in Jungian terms, she was far more emotionally driven – a feeling type of temperament that drove her words and deeds. The Maid of Orleans dealt with her vision in a very heart-felt manner and it would lead to her death by the dogmatic rationalistic males in power.

An example of her feminine guile comes from biographer, Perceval de Boulainvilles, who wrote, *"This maid has certain elegance and is a pretty woman."* These words offset those that would describe her as a malicious woman on a power trip for personal aggrandizement. She could easily have been characterized as one of the most odious persons in the arena and historians would have demeaned her rather than anointing her as St. Joan. Had she been older, she would not have been maligned.

The irony of her life and work as a warrior is interesting in that the men she led into battle in that era were typically old enough to be her father. She often humiliated them and showed that she was right in her strategy to destroy the hated British. She learned early to flatter and manage them, but was savvy enough not to come on too strong so as to demean their manhood. But, it was not enough to keep them from having her burned at the stake for being a heretic. When she was brought before the court by her British captors, she was interrogated by dogmatic, macho men from the cloth. It was the Bishop of Cauchon who would interrogate her under oath. Her testimony was as follows:

Question: Do you swear to speak the truth in answer to such questions as are put to you?

Joan: I do not know what you wish to examine me on. Perhaps you might ask such things that I would not tell.

Question: Will you swear to speak the truth upon those things which are asked you concerning the faith, which you know?

Joan: Concerning my father and my mother, and what I have done since I took the road to France, I will gladly swear to tell the truth. But concerning my revelations from God, these I have never told or revealed to anyone, save only to Charles, my King. And I will not reveal them to save my head.

The majesty of Joan was proven both in battle and in court as she daringly came attired in men's clothes. This was highly taboo in fifteenth century France. This young girl who was living in a paternalistic society, but dared play the *maternalistic maiden,* dumbfounded her prosecutors. When she mounted her horse like a man instead of a woman, the men were aghast. When questioned, she told her adversaries that she was not messing with her virginity, but keeping it intact since as a pretty teenage girl in that era she would have certainly been molested or raped. While in prison, the prospect of rape was very high and not looking female would keep the male molesters from her.

The English knew that an androgynous Joan would raise the ire of the traditionalists prosecuting her. Her showing up in pants and male clothing would be the nail in her coffin in the minds of the English who charged a case against her. It would indeed send her to the stake. One of the interesting things in life is that perception is often reality for those with less awareness. In Joan's case, it would lead to her destruction. But, when she was leading male soldiers into battle, her androgyny was crucial for success. Had she shown up in a woman's clothing and rode her mount side-saddle, she would never have found a man to follow her. Joan succeeded because she dared to be different. This is often lost on macho dogmatists.

Early Years and Trek to Eminence

Joan of Arc was christened Jeanneton Darc. Later, she would be called Joan d Arc. When put in charge of an army, she would be labeled the "Maid of Orleans." She was born in 1412, the daughter of Jacques Darc, peasant proprietor of a farm in Domremy, France. It was located between Champagne and Lorraine. Her parents were what today would be called middle-class. Joan never learned to read or write and received her sole religious instruction from her mother who taught her to recite the Pater Noster, Ave Maria, and Credo. Joan spent her early youth watching over her father's flocks in the fields of France. In her trial in 1431, she strongly resented being referred to as a shepherd girl. She had been quite exacting in everything she did. Today, a psychologist would label her a *"perfectionist."* During her childhood, she was known as a girl with incredible energy and vivacity of spirit. She was certainly not unfeminine in any way as some historians are want to say because of her androgynous nature when attacking the British. She had a strong emotional nature that Carl Jung would later label as one with *feeling,* as these types make most decisions in a very emotional manner. Joan was an exemplary child and it made her a favorite in the village where she grew up. A great deal of evidence shows that she was the classic introvert – energized from within – although the less aware think that such an overt personality is extroverted. Extroversion and Introversion are a function of how one is energized – internally or externally and not how much one talks. Joan has been seen as a girl who was a pontificating zealot, but so was Hitler—a pathologically shy warrior, and Gandhi who was also highly introverted beyond the norm. When an introvert like Joan speaks, people listen, as was the case for the introverted Ayn Rand or Danielle Steel. When these women spoke, they came across with a strong acerbic rhetoric. Joan was of a similar nature—an attractive teenager who repelled all attempts of the young men of her acquaintance to win her favor. When she was imprisoned and waiting to be tried, she agreed to wear feminine clothing, but then changed back to her male outfits when she saw males stalking her. When queried on this, she told a tribunal member, "a great English lord entered her prison and tried to take her by force." She resumed male attire either as a defense against molestation or, in the testimony of Jean Massieu, because her dress had been stolen and she was left with nothing else to wear.

Charismatic Powers Proved Prophetic

Joan used an unusual art of persuasion to convince Charles VII to give her power. Duke John II of Alençon helped her in this, but you can be assured anyone backing her had been mesmerized by her power of persuasion. Those in power would give her royal permission for her plan to recapture nearby bridges along the Loire as a prelude to an advance on Reims and the coronation of Charles VII. One point in Joan's path to glory was her ability to analyze the words of the power elite and discern when they were true and not so true. When she was counseled that the nearby city under siege was well provided for and the city should not be attacked, she saw through the ruse and refused to comply. Angry at the male military elite's lack of faith in her counsel, she told them, *"You have been at your counsel, and I at mine, and I know that my Lord's counsel will be accomplished and will prevail and that your counsel will perish."* Her charismatic words of passion would be enough to bring adversaries to their knees and disciples to her side. Despite having no educational training in the art, Joan was driven by the words of God. She would tell her patrons, *"In God's name, the soldiers will fight and God will give them victory."* Joan offered this response when asked why she needed soldiers. If God wished to deliver France, why didn't he give her the power or the men? After gaining approval from the Church theologians that examined her, Joan was given command of an army.

Charles was impressed by this teenaged girl's strong demeanor and knowledge of what was transpiring in a heated war. Prayer had become her power and Charles was shocked at how a girl without learning or heritage could be so bold. When he gave Joan the power to lead an army, she showed up clothed in a coat of mail, armed with an ancient sword, and refused to be diffused by adversaries. Upon receiving the power to lead the men, Joan entered Orleans and vanquished the enemy to the amazement of even those that had supported her. History has acclaimed that it was Joan who caused this to happen due to extraordinary pluck and a mystical sense of leadership. As she won battle after battle with a woman's demeanor, it would become her indomitable spirit that mesmerized those assigned to her. Believing would attract many disciples.

Shaman Fantasies as Motivational Mantras

Joan of Arc's shamanic Legacy provides an intimate portrait of history's most enigmatic military leader. Her elevation to power would be one of the most dramatic acts in history. She used mystical messages with surrealistic implications to make her be marked with the French aristocracy. When one believes they are right, even if they have no clue of their messages, they can do some amazing things. Examining the external and internal forces that shaped the life of this Maid of Orleans it is interesting to see how she refused to permit the externalities to interfere with her internal ideas. She would admit to having had her initial vision in 1424 at the age of twelve. At the time, she was alone in a field when angelic figures appeared to her and told her they were Saint Michael, Saint Catherine, and Saint Margaret. These angelic visages told Joan to take charge and drive out the English and bring the Dauphin to Reims for his coronation as the true king of France. She was not sure what to do once the angelic figures in the sky left and she was forced to deal with what they had told her. When she was sixteen, she asked a relative, Durand Lassois, to bring her to the nearby garrison commander, Count Robert de Baudricourt for permission to visit the royal French court at Chinon. Upon arrival, she was certainly unique. But, when she spoke, the world listened as she told them:

> **"You Englishmen have
> no right in this Kingdom of France.
> The King of Heaven sends you
> word and warning by me, Jehanne the Maid,
> to abandon your forts
> and depart to your own county,
> or I will raise such a war-cry against you as shall be
> remembered forever!"**

A final warning to the English was issued by Joan on May 5th, 1429. It was ironically on Ascension Day and she would be taken the fort at St. Loups to pursue her quest to drive out the British and lead the king to his throne. On this day, she succumbed to Catholic dogma and decreed that there would be no fighting. Her message was sent to the English through the air by a bowman and delivered on the tip of an arrow. Joan was not immediately accepted as a woman who should be listened to. She would hold her own in this paternalistic aristocracy. Later, she would tell of her being disobedient to her parents and would go to confession. She admitted that she left them to travel with the army and told the tribunal, "Since God commanded it, had I a hundred fathers and a hundred mothers, had I been a King's daughter, I should have departed to do my appointed job. Her compassion was without peer and so bizarre it was questioned by those in charge.

Once, she saw a fellow Frenchman leading away some English prisoners and saw a French soldier strike one of the Englishmen so hard on the head that it appeared he might be dead. Upset and angry, Joan dismounted and knelt down next to the dying Englishman, cradling his head in her hand as she heard his final confession and consoled him in his pain. She cried easily when soldiers died without confession or the last rites. She also refused to see those who were not in synch with her message and any women of ill-repute saying, "It was for those sins that God allowed a war to be lost." This woman of God believed in being good and in doing good for the right reasons, and not for money or power.

Epiphany that Proved Transformational

Joan was driven like an empowered missionary from the heavens, but at first no one listened since she was but a poor and uneducated farm girl. When queried about her having heard voices from heaven, she said, "*Of the love or hatred God has for the English, I know nothing, but I do know that they will all be thrown out of France except those who die there.*" While still working on the farm, she would become enamored of a life as a maiden of God saying, "*When I was thirteen years old I had a Voice from God to help me govern my conduct. And the first time I was very fearful, but then came this voice about the hour of noon. It was summer-time and I was in my father's garden. I had not fasted on the eve preceding this day.*" Joan would testify at her trial for heresy that the first voice to visit her was Saint Michael. He had come to offer her guidance and counseling.

He was soon joined by Saint Catherine and Saint Margaret on subsequent visits and she said, "*I have seen them with my corporeal eyes as plainly as I see you, and when they went away from me I wept and I greatly wished they had taken me with them.*"

It is important to understand the background of the era in which Joan lived and played warrior. Her work came toward the end of the Hundred Years War - where two rivals claimed the right to the French throne. Henry VI was a young and vibrant king of England and Charles VII was the rightful kin, but was of questionable mental veracity. Charles was very weak and confined to the region round Bourges and Henry was in London. Joan envisioned that if Charles could fight his way into Reims, he could be crowned king. It would become her life's mission. But in her heart of hearts, she knew she had to tell the king of her visionary ideas. Knowing she had to come on strong with this pathetically weak king, she donned a man's clothes and with six male companions embarked on an eleven-day trek to Chinon. It would take her two more days to finally get an audience with Charles VII. He had been crowned at Poitiers in 1422, but few, including Joan, did not consider him king. Joan was the youngest of five children, a girl who was good at sewing and spinning. From a young age, she was often in church, kneeling for hours in prayer. She was used to being subservient to those in power, but her epiphany came from visages from above and she took the power to run off the British and restore Charles on the throne of France.

Eccentric Wizardry and Empowerment

Like Alexander and Attila the Hun before her, Joan was left-handed and a right-brain visionary. In many other ways, this young girl was unique and came on so strong she would befuddle the male power brokers of the time. George Bernard Shaw writes in the Preface of his play *Saint Joan* on the driving and eccentric nature that came out of a girl on a mission to alter history. Shaw writes:

> **"She is finally canonized in 1920. She is the most notable Warrior Saint in the Christian calendar and the queerest fish among the eccentric worthies of the Middle-Ages. Though a professed and most pious Catholic, and the projector of a Crusade against the Husites, she was in fact one of the first Protestant martyrs."**

The irony in Shaw's words about this new saint is that he had been an avowed atheist for his whole life. He was a fan of the father of Communism, Karl Marx. Another, even greater irony is that he would win his one and only Nobel Prize for Literature in this work on Saint Joan. The curmudgeon would then refuse to accept it as the quintessential eccentric renegade. Like his protagonist St. Joan, he was a man willing to push the windows of conformity. Defiance was his master and thus, he found Saint Joan an ally in will and spirit. He had been the co-founder of the liberal Labor Party in England, despite being Irish and having only made it through the fifth grade in school. Shaw's first eight novels had been summarily rejected by the British publishing industry as well as his first six plays, despite having written *Man & Superman* and *Pygmalion – My Fair Lady*. He would offer insights on Joan's life in his play as he obviously felt some kinship with this curmudgeon who was willing to defy the church and societal dogmas, writing:

> **"If Joan had been malicious, selfish, cowardly or stupid she would have been one of the most odious persons known to history instead of one of the most attractive. If she had been old enough to know the effect she was producing on the men whom she humiliated by being right when they were wrong, and had learned to flatter and manage them, she might have lived. But she refused."**

Shaw would go on to draw a parallel between Joan and Napoleon. He would write, "Napoleon, also possessed of terrifying ability, but neither frank nor disinterested, had no illusions as to the nature of his popularity. When he was asked how the world would take his death, he said it would give a gasp of relief. But it is not so easy for mental giants who neither hate nor intend to injure their fellows to realize that nevertheless their fellows hate mental giants and would like to destroy them, not only enviously because the juxtaposition of a superior wounds their vanity, but quite humbly and honestly because it frightens them. Fear will drive men to any extreme; and the fear inspired by a superior being is a mystery which cannot be reasoned away." These words are written in the preface of his play on St. Joan showing that he understood the psychological nuances of what m
ade such a female warrior tick.

Influence on the World

When Joan was finally captured by the British and imprisoned in the castle of Rouen, she was exhibited in a specially-built iron cage barely big enough for her to stand upright. She was chained by the neck with both hands and feet in shackles. On January 9, 1431, Joan was given an informal hearing before a small, hand-picked court. The nine ecclesiastics were pro-English, and during the four sessions, they were often impressed by the answers given by Joan's high-minded insight into what made her do what she had done. There was testimony by women appointed by the Duchess of Bedford that Joan was a virgin - and therefore by implication not a witch. There were favorable reports on her by the royal notaries from her neighbors in Domremy, France. But there were detractors, the most devastating, Bishop Pierre Cauchon, who would draw up several articles to prove that this teenager was a heretic. Initial interrogations were held at Rouen castle on February 21 and 22, 1431, but little of note would occur.

In March, Joan would be examined in her prison cell with examinations focusing on her claim that the voices that she heard were of a divine nature and could have happened and not some ideas by a young, emotional country girl. It was the Bishop's intent to show that she had violated the Church dogmas and refused to accept the authority of the Roman Church as the only master in such matters. The implication in court was that her voices came from the Devil and were concocted by an emotional girl envisioning fairies, a holy tree, and mandrakes while catching butterflies that were unrealistic. On March 27, Joan was brought to formal trial in Rouen castle before thirty-seven clerical judges with seventy counts of heresy made against her. On May 30th, 1431, shortly after noon, Joan of Arc was burned at the stake in Rouen, France for being a heretic. It would only take a couple decades for the people of France to finally realize that Joan was innocent and her charge of witchcraft was an outright fraud of the church's leaders who had capitulated to British influence. Like many such trials, it was little more than a political game played to win their war on France. In 1920, Joan would be made a saint by the Roman Catholic Church.

Joan of Arc was a very caring and brave woman who helped France win the Hundred Years War and that is her primary legacy. In retrospect, Joan gave the French an identity of note since prior to her each person identified themselves as from a region or city in the country. A person before her was labeled by the region in which (s)he was reared or worked, such as being a *Bergundian.* After Joan, the people in France had a more nationalistic identity. Her life and work leave a legacy of *"believe and you can be:* even when that belief may be slightly beyond the pale of belief. The mind is master, and even when it is deluded, it can lead individuals to a destiny far greater than the one that otherwise could have happened.

Saint Joan endures as one of the most famous people of the Middle Ages, not because of some military might or warrior wisdom, but because of a zealous drive to chase her dreams. Her extraordinary life has engaged generations of historians, writers, and artists, as well as many Hollywood film producers, many of whom have used her image to stir an astonishing array of passions. Many works have attempted to put her words and deeds into a new art form. For several centuries, representations of Joan have reflected the historical contexts in which they were created and have been used to promote a huge variety of political, cultural, and religious views. These range from icons of martial ascendancy and nationalist unity to paragons of humble piety and maiden purity. In this work, it coincides with the warrior defying logic and rules when they take a path to empowerment.

Chapter Five

Hernan Cortes – Psyche Power

"I love to travel but hate to arrive."

The Spanish conquistador, Cortes, was a vagabond spirit who said, "*I love to travel but hate to arrive.*" Why is this so important for warrior wizards? Because it demonstrates that they are fueled by a strong need to go where others have never gone and pursue a global rather than local mission in life. Such people are happy when finding new arenas to conquer and are never called xenophobes – those that hate the unknown. Cortes just took off as a young man and landed in the new world fifteen years after Columbus had discovered the Americas. But, unlike Columbus, Cortes was far more the adventurer looking for personal power. While still in his twenties, he would conquer the Aztec empire in Mexico and it would go down in history as one of the more incredibly audacious moves of any warrior. Cortes had no training in the mission he would tackle. But, he would implement it with great majesty and an indomitable mindset. This Spanish warrior became enamored of the pioneering trips of Columbus, envisioning a chance to make his own mark in the New World. He dropped out of law school, jumped on a ship with some Spanish adventurers, and headed for the Americas in 1506. Not long after, he had landed in the Caribbean. He would take part in the conquest of Hispaniola and Cuba, receiving a large estate of land and Indian slaves for his efforts. At twenty-six, Cortés was made clerk to the treasurer with the responsibility of ensuring that the Crown received the *quinto* - one-fifth of the profits from the expedition.

Cortes was quite expressive and would later tell others of his personal power as a warrior, *"He [who] travels safest in the dark night is he who travels lightest."* Using such a strategy helped in his conquest of the Aztec Empire where Cortés was awarded the title of *Marqués del Valle de Oaxaca.* The more prestigious title of Viceroy was given to a high-ranking nobleman, Antonio de Mendoza. It told Cortes that he was not enough the aristocrat in Spanish eyes to have true power, so he kept on moving after his early successes. It would take him back to Spain for a couple years where he would attempt to get backing to become a true power broker in the New Spain of Mexico that he had been instrumental in creating. Despite having married in Cuba, he would have many lovers and wives in Mexico – a trait found in warriors from various cultures such as Attila the Hun, Alexander in Greece, Napoleon in France, Geronimo in America, and Dayan in Israel. Voracious appetites from their high dose of testosterone led them into new lands and fresh beds.

Upon arriving in the land of the Aztecs, he found a native woman, Doña Marina, to be his interpreter, as well as lover. She would bear Cortés a son. Mistress begets mistresses and it would be a gal named "La Malinche" who would mother a child, Martín, who would become his favorite. Another Aztec woman he met was Malinche who was steeped in both the Aztec Nahuatl language and Mayan. This lady enabled Cortés to communicate in both languages with both friends and foes. She would become a very valuable interpreter and counselor for him as well as bedmate. Through her help, Cortés learned from the Tabascans about the wealthy Aztec Empire and its riches. From the start, this conquistador warrior ruled with an iron fist for twelve years. He would leave for other adventures when his power had waned in Mexico. King Charles I of Spain had become the Holy Roman Emperor, Charles V, in 1519. He would appoint Cortés as governor, captain general, and chief justice of the newly conquered territory. In 1529, Cortés was rewarded and named, *"Marqués del Valle de Oaxaca"* – the Marquis of the Oaxaca Valley. It was a noble title and would permit his ancestors to reap the rewards of his work. His assets would be passed down to his descendants until 1811 since the Oaxaca Valley was one of the wealthiest regions of the New Spain. In 1528 when he was forty-three years-old, Cortés would have

23,000 vassals in his command. By 1540, he would return home to Spain to live out his life as a wealthy, honored, but embittered man.

The Path to Glory

Cortes had left Spain for Cuba with 700 men on his vessel. As such, he would become one of the original conquistadores that historians credit with settling the Caribbean nations and ending the long rule of the Aztecs in central and South America. This conquistador landed on the coast of Mexico with a small band of adventurous men and founded the settlement of Veracruz. In this, Cortes had pulled off one of the world's great psychological moves on the way to glory. His initial landing took place in a territory where he would found the city of Vera Cruz.

This man on a mission had left a few men on board his eleven ships. Once all of his five-hundred adventurers where safely ashore, he signaled back to the men on board the ships to light fires and burn the ships into oblivion. Cortes would leave his name etched in history as he looked at his men and told them, "We win or die as there is no way to go back home." That was a brave and pivotal move beyond the pale of most men. It proved this was an ambitious warrior with the temperament of a zealot. And, this was not a small contingent. Although, it was in terms of the Aztecs he would be fighting. With him were the five-hundred men, thirteen horses, and a small number of cannons. From a military perspective, his conquistadors had the advantage over the Mayans in the form of firearms and steel swords and weapons. But, the Mayans and Aztecs had the advantage of established settlements, knowledge of the territory, and a large dose of wanting to remain masters of their own domain. The Aztecs also had a huge edge in numbers of warriors that would prove successful in many of the battles where many Spanish conquistadors would perish.

On November 8, 1519, the conquistador intruders were peacefully received by the Aztec Emperor, Montezuma II. There had been a long-standing Mexican tradition of noble diplomacy in dealing with new immigrants to their land. Montezuma deliberately let Cortés enter the heart of the Aztec Empire in hopes that they could get to know each other and begin a trading agreement with Spain. That would prove beneficial to both cultures, but it was fatal move by Montezuma.

Later, Cortes would offer why he had gone, saying, "We Spaniards have a sickness of heart that only gold can cure." Cortes had entered the city in hopes of learning more about the way Aztecs thought and functioned and to learn of their strengths and weaknesses so he could crush them later. To this end, Cortes came bearing gifts and Montezuma returned the favor with lavish gifts of gold. It only enticed the Spaniards to plunder vast amounts of gold later. In his letters to Charles V in Spain, Cortés claimed to have learned to be either an emissary of the feathered serpent god, Quetzalcoatl, or Quetzalcoatl himself. But, quickly Cortès learned that Spaniards on the coast had been attacked. He decided to take Montezuma as a hostage in his own palace, requesting him to swear allegiance to Charles V. He was a man on a personal mission, as we now know that ninety-five percent of our decisions are self-serving. Cortes validates this as true of warriors like him.

Early Years and Trek to Eminence

Hernan Cortes was born in Mandelin, Spain, in 1485, the only child of Martín Cortés and Catalina Pizarro Altamirano. His birth was just seven years before Columbus would discover America. His parents were of the minor-landed gentry in rural Spain. Hernán, as a child, has been described as "a pale, sickly child" by biographer, chaplain, and friend, Francisco López de Gómara. When he was fourteen, Cortés was sent to study at the University of Salamanca in west-central Spain. It was at the time Spain's great center of learning. While accounts vary as to the nature of Cortés's studies, it appears he studied Law and probably Latin. By the time he was seventeen, he was bitterly disappointed and returned home in 1501. His grandfather envisioned the youngster studying law. However, as he saw it, he had a choice between seeking fame and glory in a war in Italy or trying his luck in the Spanish colonies of the New World. He was lured by the romantic tales of the warriors who had taken ships to the new world and returned with gold. It would inspire him. By the time he was nineteen, he would find a ship on its way to the new world and he signed on as a shipmate and warrior. Hernando arrived in Hispaniola – Santa Domingo of the Dominican Republic. By 1511, he joined an expedition force to nearby Cuba where he became an intimate friend of Governor Diego Velazquez. Diego would make Cortes a magistrate of the number two Spanish town that had been founded on the island. Cortes would then become a true philandering man. He became romantically involved with Catalina Juárez, the sister-in-law of the governor. Velázquez' became unhappy with his friend when he was told of Cortés's affairs. Cortez would finally marry Catalina, reluctantly, under pressure from Governor Velázquez.

It was in 1519 when the governor he had befriended offered him a position as captain of the third expedition to the mainland of Mexico. On the way, he would stop in Trinidad to hire more soldiers to join his small contingent of conquistadors, bringing his force to five-hundred. Once he defeated Montezuma, he would be seen as malcontent and overly ambitious. That is when he split for Mexico as a lone warrior on his own mission of aggrandizement. It would take time, but by 1522, this thirty-seven-year-old would reach his pinnacle of power in the New Spain after he had attacked and conquered Tenochtitlan. History shows that he had killed 240,000 Aztecs.

After his success, the consummate vagabond kept wandering. In 1536, he discovered the peninsula of California that is now known as Baha. The King of France appointed him governor of the New Spain and he would bring in new plants and animals and agreed to convert the Aztec nation to Christianity. In retrospect, he succeeded in his quest in that Mexico is now a Roman Catholic nation. His conquest of Mexico was not as easy as it sounds. The nation he had to overpower was a mountainous nation ruled by a very diverse people – Mayans and Aztecs – who were not compatible. Both ethnic groups were highly steeped in mystical lore, bordering on witch-doctor ideologies. Each saw Cortes as a potential savior and it enhanced his success. The following map offers some insight into the trek he took to reach the domain of the leader Montezuma.

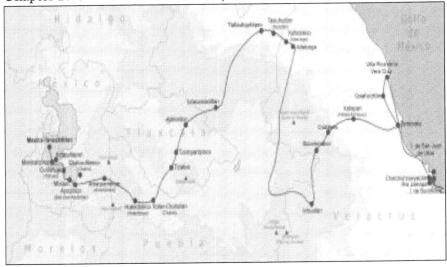

Charismatic Powers Proved Prophetic

Cortes was a very influential conquistador who had that unique ability to talk others into following him to new lands. Here was a man without credentials, education, or other political appointments. However, he would take power in his own hands, and in this case mesmerizing words of finding gold in Aztec country. His words captured the minds and hearts of many young men who followed him and became his disciples and sometimes vassals. An example of his persuasive ability was the fact that this Spanish warrior would end up with many wives from diverse backgrounds. He would father children from them. In that world, power was the aphrodisiac. He used it often and very effectively. His tumultuous battles with the power brokers in Spain, Cuba, Hispaniola, and Mexico always ended with problems that he always seemed able to escape with money and power. When Cortes got to Mexico, he tricked the Aztecs into giving him gold. They gave him plenty, as the Aztecs feared the worst. They gave him money prior to finding that he was interested in making their nation a New Spain.

The local *Totonac* from *Cempoala* greeted him with gifts of food, feathers, gold, and many women in hopes that he would be a friend and then go back to his own land. The many women he seduced were forced to be baptized before he and his conquistador soldiers were allowed to let them to fix supper for them or share their beds. It was not long before ambassadors from the Mexican/Aztec Emperor, Moctezuma II, arrived with additional gifts in order to keep him at bay by satisfying his lusts. It had the opposite effect. Cortés learned that he was suspected of being Quetzalcoatl or an emissary, a legendary man-god who had been predicted to return to reclaim his city. As men of greed tend to do, Cortes permitted the locals to believe he was a god come to save them.

Shaman Fantasies as Motivational Mantras

As discussed above, the Aztecs and Mayans were highly superstitious. They believed in mystical mavens and would consider this new conquistador as a god that had come to save them. He did not tell them differently. When Cortés arrived in Mexico, the Aztecs saw him as a mythical emissary of the feathered serpent god Quetzalcoatl. Cortes was a Catholic due to his Spanish heritage, but not so inclined. He had a very deep mythical mindset that would make him a bit enamored of being revered by this Aztec nation. Relations with the last Aztec emperor, Montezuma, became a means of employing many doctrinaire items as his heritage. He had the palace of his father, Axacayle, prepared as the home of the Spanish and their Indian allies. Cortes then asked for more gifts of gold as a vassal of Charles V from the Aztec nation and demanded two large idols to be removed from the main temple pyramid in the city. There was human blood there from the Aztec nature of human sacrifice to their gods and he demanded it to be cleaned. He then installed shrines devoted to the Virgin Mary and St. Christopher. All of his demands were met.

Epiphany that Proved Transformational

During the reign of Cortes in Mexico, there would come a night when he and his men were forced out of the royal city of Tenochtitlan by rallying Aztecs. They fled and regrouped and would return; the town was nearly destroyed. It turned out to be a two-month siege that retook and destroyed the city. Cortes had dug a one-mile canal to launch battle ships in the lake surrounding Tenochtitlan. Over 200,000 Aztecs, including Montezuma, would perish in this onslaught. Cortes would build his new palace on the ruins of Montezuma's. Cortés never could have pulled off the defeat of the Aztec Empire without a great deal of good luck. In the early days while in Aztec country, he found a man who would help in his quest for power and gold. It was a Spanish priest named "Gerónimo de Aguilar," who had been shipwrecked on the mainland several years before Cortes arrived. Aguilar had mastered the Maya language, and between Aguilar and one of his female lovers, Malinche, Cortés was able to communicate effectively during his conquest of Montezuma. Cortés also had luck in terms of the Aztec vassal states that were being governed by others, but in reality, hated them. Cortés came in as their savior from afar and would become a master of using this to gain power. Historians spoke of his being astute at exploiting this hatred between the Mayans and Aztecs. With thousands of native warriors as allies, this conquistador from Spain was able to meet the Aztecs on strong terms and bring about their downfall. It also helped that the high-priest, Montezuma, was a weak leader. He was a kind of medicine man who had to speak to a divinity prior to making any decision. Cortés came to believe that Montezuma thought that the Spanish were emissaries from the god, which caused him to wait before crushing them.

Eccentric Wizardry & Empowerment

Upon his original voyage to America, Cortes found himself on a ship commanded by Alonso Quintero. Cortes was young and impressionable and would be highly influenced by the ship captain who tried to deceive his superiors and reach the New World before them in order to secure personal advantages. Quintero's mutinous conduct probably served as a model for Cortés in his turbulent career as a warrior talking diverse cultures into giving him power. After his ship landed on today's Dominican Republic, the island nation was rife with conflict, and the various cultures were in a major rivalry with those in charge, jockeying for positions with many occasions of both mutiny and betrayal. By the time Cortes was twenty-four, he too would be found to have learned well from Quintero on that initial voyage. When the governor of Cuba saw his flaws, he decided to relieve him of his appointed duties as commander of a new expeditionary force to Mexico. Hernando slipped away in the middle of one night knowing that he was in danger of being a man without honor or opportunity. He was able to convince many men to join his expedition to the Mayan peninsula. On February 18, 1519, Cortes took the ships he was in command of and departed with over six-hundred Spanish soldiers, two-hundred Indian auxiliaries, and sixteen horses. He landed on the Yucatan peninsula and then went on to Vera Cruz.

When he became settled in Mexico, he would become bored. Between the years 1524 to 1526, he would lead a new expedition to Honduras where he had first landed. In this expedition, he would defeat the Spanish governor, Cristóbal de Olid, who had claimed Honduras as his own under the influence of the Governor of Cuba, Diego Velázquez. These two had parted company when Cortes had fled to Mexico earlier in his career. Fearing that Cuauhtémoc might head an insurrection in Mexico, Cortes had brought him along on his trek to Honduras and hanged him during the journey. Raging over Olid's treason, Cortés issued a decree to arrest Velázquez whom he was sure was behind Olid's treason. This would serve to further estrange the Crown of Castile and the Council of Indies from allegiance to Cortes. The king's court was beginning to question the faithfulness of their conquistador warrior and feel anxious about his rising power. On returning to Mexico, Cortés found the country in a state of anarchy. There was a strong suspicion in court circles of an intended rebellion by Cortés and a charge was brought against him that cast a fatal blight upon his character. He was accused of murdering his first wife and other atrocities and it would end his rule of the New Spain.

In Cortés's bold, but ghastly conquest of the Aztec empire, he would leave a trail of bloodshed that other conquistadores would follow when he left. The blueprint established by this warrior was based on pitting the Aztecs against the Mayans and making himself the maestro in the middle. This adroit exploitation would be followed later by Pizarro in Peru, Alvarado in Central America, and conquests by others in South America. Cortés's success in bringing down the mighty Aztec Empire quickly became the stuff of legend back in Spain. Most of his soldiers had been peasants or younger sons of minor nobility. Such men saw Cortes as a catalyst to their own destiny. After his conquests, these loyal disciples were given generous lands and plenty of native slaves and gold. These rags-to-riches stories drew thousands of Spanish to the New World, each of whom wished to follow in Cortés's bloody footprints. In the short run, Cortes's work was good for the Spanish crown because native populations were quickly subjugated by these ruthless conquistadores. In the long run, it would prove disastrous because these men were the wrong sort of colonizers and not the type to colonize or nurture and build towns, schools, and churches. As in the American conquest of the West, they were high-testosterone, thrill-seekers and mercenaries there for the glory and gold.

Influence on the World

The Sea of Cortes exists only because this conquistador warrior had dared what more grounded men only dream. Also, it is an arena in which he and his ships moved in his conquest of Mexico. The waterway separates Baha, California from the modern day west coast of Mexico. In the end, Hernan left the land of the Aztecs with a more positive legacy than he had found on arrival. He brought large portions of mainland Mexico under the rule of the King of Castile in the early sixteenth century. When he had captured Tenochtitlan in 1521, he had officially terminated the Aztec empire. He would spend many years marrying women and ruling the area as the New Spain. It would be in 1540 at age fifty-five that he would fall from favor with the Spanish King. He would return to his homeland to plead his case, but it would be in vain. He would die in a small village near Seville with his legacy intact, as he was one of the first Spaniards to attempt to grow sugar in Mexico and one of the first to import African slaves to early colonial Mexico.

Cortes was afflicted with wanderlust and could not just stay and manage the lands he had conquered. It was just not his forte. In the middle of his reign, he split for Honduras, but returned barely alive. Upon arrival, he was greeted with joy by a desperate, lawless population and would serve them as Governor-General. Juan de Grijalva would be the man who named the Aztec nation "Mexico." But the Castilian bureaucrats began to arrive and would name it the New Spain. When Cortes fled back to his native land, others would undo much of his work. He had left with his eldest and favorite son, Martin, on a trek to find China, but he eventually returned to Europe. Cortés died in Castilleja de la Cuesta, Seville province, in 1547. Like Columbus, he died a wealthy but embittered man without realizing his most ardent dreams as a kind of Caesar of the western world. At the time of his death, his estate contained at least two-hundred slaves who were either native Africans or of African descent. He had left many wives, mistresses, and offspring in Mexico. In his will, he requested that his remains be returned to the land he had conquered as a young conquistador. Before he died, he had the Pope remove the natural status of three of his children in order to legitimize them in the eyes of the church. This would include Martin, the son he had with Doña Marina who was his favorite.

One of Cortés' lasting legacies was the *encomienda* system that he instituted – a system of entrusting a tract of land and any number of natives to a Spaniard - often a conquistador. The *encomendero,* as it was called by the natives, had certain rights and responsibilities to maintain them in perpetuity. He agreed to provide religious education for the natives in exchange for their labor. The system he had brought to this nation was little more than enforced and legalized slavery, a means of having an *encomienda* empower the conquistadors and make them wealthy and powerful. The Spanish crown would eventually regret allowing the *encomienda* system to take root in the New World, as it would prove unmanageable from afar, and many reports of abuses began piling up. They would eventually have to give up the ghost of managing Mexico.

Chapter Six

Catherine the Great – Passionate Power

"I was ready to die rather than end up in a convent."

In Catherine's memoir, she wrote of what she saw as her attributes that had permitted her to reign in Russia for the balance of her long life. This Russian Empress was equipped with an indomitable will and far more passion than most men and it led to her seducing like a man and becoming a female warrior in a male-like manner. In her memoirs she wrote of how she managed to rise to power:

> "Here lies Catherine the second, born in Stettin, on April 21, 1729. She went to Russia in the year 1744 to marry Peter III. At the age of fourteen she formed the threefold resolution to please her husband, Elizabeth and the nation. Eighteen years of boredom and loneliness caused her to read many books. Having ascended the throne of Russia she wished to do good and sought to procure for her subjects, happiness, liberty, and property. She pardoned readily and hated no one. Indulged, easy to live with, possessed of a cheerful nature, a republican soul and a kind heart, she had friends. Work was easy for her and she enjoyed society and the arts."

Chapter Six – Catherine the Great – Passionate Power

These were the words from a German princess who wanted to live a life of elegance and power as a queen, but would learn that power has many roads to travel and many men to conquer. Catherine would become one of the most powerful women that ever lived by daring to go where most women would not and using her mind as much as her armies to maintain power over those what wanted what she had. She learned early, when in charge, take charge with an iron hand. Catherine had a mesmerizing manner that captured the hearts and guns of those in Russia looking for a wise leader. She had made friends early with the world's ambassadors who were quite taken by her majesty. After marrying the imbecile Peter she was supposed to bear a child as the future king or queen. When her husband wasn't up to the task she found a security guard who was and made it happen. During these years she had been kept in a secluded compound to insure she wasn't able to mingle or gain power. In her memoir she spoke of it as fate having dealt her a very bad hand. Kept in a remote room of the castle, she would become a voracious reader of warrior wizards like Cyrus the Great and Alexander. She was very lonely, but in her isolated introspection she would devise a plan to become empress. She found out early that her marriage to Peter was a disaster, as he was a child-like man who could not consummate the marriage and preferred to play with toy soldiers than sleep with this femme fatale. During her years alone, she had to devise a way of keeping her sanity. She would read, think, and write in her journal. It would be when her reign as an innovative dictator would become actualized in her head.

She achieved the Herculean task of becoming the Empress of all the Russia's despite being of German lineage and speaking very broken Russian. Where did such insight originate? She had delved into philosophical books and befriended Voltaire and read about great leaders from other nations. Foreign ambassadors became enamored of this beautiful and bright young woman and they entertained her and informed her of what was transpiring in the world. Their company helped diffuse her life as a virtual nun, and later her indomitable spirit came through in words like, *"It is better to be subject to laws under one master than to be subservient to many."* It worked for her to think rather than be torn by anxiety, as it might have for many lesser beings.

When Queen Elizabeth of Russia died, her son, Peter – Catherine's idiot husband took power. Most of the Russian elite knew that he was totally incapable of governing. On one drunken evening, Peter was disturbed by the way his wife ignored him and ordered her arrest as he was planning to put his mistress on the throne. In her memoirs, Catherine would write, *"I knew it was prison or poison."* The news had spread like wildfire to the guard that was there to protect the future queen. They came to her and told her she was about to be imprisoned and would probably end up in a nunnery or worse. One of the guards was her lover, Orlov. He immediately rushed to her side and asked what they should do. Catherine, the consummate warrior, went into the men's barracks and came out in a Captain's uniform—replete with sword. There was coup happening in the streets of St. Petersburg and she decided to take control of thus take power. Hearing the news that his wife was in the capital and sitting on the throne he became hysterical and when she led a band of armed guards to where he was he abdicated.

On that day, he would be killed by one of Catherine's supporters – probably her lover, Grigiori Orlov. The guard would lead her to the palace where she took power and never looked back. After the *coup de etat,* Catherine would be crowned Empress of all the Russia's. Never before had a woman dared lead a nation of the size and power of Russia that controlled one-seventh of the globe. Knowing this, Catherine very astutely maneuvered the various factions to ensure her future. It was a matter of knowing the factions looking to defeat her and take power themselves in contrast to those looking for a wise leader to guide their nation into a better future. One of her talents was having a nurturing nature with female guile. She had to let her adversaries know that she would kill if necessary and could be intolerant if pushed to the edge. This tactical strategy was crucial for disarming the chauvinists in the past aristocracy who saw a chance for them to gain power from a weak female. But, she had a masculine side, and would prove to be highly androgynous – not unlike Joan of Arc before her – and would kill if necessary. Her friend and confidante, British Ambassador, Harris, would say, *"She has a masculine force of mind and wants the more manly virtues."* This was true in the board rooms and her bedroom. In many ways, Catherine seduced men the way men traditionally seduced women. She would say, *"I have the most reckless audacity. There is no woman bolder than I, and [I] am sustained by ambition alone."*

When Catherine was older, she became somewhat prophetic in predicting the need for a titan to lead the French nation as she had become quite close with French intellectuals, Voltaire and Diderot. She financed the first encyclopedia since the Sorbonne had called it a stupid idea. She almost predicted with uncanny accuracy the coming of Napoleon. The erudite leader would correctly prophesize the French Revolution in 1788, prior to it happening, and the need for a new titan to lead France back to glory:

> **"When will this Caesar come? Oh! Come he will, make no doubt about it, there will be another Genghis. That will be Europe's fate. You can depend on it. If France survives, she will be stronger than she has ever been. All she needs is a superior man, greater than his contemporaries, greater perhaps than an entire age. Has he already been born? Will he come? Everything depends on that."**

Wow! Talk about being prophetic. Catherine's superior man had already been born in Corsica in 1760. What was the name of this titan? Napoleon Bonaparte! He was not in France, but in Corsica, which was actually under the rule of Italy. Napoleon, as a youngster, spoke Italian and would learn French in school in France. The Little Corsican would fulfill every word that Catherine had written. Ironically, it would be in Russia that he would suffer his greatest defeat when the Russians would burn the crops and kill the animals and ensure he would not benefit by invading Mother Russia. Napoleon would turn out to be a similar leader as Catherine and would implement his Napoleonic Code similar to Catherine's, freeing many of the serfs. Both took power from foreign nations and refused to capitulate to those that were in power at the time.

The Path to Glory

Princess Sophie of Anhalt-Zerbst was one of many daughters of a minor German royal house and would be selected by the Russian Queen Elizabeth, son of Peter the Great, to come to Russia and produce an heir to the throne. She arrived in 1744 when she was only fifteen. Due to a recent illness, she was seen as an *"ugly scarecrow."* Her future husband, the heir to the throne, Grand Duke Peter, was a bizarre character whose main interests were his toy soldiers and "romping" with his valets. No one, unsurprisingly, recognized in her the future Catherine II—one of Russia's greatest rulers. She would marry Peter and live in seclusion for years waiting for his mother Elizabeth to pass. She would be the woman who once in power would preside over a vast expansion of Russian territory, and build massive new palaces in St Petersburg, which would house a huge collection of European art and sculpture. She would create the Hermitage and reform local governments and make education more available to the masses.

The princess, being German, was an unlikely choice as a future empress. She had been selected by Empress Elizabeth who saw potential in this fourteen-year-old. She was a German girl who would spend her life devoted to the good of Russia. Her husband, Peter, was enamoured with Frederick the Great who had defeated Russia and was considered the consummate warrior of the era. Peter would play silly military games with toy soldiers and would infuriate the Russian army by remodelling it in a Prussian style. Despite being of Prussian lineage, Catherine was upset over this childish future king and would take on lovers to appease her seething soul. The paths she took were sometimes treacherous and often amazing insights into what was right and wrong. Her main timelines were:

1729: Catherine The Great was born

1762: Catherine becomes Empress of Russia

1763: Catherine releases a manifesto inviting immigration into Russia from Western Europe in order to bring the nation into the 18th century

1764: She would mark the Poland borders to show the demarcation line that could not be crossed or she would attack with a vengeance

1767: She formed a group of delegates to create a constitution and consider people's wishes and ideas – the thinking queen

1768: She fought a battle against Turkey, expanding the nation's borders

1775: Catherine introduced a new system of local government for Russia

1783: Treaty of Georgievsk was signed between King Herekle and Catherine expanding the borders of the Russian empire

1796: Catherine the Great died and was widely mourned by a nation she had adopted as her own

Early Years and Trek to Eminence

Catherine II was born in Germany on April 21, 1729. Her German name was Sophia Augusta Frederica, a princess and daughter of Prince Christian August of Anhalt-Zebst and Princess Johanna Elizabeth. Catherine's parents had longed for a son and consequently showed her little affection. During her childhood, she was more attached to her governess, Babette, than her distant parents. Catherine was so close to her that she described her as *"the kind of governess every child should have."* Catherine the Great ruled her adopted nation with an iron hand between 1762 and 1796. She is credited for bringing Russia "out of a small pond and into a bigger ocean - the modern world." This was a very smart woman who was quite ambitious and was called by foreign ambassadors: "beauty with brains." She improved the way Russia was organized and the political administration in the huge territory. She would expand Russia and westernize a nation that had been backward for centuries. The modernization took place within the context of her autocratic control over a nation of serfs. She encouraged education and enlightenment for all people, and was very popular for having many famous figures of the Enlightenment. This was a woman of bodily pleasures and has been described by biographers as being sexually insatiable. Under her wing, Russia grew and became stronger and rivaled the great powers of Asia and Europe.

Catherine married the young Grand Duke, Peter, in 1745. When she met him on her visit to Russia as a young teenager, she saw him as an acceptable husband. That would change soon after the marriage took place. She would convert to the Russian Orthodox Christian faith and did what she was told in order to become the future queen of the empire. There was no affection and zero love from day one as the marriage was not consummated for years. It would not be long for them to both be disloyal to each other. Biographers say she had many lovers prior to taking power and had two children who were illegitimate relative to her marriage to Peter. Paul and Anna were Catherine's children who most believe were spawned by men from the military guard who she slept with regularly. She would write that she had been more attracted to the Crown of Russia which Peter would eventually wear than to him as a husband. This sharp-witted and cultured woman showed great interest in reading, mainly French, and she was very fond of plays, novels, and verse.

Her main interest in literature was on the French Enlightenment – Rousseau, Voltaire, Diderot, and Montesquieu. Catherine was a very bold and outspoken personality and the nation flourished under her rule. As she grew older, she was in great dilemma because her son Paul was highly unstable and unable to rule. She considered naming Alexander, Paul's oldest son, as her successor, but sadly, she died of a stroke before she could do so.

Catherine had Enormous Charismatic Power

In her famous *coup d'etat,* this woman warrior pushed the windows of opportunity and traditional mores. She was an attractive, well-bred lady who was driven to the wall by an imbecile husband and an autocratic Russian system, and she was a charmer beyond the norm. As soon as Peter took power with his mother's death, she knew that the future was not only in question, but her life may also be in jeopardy. In June 1762, she was awakened in the middle of the night by the news that one of her conspirators had been arrested and that she would have to pull off a coup or be gone or end up in a nunnery. She left the palace in a hurry. As only a woman of class would do, she found her French hairdresser to make her look like a queen deserving of the throne. The woman arranged her hair while in a carriage on her way to take power. She arrived at the castle and was crowned the Empress of *All the Russia's* receiving the oath of allegiance in her lace nightcap. In her inimitable style, she was a woman with a masculine bent. She would write, *"First health, then wealth, then pleasure, and do not owe anything to anybody."* Those words would be followed by, *"The more a man knows, the more he forgives."* And on taking the throne she would write, *"My dear, I am about to seize the throne of Russia. What on earth shall I wear?"* Catherine, while awaiting her destiny, became close friends with British Ambassador, Harris, who would characterize Catherine in his notes back home saying, "*Catherine has a masculine force of mind, obstinacy in adhering to a plan, and intrepidity in the execution of it; but she wants the more manly virtues of deliberation, forbearance in prosperity, and accuracy of judgment, while she possesses, in a high degree, the weaknesses vulgarly attributed to sex - love of flattery and its inseparable companion, vanity; an inattention to unpleasant but salutary advice; and a propensity to voluptuousness, which leads her to excesses that would debase a female character in any sphere of life.*"

Madam Bigee-Lebrun was a celebrated French artist who, after visiting the Russian court, said of this powerful world leader, "*Genius was stamped on her brow. Everything about her was so majestic that she seemed to me the Queen of the world.*" Her talent was exemplified in her leadership. When once asked to reprimand a subject in public for detestable behavior, she said, "*No! That would be too humiliating for him: I shall wait until I am alone with him; for I like to praise and reward in a loud voice and to scold in a whisper.*" Her biographer, Henri Troyat, would write, "*Everything about her was measured and methodical. She knew the art of listening, and her presence of mind was so habitual that she appeared to be paying attention even when she was thinking of something else.*"

Shaman Fantasies as Motivational Mantras

Upon hearing the news that Peter had been dethroned by his German wife, Frederick the Great said, "*It was like a wife sending her child to bed.*" Catherine the Great's relationships were made with some of Europe's most distinguished intellectual giants. But her dalliances with lovers were even more bizarre. She was said to have slept with three-hundred men, but that is considered low by many. Historians wrote of her bestiality fetish and that she had died having sex with a horse. That was absolutely not true. During her lifetime, Catherine made many enemies throughout Europe. After her death, the horse myth probably emerged from the French upper class as a way to mar her legend. "*She was a woman in power with a promiscuous sex life,*" says Michael Farquhar, author of *A Treasury of Royal Scandals*. "*Her contemporaries were never comfortable with that.*" The French Ambassador in her court would write, "*Catherine's power of self-delusion bordered on the irrational – her uterine frenzies were wild.*"

Catherine was a bit manic and rose at five each morning and worked twelve to fourteen hour days. Such behavior was found in bipolar leaders such as Alexander and Patton and others like Mark Twain and Walt Disney. One of the traits in such people is a raging libido fueled by high testosterone. These types are not only driven zealots, but also have a creative bent, take big risks, and have sex drives that dwarf that of more normal leaders. They have been labeled "Big T's" by psychologists with the "t" standing for both thrill-seeking and high testosterone. Catherine fits this very well since she seldom took the time to eat, and she wore out her administrators, as she was infamous for dictating to four women simultaneously. Napoleon did the same. History has labeled him as a "Big T thrill-seeker who was manic-depressive."

When she did sit at a table with friends and guests of honor, she had finished her meal while others were still getting started. By nine in the evening, she would collapse from exhaustion from a day that would have bedazzled most men. She was infamous for firing off drafts at a speed that surprised and even vexed the copyists who were there to do her bidding. The secret agent to the Russian court was Chevalier de Eon who wrote of this powerful Russian empress:

> **"The Grand Duchess is romantic, ardent, passionate; her eyes shine, their look is fascinating, flashy, the look of a wild beast. She has a lofty brow and, if I mistake not, there is a long terrifying future written upon that brow. She is affable and obliging, but when she comes near me, I instinctively recoil. She frightens me."**

Epiphany that Proved Transformational

Catherine was feminine with a masculine nature. When her imbecile husband, Peter, told his friends that he would put her in a convent or have her killed and place his mistress on the throne, she was told of what was about to transpire; she prepared her own plan. Catherine saw the future and decided to take destiny into her hands. Her husband had been given the throne when his mother Elizabeth passed. He began wild partying with his buddies and mistress who he promised to make empress. As discussed, Catherine donned a male Captain's uniform replete with sword and she mounted her white stallion full saddle to show the soldiers that she was not only a gentle woman who could be trusted, but one with great temerity. Riding full straddle in the seventeenth century was unheard of for a woman of breeding. She rode to the palace and asked the guard to join her in a confrontation of her husband. Had Catherine taken a traditional path in traditional garb, she would have been dead. At the time, Catherine was thirty-three, and she was not only young for a woman with no Russian blood in her veins to take over a nation, but she was well-equipped with beauty and brains. With the Imperial Guard behind her, she took charge with a male-like manner and a lot of guile. During her rise to become Empress, she knew she had to look and act special. She told the soldiers, *"Any man who wants to shoot your Empress, now is your time."* No one fired. They captured Peter and this powerful woman crowned herself Empress of Russia.

Eccentric Wizardry and Empowerment

Catherine was not only clever, diligent, and well-read from her years of preparation, she was also an empress who astonished her Senate by actually joining in their sessions. This was a warrior woman who often knew more than her Senators. She was often shocked at their ineptitude or lack of knowledge. She was not the type to listen to incompetence. She took control since she had the power to do so.

She established a strict timetable of work beginning at six in the morning and worked diligently for twelve hours. It would take her many years to put in motion an innovative Codification of the Laws. The men in her court were often mesmerized by this tall warrior with power and grace but with a corpulent mind. They saw her as like them in many ways. Yet, she remained quite feminine. Something about her was teasingly unclassifiable. It made those around her keep a safe distance. She had a kind of indomitable grace and elegance. Androgyny was the word that fit her when on the throne. Catherine herself was to note in her memoirs that she possessed a "masculine cast of mind." She shocked many men as an exceptionally effective ruler in a country where women had traditionally exercised authority in private and outraged conservatives. Prince Mikhail Scherbatov would describe her as an *"egregious illustration of the monstrous regiment of women that had engineered the ruination of the morals of Russia."* French biographer, Henri Troyat, offered insight into her androgyny and empowered spirit, saying, *"She was a relentless worker, and at the same time a charmer who combined the graces of her sex with a virile authority. Everything that she desired she obtained by patience, intelligence, toughness, courage, taking incredible risks when necessary, suddenly changing course in order to reach the goal more surely."*

Catherine kept many lovers in her royal stables. Many saw her as a raging nymphomaniac. Although as discussed, this perception of her was due to her abnormally high testosterone. History has seen this often; most recently in America with such driven men as President John F. Kennedy and Bill Clinton. Her lover, Potemkin, slept with the queen for much of her life, but he was but one of many who made her whole in her chambers. Potemkin was of an intellectual bent, and that seemed to be her favourite as she did not seduce men with muscles who could not think. Many biographers spoke of her desire for *menage a trios.* Evidently, she participated in such dalliances well into her sixties. Her marriage to Peter was not consummated for years, to the consternation of Empress Elizabeth who had brought her to Russia to produce a male heir to the throne. After earnest discussions of what might be wrong, a young widow was recruited to motivate the Grand-Duke sexually. By this time, Catherine was passionately in love with her dashing chamberlain, Sergei Saltykov. During his allegiance and bedtime, she would deliver a son who was to be the future heir to the throne. He was given the name Grand-Duke Paul. It is very unlikely that Paul was the child of Peter but one never knows. Once she became the head of state, her liaisons were no longer a problem, and she chose the best available men to sate her passions. They were so numerous that many jokes were passed through the nation with one in St Petersburg saying that the canal which had cost the most money was Catherine's Canal. After she forced her feckless husband to abdicate, she was a woman on the wild side of propriety.

Influence on the World

In 1762, Catherine decreed that anyone could start a new factory, except in the two capitals – Moscow and St. Petersburg—that she found to be overcrowded. The total number of factories during her reign was increased from 984 to 3,161. It would not be long before enterprising state peasants were running large textile plants in the nation. She founded the first School of Mines in St. Petersburg and underground mines. She was a patron of mass education, funding Diderot's first encyclopedia. In many ways she was an aggressive combatant with a compassionate soul, not unlike Napoleon. Both kept journals and loved poetry and thought about the world with a philosophic bent. Both were very lonely, with their only friends being heroes from books and lovers to cavort with. They saw life through a mythical filter that made them innovative warriors of a different kind. After she had borne a male heir to the throne, Catherine, who was still a virtual captive and recluse, would write in her journal, *"I lived a life for 18 years from which ten others would have gone crazy and twenty in my place would have died of melancholy."* Catherine's Legacy was as follows:

- In June 1767, she created the Legislative Commission to modify the old laws in accordance with her "instructions." She also formed a group of delegates the same year to create a constitution and consider people's wishes and ideas, but it was considered too liberal and reaped nothing. Russia's legal system was based on a disorganized Code of Laws in use from the year 1649 until Catherine gave an idea for a very advanced legal system - Codification of the Laws. The idea was that the system would provide equal protection to everyone under the law. She also gave ideas on preventing criminal acts, rather than the handing out of harsh punishments.

- In 1775, she introduced a new system of local government.

- In 1786, Catherine made a plan that would help her create a large-scale educational system. She was very keen on expanding the country's academic structure, but unfortunately, due to some reasons, she could not carry out the entire plan. However, she did introduce some elementary and secondary schools into the country's educational infrastructure. Some of the unfinished plans were carried out after her death.

- During Catherine's reign, the arts and science were also revived. She believed that by accelerating in these two fields, Russia could earn a reputation as a center of civilization. St. Petersburg was turned into a stunning capital under her rule. Music, painting, and theater thrived with her support.

- Catherine the Great was just what Russia needed. Once she took power and attended the Senate meetings to the surprise of all, she was horrified to discover the senators' ignorance of the country they were governing. She came to discover that most of the men were inept. She established a strict timetable of work and made them adhere to it. She went to her chambers and worked for many years on the Codification of the Laws and put it in effect.

Catherine was taller than the average woman of her era but had a certain grace and style that beguiled and seduced those around her. It has been well documented that corpulence was her thing and in 1990 dollars Catherine was said to have spent the equivalent of $1.5 billion on her paramours. It would do her injustice to say she was masculine, but she was androgynous, just as Gandhi and Napoleon. Catherine was quite introspective, writing, *"For to tempt and to be tempted are things very nearly allied... whenever feeling has anything to do in the matter, no sooner is it excited than we have already gone vastly farther than we are aware of."* She exercised great authority in private and had a way of outraging traditionalists. This would make her an amazing warrior wizard.

Chapter Seven

Napoleon's Perilous Magnetism

"Keep acquiring more and more power, all the rest is chimerical."

No matter what one says positive or negative about Napoleon, one thing is consistent; he was not normal in any definition of the term and his achievements were far above normal. In his memoirs at St. Helena, he wrote, "*I grew up wild and untamable. Nothing overawed me. I wasn't afraid of anybody.*" When he spoke about his time in French military schools, he wrote, "I had confidence in my power and enjoyed my superiority. I had the feeling that my will was stronger than that of others." Wow! A psychiatrist writing on the nature of the manic-depressive Napoleon said, "*There was a fire in his veins to such a point that he came to believe he was a supernatural man.*" Pretty powerful words, but his trek to the top was that of a superman who had controlled his kryptonite. The Little Corsican was a man among men, despite his being small in stature, but very large in mental veracity. He was driven like few other men in political history. An example was his rising when most men would still be asleep for hours, much like Catherine the Great, although even she didn't get up at 1:00 am and remain awake for the remainder of the day. When questioned on his decisions such as taking off down the Mediterranean Sea to attack Egypt or other wild adventures, this man on a mission to glory said, "*I am not a man like other men; the laws of morality do not apply to me.*" His messianic nature made him very difficult to work with or deal with. Reason was not an argument against him as he was off on his own tangent, and it was far beyond the pale of even an ambitious man. Napoleon had the same disease of Hitler and Stalin, all bipolar and often suicidal. After Napoleon's father died of stomach cancer, he considered ending his own life. When older, he offered insight into his mind saying, *"There is only one thing to do in this world and that is to keep acquiring more and more power. All the rest is chimerical,"* and he finished this whole inflamed oratory saying, *"If I lose my throne I will bury the world beneath its ruins."*

When still quite young, Napoleon believed that he was destined to rule the world and that he was an omnipotent mortal unlike traditionalists. Such ideas are often difficult to fathom for those less driven. This was a man on a mythical mission to prove his destiny as a superior being. Like his hero-mentor, Alexander, he would ignore the sage advice of older men and take off in an attack on Egypt. It is without question that his mania was a fuel within that drove him on a personal mission for power. His charismatic charm attracted many powerful disciples to his side in order for him to realize his wild dreams of conquest. Validation comes from the pen of Russian commandant Count Balmain at St. Helena where Bonaparte was a prisoner of war:

> **"The most astonishing thing of all is the influence which this man – a captive deprived of his throne – wields on anyone who comes near him. The French trouble at the sight of him and the English approach him only with something like awe. No one dares approach him on a basis of equality."**

A tyrannical and maniacal work ethic enveloped his waking hours. When he became emperor, he would often keep his legislators in meetings and not permit them to go home to their families at the end of the day like most normal political leaders. Napoleon forced them to work through the night and would shout, *"Well, well, Citizens and Ministers wake up! It's only two o'clock in the morning and you must earn the wages the French nation is paying you."* That is the mania of a warrior who refuses to cower to tradition. Such eccentricity is what would make him successful and also make him hated and feared. Often this zealot would go off into a state of grandiosity where he actually would believe that he possessed supernatural powers beyond the pale of ordinary men. *"Nothing ever happened to me,"* he would claim, *"that I did not foresee. I can divine everything in the future."* Is that wild or what? Such surreal ideas came out in torrents from this man on an impossible mission. Many felt he was hallucinating or delusional, but a great deal of his antics was fueled by his ego-mania. The Corsican came to power at a young age since many of the landed-gentry had left the French nation during the revolution. By the time he was twenty-four, he was a general who was sent to Italy to wage war against Austrian-Italian forces. This little man with a big heart and uncontrollable ego personally led the charge with bayonet in hand across a bridge and it was there that he earned the affectionate nickname, 'the Little Corporal.' He won a battle he was expected to lose and would feel internally that he was a warrior on the pathway to greatness and wrote that in his tent that night.

On his return with a reputation as a man to be reckoned with, he found himself in the midst of the Reign of Terror. In such chaos, the sword and gun become masters. Napoleon would kill and maim with wild abandon. During the Reign of Terror, innocent people were being murdered in the streets with no one caring or taking notice. At the time, Napoleon was put in charge of order and told to shoot at will and frighten those around him – pretty strong words to give to a manic-depressive on a personal mission for power. It is true that few people mess with the insane or radical. His superiors saw a young man who was fearless and they gave him power that they would later regret.

Charisma was Napoleon's friend, as he had a way with words that motivated and energized those in his presence. It made him and would destroy him. For those in power above him, he looked like someone to fear and to limit. For those under him, he would become a compelling champion. Once in power, one of Napoleon's generals admitted, *"That devil of a man exercises a fascination on me that I cannot explain. He could make me go through the eye of a needle and throw myself into the fire."* That is Charismatic Power! Mothers often refuse to bow to the power of their sons no matter how high they climb. This was also true in the case of the Little Corsican. When he was crowned Emperor of France, he had a huge entourage in the palace. When the Pope came to kiss his ring, he had him kneel before him. All of the aristocrats and members of the court were told to kneel before him and kiss his ring. Then his siblings subjugated themselves to their new powerful brother. Then up walked his mother and she did not kneel, so he put his hand gently on her shoulder to go down before him, and she slapped his hand. Any other person in the court would have died, but not his mother.

The Path to Glory

Like many warriors who reach the pinnacle of power, Napoleon would become a bit self-absorbed by his new position. The delusion of those on the very top can make a man out of touch with reality. The English were shocked at how mesmerizing he could be and the absolute mastery he had over those in his presence. His mindset to make France the dominant nation in Europe was less important than his own sense of eminence. He would make dramatic statements like, *"If I lose my throne I will bury the world beneath my ruins."* Testimony to his pathological need for speed was his philosophy, stating, *"I will lose a man but never a moment."* Biographers told stories of him cheating in card games with friends and family. The ignominy of losing was intolerable to such a warrior. Once in power as the Emperor, he proclaimed himself to be invincible – a true maniac on a mission to glory. He would make delusionary statements like, *"I can divine everything in the future."* Such a statement is born of those who aren't quite sure they are real and must wax arrogant to demonstrate that they are. When a surreal dream becomes real, it warps the mind of the one having it. Early in his career he would write, *"I was full of dreams. I saw myself founding a religion and marching into Asia like my hero Alexander the Great."* Such a sense of drama borders on the supernatural. Studies show that manic-depressive personalities have a tendency to go far beyond the norm in risk-taking, hypomania and seduction. They are not normal. But once they buy into being beyond normal, they start believing their own hype. Bipolar personalities experience wild mood swings that lead to exhilaration followed by deep depression. They vacillate between the invincible warrior and the loathsome loser. When grandiose, they have a decreased need for sleep and are armed with quick ideas, fast with the fists, and aggressive moods. When down, they suffer from severe melancholy, apprehension, and depressed feelings that sabotage everything they do. In *Touched with Fire* (1993), Kay Jamison wrote, *"Hypomanics have increased energy, intensified sexuality, increased risk-taking, persuasiveness, self-confidence and heightened productivity all linked with increased achievement and accomplishment."*

Jamison used Napoleon in her writings on the bipolar personality. Napoleon was the quintessential poster boy for her definition: *"a man who was sometimes mesmerizingly euphoric and then suddenly turned into a very depressed psychopath."* When manic, he was spellbinding. When depressed, he would escape into his tent or room and refuse to come out. On his memorable march across Europe, he pulverized the Austrians, Prussians, and Russians. But when his Grande Army walked into Moscow expecting to make a grand entrance, he was devastated to find the Russians had been devastated and was devoid of people to idolize him or food to feed his hungry army. The Russians had burned the city, and fled with the food, women, and animals, leaving no spoils of victory. His megalomania took over and he was a broken man who went into his tent and stayed there for weeks while his men were dying by the thousands. In deep despair and fundamentally incapacitated, his Grande Army was without a leader. The cold and lack of food would cost them half a million men. Their leader finally emerged from his tent, mounted a horse, and made a mad dash across Europe to France. Biographers Hermann & Lief wrote, *"The very mania that gave him such advantages in battle doomed him to waste his victories and destroy his empire."* When depressed, he would become a shadow of his state when elated. On that return trek from Russia, he killed five horses in five days. His valet, Constant, would later write, *"I never comprehended how his body could endure such fatigue, yet he enjoyed almost continuously the most perfect health."* At Elba, one of his captors, a British Colonel, told the press, *"I have never seen a man in any situation of life with so much personal activity. He appears to take much pleasure in perpetual movement and in seeing those who accompany him sink under fatigue."* (Hermann & Lieb 1994 p. 145)

Early Years and Trek to Eminence

Napoleon was born in Corsica on August 15, 1769. His birth came just after the island's cession to France by the Genoese. His father was a lawyer and his mother, Letizia, was a beautiful, strong-willed woman who married Napoleon's father, Carlos when she was only fourteen. Napoleon was the fourth and second surviving child of a total of eight. The French occupied Corsica and led to a long civil war led by Pasquale Paoli who would become one of Napoleon's heroes. His father had fought with Pasquale. When Paoli had to flee the country, Carlos Buonaparte came to terms with the French and was appointed assessor for the judicial district of Ajaccio in 1771, when Napoleon was two years-old. In 1778, Carlos obtained the admission of his two eldest sons, Joseph and Napoleon to the Collège d'Autun in France. Napoleon left for his French education during a time when the French considered him a foreigner since Corsica had been under Italian rule for centuries. At age ten, he would enter the military academy at Brienne, France. During his first couple years there, he was teased unceasingly by the French students about his strange name, his foreign accent, and his diminutive size. Napoleon coped by concentrating on his studies.

Napoleon attended three different military schools; first, in Autun, then in Brienne for five years, followed by one year at a military academy in Paris. It was during Napoleon's year in Paris that his father died of stomach cancer in February, 1785. Napoleon returned home for a brief time as he would assume the position of head of the family when just sixteen. He graduated a short time later ranking 42nd in a class of 58. But, he did so in one-third less time than the other students. He was made second lieutenant of artillery in a training school for young artillery officers in Valence. Napoleon was a voracious reader and fan of grand military men such as Alexander the Great. It was during this period he would write Lettres sur la Corse - Letters on Corsica - in which he speaks personally about his strong feelings about his native island. He would return to his homeland in September 1786, but an emotional foment of the French Revolution was in motion. He saw an advantage to find his mark as a military man as the nation needed warriors to quell the violence. Voltaire and Rousseau were Napoleon's intellectual heroes. They would ultimately influence his Napoleonic Code. Napoleon's regiment was stationed in Auxonne when the French Revolution broke out. He approved of the Revolution, in principal, but deplored the violence of the common people. In 1792, he witnessed the second storming of the Tuileries and the arrest of King Louis XVI along with the slaughter of the Swiss Guards. From this point on, Napoleon both hated and feared the common people of France.

In 1795, Napoleon was asked to quell the Parisian mobs under royalist leadership. They were preparing to storm the Tuileries and Napoleon was placed second in command. He took charge as only a warrior wizard could do. In predictable style, he ordered the storming crowds to be annihilated with forty cannons. This act established Napoleon as a hero of the Revolution to those in power. It would lead to his entrance into Parisian society where he would meet Josephine de Beauharnias. On March 9,

1796, they would marry, as he was enamored of her court connections. The truth was that his new wife had slept with many men in the social world of Paris. The couple would become new young socialites in the court and the contacts at the top would lead to his appointment to lead the Army in an Italian engagement. He was then made a general at the young age of twenty-four. In quick succession, Napoleon achieved victories, and in February 1797, he would take his army across the Alps toward Vienna. The Austrians sued for an Armistice before a single shot was fired. His return to France was triumphant, and by twenty-eight, he had established himself as the greatest French general of all time. In honor of his achievements, he was elected to the prestigious Institute. He would then set his sights on achieving total power. An early move was to derail the British sea power by attacking one of their principalities, which was in Egypt. A far deeper reason was that his hero, Alexander the Great, had attacked that nation millenniums earlier. He decided on a rearguard action to attack Britain's resources by occupying Egypt and cutting off her trade routes with India and the Far East

On June 10, 1798, his forces took the island fortress of Malta. Three weeks later he seized Alexandria. Within days the entire Nile Delta was in French hands, but it was not to last as his first defeat occurred on August first, when his entire naval fleet was destroyed by the British navy. In February, 1799, the French were again defeated; this time on land at the battle of Acre. Napoleon retreated to Egypt. Here, he handed his command over to General Jean Baptiste Kleber and he sailed for France, but not until after he had been regaled in Alexandria by the Egyptians. Upon his arrival in Paris, he was dismayed to find that France had lost control of most of the territories he had won in Italy. Now the empire was in a state of chaos. Many saw this young military genius as a potential savior for the nation. Two Directors approached him with a plan to overthrow the Directory in a coup d'etat. It was a wildly audacious game, but it worked faster and better than they would have imagined. In November of 1799, a new government was established and Napoleon had achieved his dream of becoming the power broker of France. Napoleon began immediately to start a reformation of the government and the nation's educational system. He quickly proved himself to be a viable statesman and administrator. In 1802, he was voted consul for life. In May of 1804, he crowned himself Emperor of France.

Charismatic Power – Napoleon's Fuel to the Top

Prince Tallyrand, an aristocrat who Napoleon had deposed and exiled was the Little Corsican's mortal enemy. However, he would write the ultimate tribute, *"His career is the most extraordinary that has occurred for one thousand years. He was certainly great, an extraordinary man and clearly the most extraordinary man I ever saw and the greatest that has lived in our age or for many ages."* Pretty strong words from a man who hates you! Another of Napoleon's mortal enemies on the field of battle was the Duke of Wellington who had beaten him in the historic battle of Waterloo. The Duke would say of his nemesis, *"Napoleon was not a personality, but a principle. The Corsican's presence on the field of battle was equivalent of 40,000 soldiers."* Madame Germaine de Stael also despised Napoleon, but still said of him, *"That intrepid warrior, the most profound thinker, the most extraordinary genius in history."* Those are some powerful words from one's adversaries. When Napoleon was captured by the British forces and imprisoned on the island of Elba, his charisma would become a cornerstone of his ideological role as one of the greatest warriors that ever lived. His charismatic flair was never more dramatic than on that memorable day when he and a small band of men boarded some boats and landed on the coast of France to start a march to retake the throne. After ten months in captivity, this zealot was willing to die rather than remain docile in captivity. On March 1, 1815, he and his men boarded a ship without notice and landed in France to begin a march on Paris to dethrone King Louis XVIII. Along the road, disciples joined his tiny band of men. Hearing of his escape, King Louis became alarmed and picked one of Napoleon's enemies, General Ney, who Napoleon had abandoned in Moscow, and told him to capture him or kill him. General Ney had a regiment of 1,000 men with heavy artillery and he would meet Napoleon and their small band in Grenoble. This engagement would go down in history as one of Napoleon's grandest moments. Here was a captive trying to retake a nation of which he wasn't even a citizen, faced with death at the hands of a general commanded by the king. Napoleon stood there looking at a dire situation in which he had no chance of winning. He told his followers to drop their weapons as he dropped his and started walking toward the men sent to kill him. Ney commanded him to stop. He kept walking. Then he screamed at his men to raise their muskets and ready them to fire. Ney commanded Napoleon to stop walking and to surrender. Napoleon kept walking and looked at the men formally in his Grande Army and shouted with the pomposity of a reigning sovereign, *"Kill your emperor if you wish, but I am here to take you back to power with me."* Napoleon then waited for the gunshots that would end his life, but none came. He then looked at Ney as he ordered his men to fire. The soldiers did not fire on a man who had led them in battle after battle and then one dropped his musket and that was followed by others. In one grand moment, the soldiers screamed back at their mesmerizing leader, *"Vive l' Empereur,"* and joined him in the march on Paris. Ney had no choice but to join his former leader and now they had a formidable force to take Paris. King Louis heard the news and fled the country. At St. Helena, Napoleon would write, *"Before Grenoble I was an adventurer; at Grenoble I was a reigning prince."* (Landrum 1995 p. 132. Such was the awesome charismatic power of the Little Corsican.

Shaman Fantasies as Motivational Mantras

Napoleon was certainly different—a man often lost in his own reveries that bordered on the arcane. He was very bright and thought like a philosopher and poet. He would often write of his battles and his own emotional turmoil. In his sonnet *The Sorrows of Young Werther,* it would be a soliloquy offering insight into his manic needs and feelings that were far beyond the norm, as he being the Young Werther:

> **"Always alone in the midst of men, I come to my room to dream by myself, to abandon my melancholy in all its sharpness. In which direction does it lead today? Towards death! What fury drives me to my own destruction? Indeed what am I to do in this world? Since die I must, is it not just as well to kill myself? Since nothing is pleasure to me, why should I beat days that nothing turns to profit? Because the men with whom I live and probably always shall live, have ways as different from mine as the moon from the sun. I cannot pursue the only way of life that could make life tolerable – hence distaste for everything."**

"Mania was the secret behind Napoleon's great success," wrote Hershmann and Lieb. In one sense, it is what made him special and made him weird. One example of his mania took place in 1809 when he became concerned about his wife, Josephine's, inability to bear him an heir. She was not only impotent, but six years older and she slept with everyone in

his cabinet. Napoleon would at one time attempt suicide, but since there was no one to take power when he was gone, he decided to stay the course. In December of 1809, he would divorce Josephine to marry a younger woman who could bear him an heir. In April of 1810, he married the eighteen-year-old Archduchess, Marie Louise, daughter of Emperor Francis I of Austria. They would have a son named Napoleon II, but it would all be for naught as Napoleon kept permitting mania to interfere with a normal life. It is kind of paradoxical that when a young man slept with much older women, a few old enough to be his grandmother. One of these ladies was Mademoiselle de Montansier who was sixty at the time. Another of the eccentricities of Napoleon was his bi-sexual nature. He was quite tolerant of homosexuality during his reign. He often refused to tolerate prosecution against its practice in France.

To Napoleon's credit, he took power and used it, whereas Alexander the Great inherited an army from his father, Philip. Julius Caesar rose to power through political liaisons due to his status. Only Genghis Khan was somewhat comparable, as he conquered the world from the middle of nowhere like the Little Corsican. Kahn's victims were relatively defenseless. His main weapons were brutality and terror, whereas Napoleon's weapons were words and actions on the battlefield leading men to victory after victory. It was the ability to impose an indomitable will on those above and below that made Napoleon truly special. He commandeered the rest of continental Europe as a maniacal head of state with imperial majesty through the sheer power of his personality. An example of the legacy he leaves was that after his passing, Louis-Philippe in 1840 had one of his sons to St Helena to bring the emperor's remains back to Paris. They are buried him with much ceremony in a place of exceptional honor - in the central spot, beneath the dome, in the church of Les Invalides in midtown Paris.

Epiphany that Proved Transformational

Napoleon experienced his epiphany at age twenty-four. He was sent to Italy to fight against incredible odds since many Parisian leaders felt it would tame the ambitions of this arrogant young upstart. The Austro/Italian forces outnumbered the French forces by over two to one, and he came away the victor, when in a very visionary style, he concentrated fire on one area. When that was breached, the equilibrium is broken as well as will power. He won a battle no one expected him to win. It was April in 1796 when he was sent there with 30,000 men against the Italians with 70,000 men. With brilliant tactical maneuvers, he won a stunning and decisive victory to the shock of everyone in Paris. In his memoirs, he said that he walked back to this tent and wrote in his journal, "I am a superior being," and he would later say that was the metamorphoses of him into a man to be reckoned with. In St. Helena, he wrote of the epiphany that took place that prophetic day. He now saw himself transformed from a wannabe into a military genius with destiny waiting in the wings. He spoke of walking back to his quarters and writing of his transformation – in what Joseph Campbell would later define as, "The symbolic way a man will discover his true identity." Napoleon wrote:

"It was only after Lodi that I realized I was a superior being and conceived the ambition of performing great things which hitherto had filled my thoughts only as a fantastic dream." (Landrum 1995 p. 127)

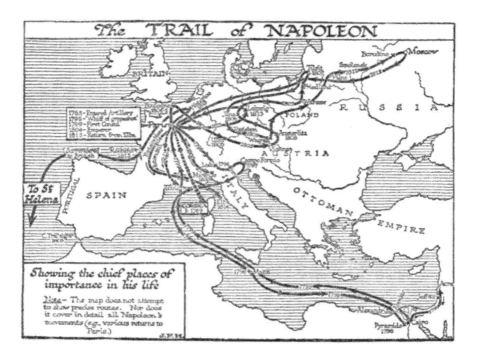

Eccentric Wizardry and Empowerment

Both Napoleon and his first wife, Josephine, were left-handed and both were passionate to a fault. Each saw the world through a unique perspective. Napoleon's General de Segur wrote, "In moments of sublime power, he no longer commands like a man, but seduces like a woman." What he was saying is that Napoleon had an androgynous manner that was both masculine and feminine depending on his environment. He was one of those people who came across with boundless sexual energy; a man who would write, "Imagination rules the world." When the heart rules the head, most associates will see you as odd or worse. Napoleon liked to tell his disciples "Never interrupt your enemy when he is making a mistake." The retreat of the Grande Army from Moscow in 1812 has become one of the classic images of this man's strange behavior under duress. It would document for history the wild megalomania in the mind of the emperor. He and his men had been harried by Russian troops doing guerrilla warfare and that was not his style. With snow coming down in torrents and hostile villagers preying on is men, Napoleon's Grande Army came face-to-face with a Herculean task and would capitulate. History shows that he lost about half a million men of the 600,000 that had marched with him into Russia. The effect on Napoleon's ability to raise another army would prove devastating, and many of his generals came to hate him, including General Ney· discussed earlier at Grenoble.

Napoleon's lust for power would become his Achilles Heel with one of his most chilling maxims. "As a Roman emperor once said: The body of a dead enemy always smells good." Had Napoleon stopped his onslaught in 1803, he could have lived in peace and tranquility like a king with a harem of adoring fans and supporters. This little man with a big ego would undoubtedly have enjoyed a long and prosperous reign. This would have been true of Hitler in 1936 when he had rescued German from horrid inflation, unemployment, and horrid reparations for World War I. But, both bipolar personalities would perish due to their own imperious style. Both men lost everything due a need for power and grandiosity. Fighting unnecessary wars and causing needless slaughter cost them their lives. As Napoleon had done in Egypt and later at Waterloo, he would abandon his army and flee to the safety of France. It took two more years for the allies to defeat and depose him. When he escaped from the island of Elba, in the famous Hundred Days, he recaptured control of France and threatened European peace once more until defeated by Wellington at the Battle of Waterloo.

Influence on the World

Historians agree on the fact that Napoleon was a dynamic, yet indomitable personality. Here was a small man with a big need for power. His hypnotic command on the men and women in his life was amazing. Even the aristocracy and intellectuals were taken with him. There is little disagreement that he was brighter than most and possessed a photographic memory for facts, people, events, numbers, military units, and maps. Here was a fanatic for detail, despite his gestalt mastery of battles and his adversaries. He was known to pour over vast amounts of statistical information and reports. Like most left-handed people, this right-hemisphere man saw the big picture. That ability to flip-flop between the data and the essence – the global and the local – is what made him special. He had a thorough command of military technology as well as the financial and diplomacy necessary to rule a land whose most adept leaders had left in the French Revolution. This was a man with brilliant insights on complex missions who was notorious for seeing the whole battlefield and not just one facet of it. Due to a manic nature, he proved faster than his adversaries and made decisions instantly with rapid dictation of complex commands. The ability to multi-task was his forte. In many respects, he was akin to a chess master who sees way ahead of the immediate plays. The true masters begin at the end and then know where they are headed as they proceed. As discussed above, he had inexhaustible energy and wore out those in his presence. Napoleon made his own rules and strategies on the spot and never questioned his actions.

After 1812, Napoleon seemed to have lost some of his verve and was not nearly as empowered for winning at all cost. Some historians suggest he might have been becoming physically impaired. Napoleon's personal insight into his life and career was captured in St. Helena when he wrote:

> **"I closed the gulf of anarchy and brought order out of chaos. I rewarded merit regardless of birth or wealth, wherever I found it. I abolished feudalism and restored equality to all regardless of religion and before the law. I fought the decrepit monarchies of the Old Regime**

because the alternative was the destruction of all this. I purified the Revolution."

When the British restored order to the French throne, they were quite generous. They gave Napoleon the island of Elba, an island Napoleon looked at from Corsica as a child. It was his to rule with a toy army of 400 men plus an annual income of two-million francs. What a life! Most men would have jumped at such an opportunity to live life in the grand style with servants and your own island. Not Napoleon! In the minds of many at that time, he was like a saint and he could not stand monotony – due to a bi-polar affliction.

Chapter Eight

Geronimo–Peripatetic Prairie Power

"I'm not a chief. I'm a military leader."

Why did Geronimo become the most famous of the Apache Warriors? Easy! He was a man's man on a mission to be free while both Mexicans and American soldiers kept trying to put him in his grave or on a reservation where he could live life like they were. Not smart! For over twenty-five years, the American military machine was unable to catch him or kill him. He finally surrendered, but not until he was aging and tired of fighting, and he discovered that his family and children were interred by the white eyes on a Florida reservation. He was attacked by those with weapons he had never seen, but was never beaten.

As a young man, the Mexicans killed his mother, his wife three children in a raid on their camp while he was out finding food. Talk about a warrior on a mission of revenge. This Apache warrior went out and sat by a river and thought and thought and meditated in the Indian sense. When he finally got up to leave he had been transformed from an ascetic Apache into a zealot wanting retribution for an insidious act. Geronimo had married at seventeen and they had the three children murdered by the Mexican banditos. It took place on March 6, 1858 when a band of four-hundred Mexican soldiers from Sonora attacked his camp. It was here that an epiphany would occur for Geronimo and he would never be the same. He visited the great chief Cochise and asked for advice and men and came back armed for battle. After one vicious attack where he left many Mexican scalps on the pathways they were aware that this Apache was not like other Indians and screamed for help from the gods. In that time and Spanish language it was not his birth name Goyahkla that they screamed but *Cuidado! Watch out, it's Geronimo."* From that day on they screamed the name Geronimo and soon his own men began calling him by that new epithet of power and glory. He had told other Indians what had happened to his family and many of them were now with him on a warrior's mission of revenge. After his tragic loss he was wired with a different set of values and a strong mental malice and an inner fire that would never be quenched. After the first few battles, the Mexicans became aware that this Indian with a band of wild warriors had better not be messed with. His band of Indians called him "Chief," but he didn't want the title. Those who would see what a real warrior was like made him their chief, but he refused. Goyahkla only wanted revenge and did he get revenge! In the big picture, all he wanted was freedom for himself and his people. However, after the Mexican-American War in 1848, America took control over Apache territories of California and what would become Arizona and New Mexico. An Apache warrior would later observe: *"Geronimo seems to be more intelligent, resourceful, vigorous and far-sighted than other men."* These would prove to be the qualities that fueled his drive to immortality.

How did Geronimo and other Apache warriors become so gifted at what is now called guerilla warfare? Easy! When he turned seventeen, Goyahkla was sent into the mountains to earn his stripes as an Apache warrior and be admitted into the Chiricahua Apache Council. He passed the rituals by learning the art of survival, how to find food when lost and alone on a mountain range, and how to build a fire and get smoke above the hills so he could be found. He learned that it was necessary to hide in the brush so that he could discern if the men were friend or foe. In that era, it was often another Indian tribe or the hated Mexican banditos still known as Aztecs. Soon it would be white eyes looking to farm their land. When older, on an Oklahoma reservation he would tell his biographers, *"I was born on the prairies where the wind blew free and there was nothing to break the light of the sun. I was born where there were no enclosures."* He was crying out for the right to return to his heritage. He would turn to alcohol due to wanting out of the Euro-American enclosures that were barriers to his freedom. When the white-eyes kept calling him a chief, he responded, *"I'm not a chief. I'm a military leader."* The Apache would be anointed by historians as the greatest guerilla fighter the world had ever seen. And, the Apache with the name "Geronimo" was the head warrior when faced with adversaries or banditos. For twenty-five years he showed his mettle at escaping from American soldiers and refused to be taken prisoner. When he finally surrendered in 1886, he had but a small band of sixteen Indian warriors that consisted of fourteen women and their six children. The army had been pursuing this small band with 5,000 troops that composed one-fifth of its entire regular army. They had spent over $1 million dollars a year to fight him, but when he finally was in a state of exhaustion, Geronimo voluntarily surrendered. In 1882, Geronimo and his small band of Apaches were interred in the San Carlos Reservation on the banks of the Gila River in eastern Arizona. It was called "Hell's Forty Acres" with 5,000 Apaches. The fates interfered and the white-eyes discovered valuable deposits of copper, coal, and silver. Then many white squatters showed up on the land they had been given and suddenly even that land was no longer theirs. Talk about getting pissed off? An Apache shaman named "Noch-ay-del-klinne" began preaching and the reservation police killed him. That led to a revolt by Geronimo who fled the reservation with twenty-four followers. They went on a two-year assault on those that had betrayed them and their dignity. Among those killed were, ironically, a federal judge and his wife.

The Geronimo legacy is far more than most people realize. The valiant exploits of this Apache warrior would inspire World War II paratrooper Aubrey Eberhardt to use his name when he was jumping from a plane behind enemy lines. Eberhardt was in a training camp to learn how to successfully parachute when he was bored one night and he and other paratroopers went to see the 1939 movie *Geronimo*. This was the first ever United States parachute test platoon that consisted of fifty volunteers who trained in the sweltering heat of Georgia's Fort Benning. In an attempt to avoid the scorching heat, Private Eberhardt and three friends watched the movie on this valiant Apache. When they left the movie, they held a meeting to discuss using the name "Geronimo" prior to jumping from the plane. Why? This brazen warrior was without fear and survived superior forces to make his mark in the world. The next day, Eberhardt would be the first to jump from the plane, and when he left the plane, he screamed, "Geronimo! " His men jumped screaming the label and it caught on quickly with other soldiers in World War II. The screaming would be repeated by his men and would take hold in that period of high anxiety as they wanted to show that they too were like this Apache warrior, without fear and armed with exuberant ferocity. After some time, it would become a war chant in France and Italy. Later, in World War II, the aphorism would be outlawed because commanding officers felt it would draw unwanted attention to paratroopers landing in hostile territory. But the Geronimo motto is still seen on certain military insignias so Eberhardt's legend lives on.

The Path to Glory

Geronimo's life is akin to the lifelong struggle of Native Americans having to learn to cope with conflict in addition to the harsh conditions for finding food and shelter in the American Southwest. This warrior wunderkind was reared in present day Arizona. When young, he was considered indolent since his birth name Goyakla meant "He Who Yawns" in the Apache language. On his trek to adulthood, all this would change when the Treaty of Guadalupe Hidalgo was signed and it ceded much of the Southwestern, United States to the Americans; a territory once owned by Mexico. This frontier had been inhabited by both Indians and Mexicans for many years. The two cultures hated each other and had spent their lives killing each other. The land was originally New Mexico territory, but Arizona was split off and ultimately would become a separate state. America owned it as a territory and decided to open it up for pioneers looking for land to farm or to form new cities. For them, the Apaches had to be run off or put into reservations. As new settlers began to arrive and build their own ranches and towns, there were many skirmishes. They had guns while the Apache only had spears, bows, and arrows. If the new settler found a stray Indian kid on their land, they would kill them. For the Apache, this had been their land, and they found this foray into their territory uncalled for. They had been trained to survive, and that is what they did to the chagrin of the American military. The ranchers soon began to build fences to keep the Apache intruders off their property. This new intrusion into their territory did not sit well with the Apaches. Geronimo was their leader who chose to resist the white-eye laws. At this time, some of the new settlers gave land to the Chiracahua Apaches, but that was not what the Native Americans wanted or understood. They wanted freedom to roam, fish, and hunt. It was being taken from them and they were not happy campers. Eventually, even their reservation land was taken from them in 1872 when the

Chiracahuas were forced to leave their reservation and live among other Apaches on the San Carlos Reservation in Arizona.

In 1874, Geronimo and his people faced an even greater challenge. The U.S. government forced 4,000 Apaches to move from their encampments into what was called San Carlos Reservation – a five thousand acre tract of land on the Gila River. Without rights or their way of life, the Apache began to suffer from a restricted life and were made to live on a white-man's reservation. Geronimo refused, and he and a band of Apache warriors left and would fight U.S. troops for many years.

In 1881, Geronimo and his men left the reservation and hid in the mountains in Mexico. From his camp, he led attacks in the United States and Mexico, but by 1886, the American government decided to bring him in and sent 5,000 soldiers to complete the task. For the next fifteen years, his role as Chief rose, and the Apaches would kill and flee and become an impossible force. This was their kind of warfare and the U.S. troops were at a disadvantage when in the Rocky mountains trying to catch a man who had learned to survive there as a young man. Apache agent, John Clum, finally arrested Geronimo in 1877 and would describe him as, "erect as a mountain pine, while every outline of his symmetrical form indicated strength and endurance. His abundant ebony locks draped his ample shoulders, his stern features, his keen piercing eye, and his proud and graceful posture combined to create in him the model of an Apache war-chief." This kind of inner resolve and instinct would make him special and a very tough adversary.

Early Years and Trek to Eminence

Goyahkla was his birth name given to him in June of 1823. It was at the time when the New Mexico Territory was a province of the nation of Mexico. It was where Montezuma and the Spanish Conquistadors had lived and built a unique culture. He was born into a community of Apaches that were known as a predatory Indian tribe. In his youth, he never saw a white man. In such a world, one's wit and speed were key to survival. They had to learn early how to survive on the spoils of the land. To this end, he was taught to know every watering hole and place to hide as well as how to kill the animals needed to eat. He learned to ride a horse at a very young age and how to feed that animal. When it could go no further, they killed the horse and ate it in order to keep on living. This tough life was made tougher in 1835 when he was a teen and the Mexican State of Senora passed a law that offered one-hundred pesos for every Indian scalp brought to town. Two years later, the neighboring territory of Chihuahua offered one-hundred pesos for a male's scalp, fifty pesos for an Indian woman's scalp, and twenty-five for child's.

Goyahkla grew up in the wilds of the southwest where survival was a way of life. Geronimo's grandfather had been a chief of the Bedonkohe Apache tribe and he grew up with three brothers and four sisters. He wrote of his childhood in his memoir:

> *"When a child, my mother taught me to kneel and pray to Usen for strength, health, wisdom and protection. Sometimes we prayed in silence, sometimes each one prayed aloud; sometimes an aged person prayed for all of us and to Usen."*

To the Apaches, Geronimo embodied the essence of Apache values. They were necessarily aggressive as it was the only way to survive and it took great courage to be an Apache warrior. These qualities inspired fear in the "white-eye" settlers of Arizona and New Mexico. When food was scarce it was their custom to raid neighboring tribes. Raids and vengeance were an honorable way of life among the Apache nation, something that Caucasians did not understand. For the remainder of the 1870s, he and some of his friends led a quiet life on the reservation. However, with the slaying of the Apache prophet in 1881, they would return to full-time aggressiveness from a secret camp in the Sierra Madre Mountains. Sensationalized American white men's press exaggerated Geronimo's activities, making him the most feared and infamous Apache of all. Though Geronimo was usually outnumbered, he fought valiantly against both Mexican and United States troops. It would be this daring and a mentality that would make him famous - even among the Apache tribes.

During his life, he would experience many wild soirees and had numerous escapes from capture between 1858 and 1886. One escape was a kind of Hollywood scene beyond the purview of ordinary men. It took place in the *Robledo* Mountains, southwest New Mexico. When cornered, Geronimo and his warriors entered a cave and would be surrounded by American soldiers. They waited outside the entrance for the Indians to run out of food and would have to come out and be captured. But, they never came out. After many days, the soldiers went in to find the dead or dying Apaches. Geronimo was not there, and later it was heard that Geronimo was spotted nearby. That perplexed the American soldiers and it was obvious this warrior among warriors had known of a secret passage out of the cave, unknown to the "white-eyes." This cave has remained a symbol of his mythical magic and is still known today as *Geronimo's Cave*. At the end of his legendary time escaping American soldiers, he led a small band of thirty-six men, women, and children, evading thousands of adversaries. He did this for over a year, and it would make him the poster boy for rebellious solitude. It caused historians to make Geronimo as the "worst Indian who ever lived." His band was one of the last major forces of independent Native American warriors who refused to acknowledge the United States' occupation of the American West, and that would add to his legacy and warrior wunderkind image.

Charismatic Powers Proved Prophetic

To the Apaches, Geronimo embodied the essence of Apache values - aggressiveness and courage in the face of difficulty. Such qualities and traits have been labeled charismatic powers by psychologists. For them, a charismatic has intrinsic powers manifested extrinsically via magnetism or what they label "psychic energy." This kind of inner power is possessed by only a few, but Geronimo would exhibit it far more than most. About one-hundred years after Geronimo's reign as a warrior wizard, visionaries in Big Sur California would come up with how to have this magical power. Mike Murphy would lead Esalen for some years and labeled such powers as entering a kind of "zone." Murphy wrote, *Stepping into the terra incognita by deed seems to trigger opening the terra incognita of meta-normal experiences.* Anthony Storr, a British psychiatrist, wrote on the nature of gurus and came up with a list of behaviors that defined such men like Georgei Gurdhieff, Hitler, and Carl Jung and came up with their special qualities that were magnetic like Geronimo as follows:

- Gurus tend to be intolerant of any kind of criticism
- Gurus tend to be elitist and anti-democratic
- Gurus attract disciples without acquiring friends
- Gurus seldom discuss their ideas; they only impose them

Geronimo was a guru in the Storr likeness. He was highly intolerant of the Mexicans and Americans trying to force his people to live, love, and eat like they did. For him, this was "anti-democratic" and "elitist." They had no right to take his land or make the Apaches fit their lifestyle. He had disciples that followed him religiously no matter the risk. He imposed his rules and was not one inclined to call a meeting to discuss their destination. He was mesmerizing in the eyes of both his enemies and his disciples. Geronimo was wounded many times by both bullets and buckshot and he miraculously survived. It led the Apache to believe their leader was special and a Chief. They saw him as possessing many powers beyond the pale of a man being hunted. The Indians felt he was favored or protected by the Apache High God, *Usen*. For this accolade, Geronimo would paint the faces of his disciples as a means of godly protection. During his career, Geronimo was notorious for consistently urging raids and war on Mexican Provinces and would annihilate their towns and villages in revenge for their despicable acts on his people.

Shaman Fantasies as Motivational Mantras

Geronimo would sit alone and meditate after the unexpected deaths of his family and children. It was his mortal enemy, the Mexicans, and he went into a mystical state before annihilating many of them. In his memoir, he would recall having heard a voice, not unlike that of Joan of Arc that told him, *"No gun can ever kill you. I will take the bullets from the guns of the Mexicans and I will guide your arrows."* This mystical message was like an omen and was an inner-armor for the years as he would avenge the despicable acts. He became an icon since his psychic energy was bedazzling and his people saw him as a very powerful medicine man and shaman that could foretell the future. They made him their leader due to his magical powers. Geronimo was rumored to have had mysterious powers of the mind and an ability to see into the future. It may or may not have been true, but he was treated as a mythical magic-man. Many of his Apache warriors said that he could walk without creating footprints and even hold off the coming of the dawn to protect his own people.

Geronimo felt that he was at war with those that would kill him and his people. Raids and vengeance were an honorable way of life among the tribes and would be his anthem. The very name "Apache" has mystical connotations with it being a Zuni word meaning "enemy." With this as his cultural support, it is not a surprise that this Apache would see life as death or defiance. The Mexicans and then American soldiers were trained to understand that Apache was akin to "enemy," and thus, they were fair game and should be eliminated. Consequently, many were massacred by Mexicans and American soldiers. Geronimo decided to fight. Geronimo's repeated escapes embarrassed and provoked politicians, officers, and the non-Indian populace of the Southwest. His very name brought terror to the people who continually heard of his evading capture and his occasional killing of Anglo-Americans and Mexicans. Territorial newspaper headlines screamed his name, time and again. Self-Efficacy—a term meaning to know within what makes you tick—was strong in the Apache culture. Geronimo would attest to this in his memoir, writing, *"The soldiers never explained to the government when an Indian was wronged, but reported the misdeeds of the Indians. We took an oath not to do any wrong to each other or to scheme against each other."*

Epiphany that Proved Transformational

At the age of seventeen, Geronimo was sent to the Apache Council of Warriors to earn his stripes as a warrior and was taught to fight and find food to survive. These were tough environs and the young Indians were sent there to learn to cope with the mountainous terrain and taught how to find their food and kill if necessary. In one drill they were forced to race up a steep mountain trail, without breathing, and with water in his mouth so that he would learn to breathe only through his nose. Survival was one of the important skills to learn. If lost, he learned how to build a fire and send smoke signals to others so they could find him. Since there was always a chance an adversary could show up, they were told to hide and watch and see if it was a friend or foe. Biographer, Angie Debo, wrote, *"Being a warrior was a religious matter. In their world the #4 was sacred in the Usen – the supernatural of their clan."* For background on his metamorphoses, in 1846, when Geronimo was twenty-three, the Mexican-American War took place. When the Americans won and took over the Southwestern United States, they agreed with the Mexicans that American troops would restrict Indians from raiding their villages.

Geronimo's transformation would take place when he was twenty-eight on the day when his mother, wife, and three young children were killed while he was on a scouting trip to Kas-Ki-Yeh. While gone, a band of Mexican men came in and massacred many, including Geronimo's family. Later in life he would describe this horrid day, *"Late one afternoon when returning from town we were met by a few women and children who told* us that Mexican troops from some other town had attacked our camp, killed all the warriors of the guard, captured all our ponies, secured our arms, destroyed our supplies, and killed many of our women and children, I found that my aged mother, my young wife, and my three small children were among the dead. I was never again contented in our quiet home." He went into shock and was left to sit on a riverbank to think. He would later say, "I stood silently staring at the river. How long I stood there I do not know. I had no purpose left as I found my family there in a pool of blood." In his biography, Geronimo would tell about going back to his encampment and would burn all of his kid's toys, his mother's tepee, and his tepee. And, the rest of his fabled life would be summed up when he said, "I vowed revenge on the Mexicans who had wronged me." He would do like few warriors in history.

From that day in 1858, Goyahkla was a driven zealot on a mission beyond the pale of the ordinary. Mexicans had murdered his whole family and they would pay dearly for what they had done. After his sojourn on the river alone, he would travel to see the great chief, Cochise. There, he would align a group of Indians who would join him in a war party to seek revenge. He told Cochise, "No bullet can kill me." His first battle was against two Mexican companies of both cavalry and infantry. They had guns and swords. The Apaches had only bows, arrows, and knives. Historians speak of how he outflanked them, not unlike Napoleon had done against superior forces, and would call it a scalping orgy. It would be that momentous day that he would be given his name when the Mexican saw the ferocity in his eyes and the invincibility in his moves and they screamed, "**Cuidado! Watch out! Geronimo!**" It caught on and the Apaches in his tribe picked it up and began calling him Geronimo. The second thing that happened that momentous day was he was now the Chief of the Apaches in America. It would be a few years later when Geronimo would remarry and have another child that Mexicans once again came into his camp and killed. After this second atrocity, he would later write, "I now wanted more revenge." And he got it, big time.

Eccentric Wizardry and Empowerment

Later in his life this warrior found himself on a reservation and would tell his captors, "The soldiers never explained to the government when an Indian was wronged, but reported the misdeeds of the Indians." It was true in that the attempt to force cultural adaptation on the Apache was not about to work. Geronimo resisted the forced colonization. While on the reservation, Geronimo would tell the Americans of the cultural anomalies between the Apache and the Americans saying, "*Sometimes we prayed in silence, sometimes each one prayed aloud; sometimes an aged person prayed for all of us and to Usen.*" This was a long tradition of Apache warriors and something the Americans never understood. They were attempting to corral a man that was not capable of being corralled.

In 1874, some 4,000 Apaches were forcibly moved by U.S. authorities to a reservation at San Carlos, a barren wasteland in east-central Arizona. Deprived of traditional tribal rights, short on rations, and homesick, they turned to Geronimo and others who led them in the depredations that plunged the region into turmoil and bloodshed. By the early 1870s, Lieutenant Colonel George F. Crook, commander of the Department of Arizona, had succeeded in establishing relative peace in the territory. The management of his successors was disastrous and spurred on by the power of Geronimo. Hundreds of Apaches left the reservation to resume their war against what they called the "white-eyes." In 1882, Crook was recalled to Arizona to conduct a campaign against the Indians. Two years later Geronimo would surrender in order to join his family on a reservation. He left again, but in May of 1885 and with thirty-five men, eight boys, and one-hundred and one women, he hit the mountains. Crook threw his best men into a campaign against him and ten months later, on March 27, 1886, Geronimo surrendered at Cañón de Los Embudos in Sonora. Once again, Geronimo, the consummate rebel bolted with a small band of warriors.

A cultural dichotomy took place in America's wars with the Indians in the Western United States. Americans tried to make them live like them in reservations they provided. Not good! What gave them that right? Nobody, and Geronimo refused to be told what to do and where to live. The "white eyes" assumed they had a right take lands that had been Apache land for centuries. In the larger sense, it was pure idiocy. The southwest was their territory, where they lived, hunted, and raised their children. White settlers came in and took those lands and saw the Indians as fair game. They shot them if they resisted. Geronimo would tell the U.S. military, "*The white eyes will never catch us on our land,*" and he was prophetic as he would never be defeated. Then he told his pursuers, "*We didn't start this war. Why do the white eyes want all the land? We just want freedom to live our life without war. I am not a farmer and we fight white eyes and are willing to die because we just want to be free and are willing to die to be free."* In many ways, the era is one of the travesties of the American legacy. When some Indians bought the American way and settled on a reservation, the white men found silver and copper mines and retook their lands. The Americans ignored the rights of the Apaches and passed laws and then prosecuted the Indians for violating those laws. Geronimo was the last leader who dared defy this odious faction. In many ways, he was a sage beyond his time telling a commander, *"Your men came and burned our villages. Then we moved to the mountains. That is why we killed your men and why I will never surrender."*

Influence on the World

After the death of the Great Apache Chief, Cochise, in 1874, the Americans wanted to move the Chiricahuas to the Arizona desert. Geronimo and hundreds in his tribe bolted and started a war against these intruders that would last for the next twenty-five years. Geronimo would become a true symbol of the American Wild West due to his an indomitable will. Geronimo was the last warrior who was defiant and refused to capitulate to the American soldiers sent to tame him. He was willing to fight against daunting odds. He would hold out the longest and it would leave him as a legend and the most famous Apache in American lore. To better understand this warrior among warriors, let's look at his final surrender in 1886. At that time, his small band consisted of a few against many. Despite a huge expenditure of time, money, and soldiers, Geronimo gave up the ghost. Ironically, when he finally gave in to the white-eyes, it was due to a renegade band of one-hundred Apache scouts. His surrender brought an end to the Indian wars and the violence accompanying them. Geronimo was nomadic with a ferocious nature that would not be happy on any reservation. Like many visionaries and successful warriors, Geronimo was not one to take the paths taken by others. This would prove to be a success attribute of other visionaries such as the greatest American architect, Frank Lloyd Wright. Like Geronimo, Wright would live in ten states before he was ten years-old. What has that got to do with visionary eminence? A lot! He and Geronimo were able to learn early to cope with new arenas, new people, and they had to make new friends. No one of this ilk is ever xenophobic, and they learn early to adapt to new milieus. That same learning experience would empower the world's first female anthropologist PhD,

Margaret Mead. This lady would do research in the jungles of New Guinea alone in her early twenties. How was she able to do this? She had lived in sixty different homes before she was ever in a classroom. That is what programmed her to go where traditionalists would never go. She had been programmed to love the new and foreign and to tread new paths. This same early training is what made Geronimo a wandering warrior who was never afraid no matter where he found himself. After more than twenty years as a prisoner of war, Geronimo wrote this to the United States president, saying:

> "It is my land, my home, my fathers' land, to which I now ask to be allowed to return. I want to spend my last days there, and be buried among those mountains. If this could be I might die in peace, feeling that my people, placed in their native homes, would increase in numbers, rather than diminish as at present, and that our name would not become extinct."

During the last few months of this warrior's time as his own man, he and his forty Apache Native Americans were chased by over 10,000 men. They were unable to catch them or find out where they were hiding. Finally, General Nelson Miles caught up with them and offered them a conditional surrender with benefits. Geronimo and his followers were promised only two years imprisonment and then they would be allowed to go free. It was bullshit, as it would never happen. Some wonder why iconoclasts are reticent to surrender. Geronimo and his men were not required to do prison time, but they were never fully released as "prisoners of war" by the U.S. government. The Apache people on reservations were permitted to live life as farmers, and Geronimo, due to his status, was sent on tours to sell photographs and mementos in Wild West Shows and other expeditions. Geronimo would appear at the 1904 St. Louis World's Fair as an iconic celebrity. It is unfortunate that his end would come when on a drinking spree in 1909 as he was approaching age 80. Still riding his horse, he would fall and lay on the ground all night. The warrior would catch pneumonia and died a few days later. A great American native warrior had crashed in the ashes of history.

Chapter Nine

Mao's Perseverance Power

"Power comes out of the barrel of a gun."

Tenacity is magical. For those that never give up they don't really lose at least in the mind of warriors with such a mindset as Geronimo and Mao Zedung. The latter was tenacious to a fault and it would be his legacy as a savior of China during the Great Depression years and in World War II. Others who have reached the pinnacle of power had a similar perseverance that is seldom, if ever, found in the world's traditionalists. Walt Disney was such a man. Uncle Walt's Disney Studios were insolvent for thirty years during which Walt once hocked his car to make payroll and another time sold his Palm Springs home to stave off bankruptcy. To launch Disneyland, he sold investments to buy the land in Anaheim when his Board of Directors refused to fund what they thought was a "very stupid idea." Wow! Winston Churchill personifies the power of perseverance when he refused to surrender under the torrent of Nazi bombs in the Second World War. It left its mark on this warrior when later as a commencement speaker at a major university he would tell the students the secrets of success. He walked to the podium and said, *"Never, Never, Never, Never, Never, Never give up,"* and he returned to his seat. The great aviator, Amelia Earhart, was once questioned about her skills as a pilot. She responded, *"I am not the best pilot. What I have is tenacity."* The tenacious warriors like Zedong are never worried about failing, being captured, or losing a battle. They worry about how to win, not about the possibilities of losing. That separates them from the herd, as most try not to lose rather than try to win. A quintessential example of this concept is Soichiro Honda whose parts factory was destroyed by American bombs in World War II. Honda was broke and suddenly without a business and without transportation. What does he do? He picks u pa discarded GI motor, mounts it on his bicycle and rides his new vehicle from home to the ruins of his factory. Friends paid him to make them one of his new motorbikes. He built them one, and then he built dozens and then thousands and within a decade he was a titan of motorcycles. Within ten years, this man without a job was the largest motorcycle titan in the world. The Honda Motors Empire was born. Crisis was the mother of his creativity and success.

In Mao Zedung's case, he knew he could never win in his battle against the well-funded and backed adversary Chiang Kai-shek. This man would become his mortal enemy in the 1930's and then they joined forces against the invading Japanese but when that conflict was over they were back at it. It was in the early days that Mao took his men on a backwards march that would later be labeled the Long March of 6000 miles in which he would lose 90,000 men and come close to losing his own life many times. Mao went days at a time without sleeping. He would learn from this retreating strategy to stay the course and your time will come. In 1926, he was thirty when he retreated into the hills of the hinterlands of China and co-founded the Communist Party. He would spend the next twenty-two years of his life fighting for his Communist cause. During this time, he would assemble a group of renegade warriors who shared his political philosophy. A litany of examples of the tenacity of this warrior is found in his life and success. One example is of a man who would stop bathing since it took too much of his time saying, *"I stopped bathing as it is a needless waste of time that I cannot afford."* The mantra of a warrior with tenacity was, *"Keep men and lose the land, since the land can be taken again."* That is the warrior's survivor mentality.

Mao's physician, Dr. Li Zhisui, wrote the archetypal biography of this tenacious and driven zealot. Few men knew him as he was driven by some inner fires that were not easily quenched. After years as the people's savior, he would be honored as if he were a god. There were as many who feared him as loved him since he had risen to glory out of the barrel of a gun that had killed as many as it had saved. Biographers say that he killed more men than Hitler and Stalin combined. For his detractors, he was the reincarnation of the devil. Mao was notorious for an expertise in manipulating both friend and foe. When his army marched victoriously into Beijing in 1949, his path was set for life. He was fifty-seven at the time when he would rise to the pinnacle of power as the head of China's Communist Party. Mao would become the master of his domain and it would peak during the "Cult of Personality" in the 1960s. There were 850 million Chinese paying him homage as their savior for bringing them communism where the government would give them free housing, jobs, and a safe existence for the rest of their lives. Under this modern Robin Hood's rule, industrial production increased dramatically, and the problem of feeding the second largest nation in the world was suddenly solved. Mao's ideology was to create a nation for a "new man" that "served the needs of all the people." It won approval and he was made head of state for life. Once in power, he told subordinates, *"When dealing with a tiger, use a long stick."*

Mao was a hand's-on leader, a trait that has been found to be important in visionary leaders in all disciplines. They are not sitting in some safe office, but are in the factory or field in which they function. Mao never used his office when in power except to take pictures. He actually ate most of his meals in bed alone surrounded by thousands of books. Mao was never interested in hygiene and despite being a chain smoker never brushed his teeth and would ultimately die of emphysema. He had seen so many people die when young he became quite callous when in power and others felt him to be quite insensitive to human suffering. Mao would have been a successful entrepreneur in today's world as he seldom wanted to take the same path and was never lost no matter where he was, even when he had no idea where he was. Testimony to his strong egomania was is telling American author Edgar Snow, "I am a god and a law unto myself," and that is why he was able to effectively implement new cultural concepts in a very old nation steeped in tradition. His methods would become ritualistic in his era and would be known as Maoism. In his system, "Knowledge was at the core of knowing and if you have not investigated, you have no right to speak."

The Path to Glory

The path to the very top for this warrior was books, ambition and incredible energy. He would not let himself be dominated by his father or his nation's heroes like Chiang Kai-shek. He was willing to outwork and often would outthink his adversaries as he was without doubt a visionary with a dominant right-hemisphere brain proclivity that was beyond the norm. The Marxists ideology that he would preach to all who would listen was very philosophical in respect to how a true warrior takes power and keeps it. He would write of this in his famous Little Red Book of advice, *"Marxist philosophy holds that the most important problem does not lie in the understanding the laws of the objective world and thus being able to explain it, but in applying the knowledge of these laws actively to change the world."* His early words of philosophical wisdom would attract a legion of followers with rhetoric from his pen saying:

> **"Our principle is that the Party commands the gun and the gun must never be allowed to command the Party. The masses are the real heroes, while we ourselves are often childish and ignorant, and without this understanding it is impossible to acquire even the most rudimentary knowledge."**

In the autumn of 1933 Chiang Kai-shek launched a huge attack against the Communists who were then based in the Jiangxi and Fujian provinces in south-east China. The German general Hans von Seeckt advised Chiang Kai-shek not to launch a full frontal attack but to make a slow advance building trenches and blockhouses as they went to give the troops some protection. The Long March ended in Yenan, China. One hundred-thousand set off on the march but many would perish. The Red Army started the Long March carrying whatever it could with 87,000 soldiers starting the retreat carrying such items as typewriters, furniture and printing presses. They also took 33,000 guns and nearly 2 million ammunition cartridges. It took the Red Army 40 days to get through the blockhouses surrounding Jiangxi but no sooner had they done this than they were attacked. In the Battle of Xiang, the Red Army lost 45,000 men – over 50% of their fighting force. Mao, supported in his work by Zhu De then adopted new tactics. Mao wanted the Red Army to in a completely unpredictable way. As it moved away from Xiang it employed wacky twisting movement patterns that made predicting its direction very difficult. Mao also split up the army into smaller units. In theory this made them more open to attack – in practice, they were more difficult to find in the open spaces of China. In some sense it was guerilla warfare that years later would be the war in the Middle East where hit and hide tactics were the order of the day. It was Mao's nature to take a different tack and it often confused his adversaries.

Mao also had a new target – Shaanxi province towards the north of China. The journey was physically demanding as it crossed very difficult terrain and mountainous roads. They would cross snowy mountains and some of the highest mountains in the world. In the Chinese Grassland - an area of deep marshes –would claim hundreds of lives. The Red Army had to contend with the enemy as well as the treacherous environment. The lands at this time in northern China were controlled by local warlords. Even the armies of Chiang Kai-shek failed to break their power. By October 1935 there was not much left of the original 87,000 Red Army soldiers. Less than 10,000 men would survive the march. They had travelled over 6000 miles and the march had taken 368 days. The Long March is considered one of the great physical feats of the Twentieth Century. Mao Zedong eulogized the Long March in a poem titled The Long March (October 1935):

> The Red Army fears not the trials of the Long March,
> Holding light ten thousand crags and torrents.
> The Five Ridges wind like gentle ripples
> And the majestic Wumeng roll by, globules of clay.
> Warm the steep cliffs lapped by the waters of Golden Sand, Cold the iron chains spanning the Tatu River.
> Minshan's thousand li* of snow joyously crossed,
> The three Armies march on, each face glowing.

The Long March would become a manifesto for Mao's intense zeal and tenacity to never, ever concede failure. Later he would use this resolve to help the Chinese masses to believe in their own salvation. Chinese historians would proclaim the Long March as testimony to an army of heroes, while the imperialists and their running dogs led by capitalist Chiang Kai-shek were impotent aristocrats. When Chiang's armies were unable to encircle them or capture them, they gained resolve and felt anointed with power. The Long March is shown below in the map of his trek across China.

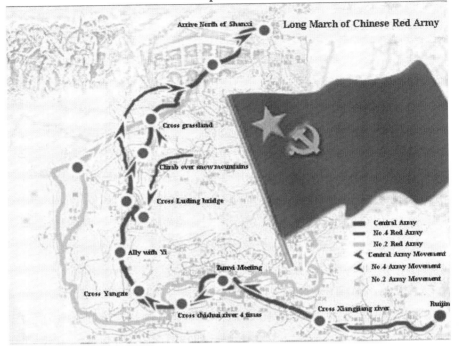

Early Years and Trek to Eminence

Born in Hunan Province in China in December 1893, Mao was a boy on a farm with a dictatorial dad. Farm work was never the life for an only child of a doting mother and an abusive father who he hated. Mao would remember his mom as being generous and sympathetic. She was not strong enough to confront her husband when he hit his son. Mao's mother believed in many traditional ideas and told her son that his ideas of wild abandon were not the Chinese way. In his interviews with historian Edgar Snow, Mao told him that he had tried to escape his traditional Chinese upbringing. How? He ran away a couple times. His mother's traditional values would stay with him all the way to when he was Chairman Mao. For him the traditional values were deeply ingrained shaping his political and personal persona. His father's harshness with dealing with opposition, his cunning, his demand for reverence from subordinates and his wild uninhibited ambition later would be the same qualities that adversaries would see in Mao. Mao would demand harmony, order, and reverence as a ruthless dictator. It would not be all that different from what he had learned as a child. In his teens he would escape in books, as is often the case for only children. During this period he became fascinated by accounts of the rulers of ancient China, men like Yao, Shun, Ch'in Shih Huang Ti, and Hu Wu Ti. He read of their heroic deeds and put them in his memory bank to mimic later when he would recall that these warriors of the past had a certain grandeur, elegance and power. It was quite a divergence from the life he was seeing in early 20th century China. Yao and Shun had been credited with forming the first Chinese society in the Yellow River Valley and it would be Mao's destiny to try to repeat their victories.

One aphorism would be born in that period he spent on a remote China farm when he wrote in his Little Red Book, *"The most important thing is to be strong."* When he left he spent days and weeks in the Beijing library and was enamored of the heroics of the British fantasy hero Robin Hood. The man who stole from the rich to feed the poor was not a big divide from the Communist Manifesto. His father forced him to marry a 20-year old when he was just 14, but he ran away again and never lived with the girl or returned home. His father then passed and he was now on his own and he would remember, *"I hated my father and he was the first capitalist I knew."* Once he would spend six months in a library reading voraciously, despite never having even read a newspaper until he was 17. He would marry four times and have four children, one of which was murdered and another committed to an asylum. He was a chain smoker and womanizer from an early age and it would cause many health issues.

Charismatic Powers Proved Prophetic

"Laziness," he would say, *"is the grave of life,"* from a manic-depressive who was always on a roll and mesmerized many of those below him. It was 1934 when Mao first encountered the power of armies led by his arch-enemy Chiang Kai-shek. He had already co-founded the Communist Party and Chiang was a democratic leader who vowed to destroy Communism. Thus began the historic Long March with Mao leading his followers in a systematic retreat in order to survive. His army would walk the rocky hillsides of central China and reached their destination a year later with only one-tenth of the men still alive – losing 90,000 in a march of death. Their leader never gave up and would later tell his side, *"Zealots are like bamboo – sharp mouth, thick skin, hollow minds."* This charismatic power broker went on to say, *"Our army has always had two policies. First, we must be ruthless to our enemies, we must overpower*

and annihilate them. Second, we must be kind to our own, to the people, to our comrades and to our superiors and subordinates, and unite with them." Mao was a master with the media and told them, *"We, the Chinese nation, have the spirit to fight the enemy to the last drop of our blood, the determination to recover our lost territory by our efforts, and the ability to stand on our own feet in the family of nations."*

Mao's personal physician would reveal many of the underlying factors that drove his leader. One shocker was that this most loved man in China would be without a friend. But he knew the ways and wiles of a leader. Swimming was always one of his loves and he would swim across the three great rivers in China to make a statement to followers and adversaries. The three rivers are the Pearl, Xiang and Yangtze and were signs of power in the minds of the Chinese who depended on them for fish, water and health. Mao promised to swim all three rivers in the spring of 1956 when he was a man in his sixties. Mao's security staff opposed the swim but as he was not easily dissuaded from anything and swam anyway to show the populace that. Chairman Mao was as mighty as the rivers. His propaganda posters depicted him swimming like no other world leader. One staff member, Yang Shangkun said, *"No other world leader looks down with such disdain on great mountains and powerful rivers."* It was then that he decided to show the world the temerity of a Chinese warrior when he epitomized his mental and physical superiority in swimming the Yangtze River near the area of the Three Gorges. Just after he swam the Yangtze in July of 1956, Mao told Dr. Li that he wanted to dam the Yangtze. The dam was to be like Emperor Qin Shihuangdi's Great Wall. In 1962 Mao advocated the Socialist Education Movement (SEM) in an attempt to 'inoculate' the peasantry against the temptations of feudalism and capitalist idealism. Large doses of his personal philosophy and didactic pontificating would be emblazoned on the psyche of the Chinese people. The Party organization saw the initiatives proposed by Mao and his even more radical followers as interfering with its successful program of economic rehabilitation. Mao turned towards the People's Liberation Army, the only organization he still deemed ideologically correct and in that way stayed ahead of his detractors.

Shaman Fantasies as Motivational Mantras

In a likeness of his hero Napoleon,, Mao would write when still just eighteen, *"I am the universe."* This would come shortly after he had encountered survival at seventeen when he assisted the Manchu government overthrow some dissidents and he would become enamored with war and would then enlist in the revolutionary army. His teachers said that he had a sense of his legacy at a very young age and insisted on dating every essay he wrote for posterity. Mao was self-educated man who would mimic one of his mythical heroes to win the day. That was very similar to Alexander the Great who did the same with Achilles. Mao had read extensively on the lives and successes of Alexander the Great and Catherine the Great as well as Marx and Lenin. But as discussed above his heroes were mythical characters like Robin Hood as well as Napoleon, Charles Darwin and Adam Smith. Mao was also an avid swimmer and often would swim in dangerous waters. When his timid companions would warn him of the danger Mao would respond, *"Maybe you're afraid of sinking. Don't think about it. If you don't think about it you won't sink.. If you do, you will."* That is quite profound for such a self-educated man but it is exacting in the sense the mind is the power behind the man.

It was Mao's marriage to a former actress that led him into the Cultural Revolution. It would be his philosophy and her works of art that were used to motivate the masses to grow and expand. Mao's wife Jiang Qing supported the artistic direction set by the PLA. The conceptual dogmas and theatrical conventions provided by the model operas that she supported also became the standard in the visual arts As the *Great Teacher, the Great Leader, the Great Helmsman.* But it would be the Supreme Commander Mao who would dominate the propaganda art of the first half of the Cultural Revolution. His image was considered more important than the occasion for which a particular work of propaganda art was designed. In many cases identical posters dedicated to Mao were published in different years bearing different slogans, i.e., serving different propaganda causes. In one he would he appear as a muscular super-person. One of the important factors that started the Cultural Revolution is power concentrated on one person.

Personality cults go against the basic ideas of Marxism. Past personality cults, such as was the case in Napoleon, Hitler and Stalin was also what would happen with Mao. He would talk aggressively against personality cults and had prohibited celebrations for the birthday of Party leaders since the Republic was established. It worked. Mao spoke of this at the congress in Chengdu in 1958 saying, *"There are two kinds of personality* cults. One is a healthy personality cult, that is, to worship men like Marx, Engels, Lenin, and Stalin, because they hold the truth in their hands. The other is a false personality cult, those not analyzed and with blind worship." From 1957 all power was concentrated on Mao Zedong and no one else. However because of the repressive laws he made, nobody dared criticize him. The people admired Mao enthusiastically as a hero of the new China on a new mission. A statue to him was built in his hometown and Mao's little Red Books were distributed to the people. How was this crazy cult of Mao developed, and how did it connect with the Cultural Revolution? Easy! Here was a man being worshipped as an icon and when in charge he took charge with an iron hand.

Epiphany that Proved Transformational

Mao hated his domineering father, a peasant from the hinterlands, and it would fuel his trek to the top. Mao never even saw a newspaper until he was seventeen, and when he ran away from home at age ten on his return his vicious father told him five years of formal education was enough. That is when he left for good to attend a school at Changsha in Hunan's capital. Upper school was a reawakening for a dirt poor teenager hanging with educated with wealthy classmates. It led to his becoming enamored with learning and books,, a major factor in his becoming a successful leader of men who were not quite as learned. It would lead to his becoming a co-founder of the Communist Party in his late twenties. While fleeing from Chiang Kai-shek's troops both his wife and sister were executed and such breakdowns do lead to breakthroughs. It would not be long before he would almost die of malaria while fighting guerilla warfare. These events would leave an indelible imprint on a man who would never again trust anyone, especially political adversaries. Here was a man born with nothing and learn to have a heart of steel and a passion for living and loving. He summed up his ability to survive in that period saying, "The enemy advances, we retreat, the enemy camps and we harass, the enemy tires and then we attack." Due to his love of books some historians have labeled Mao as an intellectual revolutionary. That is probably a bit strong but he would write in his Little Red Book of philosophical advice he would say, "To rebel is justified." That was because he had been transformed in his youth when war became a way of life.

Eccentric, Wizardry, and Empowerment

From a young man, Mao would become rebellious. When in school, he had refused to stand up and recite a lesson and he would be labeled a "renegade." This is the classic behavior of a passionate introvert with the guts to say no. His physician biographer would write, "*He was not a healthy personality and had no friends or anyone he loved.*" This has been a quality found in most of the subjects in this work. Attila was a loner as was Saint Joan and Napoleon who also said that he loved no one including his siblings. At age eighteen he walked to Beijing to begin a life of a modern man. By 1921, when he was twenty-eight he would join the Communist party as one of their very first men of passion. An example of the eccentric behavior of a warrior on a mission to the impossible he stopped bathing, saying, "*It is a needless waste of time that I cannot afford.*" This renegade warrior never took the same path twice and was fearless of new people under his control. Mao was an insomniac with a penchant for staying up all night for many causes. This combative personality was not normal, according to his physician, Dr. Zhisui, who wrote, "*Mao was devoid of human feeling, incapable of love, friendship or warmth.*" During the war years, Mao went for days without going to bed. Zhisui would write the quintessential words on what made this warrior tick, "*His quixotic crusades may have killed more people than the mass exterminations of Hitler and Stalin combined.*" (Zhisui p. 75) He would rule 500 million people as a kind of potentate with a Machiavellian sense of power. The bottom line was Mao took no prisoners and those around him were aware of his potential for destruction, with his biographer saying, "*He was a man of tremendous energy who was happiest when he had several young women simultaneously sharing his bed.*" That is a man devoid of feelings who would kill more people than either Adolph Hitler or Joseph Stalin, but he never got the media exposure, so few knew about his climb to power over dead bodies due to the closed nature of China. Dr. Li Zhisui admitted in his biographical work in 1993 that Chairman Mao was very manic-depressive and would go for days without sleep. When hyper he would go off into an orgiastic state and when depressed go his quarters and not emerge for days.

Influence on the World – Maoism

For millions of Chinese during his reign, Mao was more god than man and the media called his leadership style "Maoism." It would become the marching orders of half a billion people and it would lead to Mao being selected as the Man of the Year by *Time* magazine's cover on February 7, 1949. He was idolized at the time by the Asians and eulogized in China as the man who made the nation a world leader. When he passed away at age 82 on September 9, 1976, he was Chairman of the Central Committee of the Communist party and considered a hero to be worshipped. When he met with Indian leader Jawaaharlal Nehru and discussing the threat of the atomic bomb he would say, *"The atom bomb is not to be feared. The death of 10 or 20 million or even 300 million can be tolerated since they can be replaced. Lives have to be sacrificed for the cause of the revolution."* Wow! Mao was not a man of compromise in words or deeds. When he communicated, the world knew what he was about, no matter the gender. During the feminist movement of the 1960s, the media asked about his position in China, and he stated emphatically:

> **"In order to build a great socialist society, it is of the utmost importance to arouse the broad masses of women to join in productive activity. Men and women must receive equal pay for equal work in production. Genuine equality between the sexes can only be realized in the process of the socialist transformation of society as a whole."**

In a Moscow speech, he would say similar things that he had told Nehru, *"I am prepared to lose 300 million men if necessary to win."* Are those dramatic words for developing a rapport with an ally? But he was and would always be a guerilla willing to kill to win and it was never said more dramatically than his political philosophy to the people, *"Political power grows out of the barrel of a gun."* Mao had become the head of the Chinese Communist Party in his fifties and power lasted until his death in 1973. He would launch the Big Leap Forward at age 66 and implement the Cultural Revolution when in his 70's. In his Little Red Book Mao would write the laws of being a warrior as he told the people *"We must affirm a new discipline of the party namely"*:

Warriors Who Win

(1) the individual is subordinate to the organization;

(2) the minority id subordinate to the majority;

(3) the lower level is subordinate to the higher level; and

(4) the entire membership is subordinate to the Central Committee and whoever violates these articles of discipline disrupts Party unity.

On his passing, an enormous red flag draped his coffin, like a red sail unfurled on a Chinese junk. It was the consummate symbol of the dualism of traditional China and the present Communist China. Such dualisms were synonymous with the life and frenetic nature of warrior Mao. The people flowing past his casket seemed never to stop while he lay in state on that week in September 1976. Workers, peasants, soldiers and students and many of his female liaisons were united in grief. Mao was the helmsman guiding the good ship lollypop for China to emerge as one of the world's major powers. Community, harmony and order were the mission of this hero of China's transformation from an ancient culture into a modern dynasty. Mao's cult of personality, party purges, and political policies reflect his monumental ego. China was a "predominantly rural society with more than 80% of its people peasants when he took power. Their economic problems were so big that the totalitarianism with which Mao reigned was necessary. The collectivism and industrialization that would happen decades later show that sometimes it takes time for big changes to occur. Mao's methods were often ruthless and despotic but sometimes that must happen for political paradigm shifts to occur. When China passed Germany in GDP in 2010 they became the number two economy in the world behind Japan and the United States. Economists now predict they will be number one by 2016. It is a nation with more natural resources, human resources and a dominant work ethic and that will prevail despite Mao being gone.

Chapter Ten

Mahatma Gandhi's Paradoxical Power

"That government is best that governs the least."

Gandhi was featured on the cover of *Time* magazine as their Man of the Year on June 30, 1947. They had characterized him as a *Soul Force* that had been extracted from the meaning of Mahatma – Great Soul. This was one year before he would be assassinated by an extremist editor of the newspaper *Hindu Rashtra Nathu*. Mahatma was shot three times at close range. He died twenty-eight minutes later. His assassination was due to religious animosity between the Buddhists – Gandhi's persuasion - and the Hindus. Mahatma would go to his grave in New Delhi believing he had failed in bringing independence to India but it was not the truth since his death would precipitate the British withdrawal within the year. It was Gandhi's strategy of Satyagraha – a non-violent opposition of authority – that he described as, "My moral principle and rally cry for truth and freedom," that had brought the mighty British Empire to its knees.

The British were quite frustrated with this passive zealot on a mission for India's freedom to be their own nation with their own laws. Gandhi had a strong education in law from Oxford University but was so shy could not cross-examine witnesses and gave up his profession while in South Africa. Winston Churchill would show the bitterness in England describing Gandhi as *"a half-naked sedition fakir."* But Gandhi was not a man who listened well as he already had a program in his head about what was right and what was wrong with the system of British governance. He had learned a lot from the nation of his birth but wanted freedom for Indians to pursue their own destiny. Gandhi had a unique way of inspiring all of the cast members by addressing them in positive terms with a desire to drive the colonists back to their own homeland. Such passion often leads to heated and hated controversial words but Gandhi never spoke about how bad British were, but only how much the Indian nation needed to be independent. The paradox of Mahatma was his ability to write with both hands equally well and to think from both sides of his brain – the left when he needed structure and rationality and the right-side when he was in need of conveying a larger picture of what is right and wrong. For Mao Zedung, power came out of the barrel of a gun, but not Gandhi whose power came out of the words and deeds of a driven man. An example of his pacifist nature was when British Isles were about to be invaded by Nazi Germany he would offer this advice to them:

> **"I would like you to lay down the arms you have as being useless for saving you or humanity. You will invite Herr Hitler and Signor Mussolini to take what they want of the countries you call your possessions. If these gentlemen choose to occupy your homes, you will vacate them. If they do not give you free passage out, you will allow yourselves, man, woman, and child, to be slaughtered, but you will refuse to owe allegiance to them."**

Later, after the Nazi's had been defeated, he would become even more extreme, saying, "Hitler killed five million Jews. It is the greatest crime of our time. But the Jews should have offered themselves to the butcher's knife. They should have thrown themselves into the sea from cliffs. It would have aroused the world and the people of Germany. As it is they succumbed anyway in their millions." He went on to tell the media that there is always a choice between cowardice and violence, and if necessary, violence was quite okay. Gandhi was a simple, frail and timid man of the mind and heart. He had been a distinguished student or great lawyer but he would be an outstanding warrior on a mission of independence. Despite being such a very shy man he led 300 million people in a long fight against the British imperialists and would be out front in all of the difficult confrontations. Gandhi utilized a simple weapon of passivity known as Satyagraha. It was a non-violent weapon against a world that had become enamored of guns and military might. His methods did not demand armed soldiers carrying weapons of mass destruction. Gandhi was a servant leader who helped a backward nation come to the fore from the depths of 1,000 years of tyranny, oppression and invasion.

The Path to Glory

An Oxford professor, Gilbert Murray, summed up the problem for the British in trying to motivate and remove this man who was devoid of malice, *"Be careful in dealing with a man who cares nothing for seminal pleasures, nothing for comfort or praise or promotion, but simply determines to do what is right. He is a dangerous and uncomfortable enemy because his body, which you can always conquer, gives you so little purchase over his soul."* Sleep was never crucial to this warrior who refused to listen to medical practitioners who insisted on a good night's sleep in order to fight your battles. Sleep for most dynamic warriors was not important as was found in studies on Catherine the Great, Napoleon and Mao who would go days without hitting the bed. Gandhi had a similar propensity and would sleep sparingly. This man came to believe that he could live until age 125 due to his sacrifice of the heavy eating styles of many leaders and their need for romance. Had he not been assassinated at 79 he may have pushed the limits of his life expectancy. But his assassination was not without precedent as in the summer of 1934 there were three unsuccessful attempts on his life. Despite his growing old he would still walk many miles in only a loin cloth and ate sparingly and often slept even less. Gandhi spent World War II attempting to convince the Brits to leave and spend their energies fighting the German war machine. It did not happen as it had been a very long struggle to gain independence. When that radical editor interviewed him and then shot him his parting words would be, *"Oh God!"* Jawaharlal Nehru went on the radio to tell the nation of Gandhi's passing:

> **"Friends and comrades, the light has gone out of our lives, and there is darkness everywhere, and I do not quite know what to tell you or how to say it. Our beloved leader, Bapu as we called him, the father of the nation, is no more. Perhaps I am wrong to say that; nevertheless, we will not see him again, as we have seen him for these many years, we will not run to him for advice or seek solace from him, and that is a terrible**

blow, not only for me, but for millions and millions in this country."

This Indian warrior went to his grave not knowing that his work had not failed. Within a year, the Indian nation would be independent of British rule. Gandhi had been the most instrumental player in having the British finally capitulating after having ruled their colony for 200 years. Gandhi used a very passive system of arguing his case that was pioneering methods of civil disobedience and noncooperation that have since been copied by other nations to gain their independence. Civil disobedience means not obeying laws that are unjust, cruel or inhuman, even in the face of imprisonment and torture. That would be the forte of Mahatma Gandhi. Those he inspired were men like America's Martin Luther King and South Africa's Nelson Mandela. King admitted having read and absorbed Gandhi's teachings and applied the civil disobedience techniques saying, *"Gandhi was inevitable. If humanity is to progress, Gandhi is inescapable. We may ignore Gandhi at our own risk."*

Early Years & Trek to Eminence

Mohandas Karamchand Gandhi was born on October 2, 1869 in Porbandar, a coastal town that had been a part of the Bombay Presidency in British controlled India. His father was Karamchand Gandhi, a Hindi magistrate who worked for the Prime Minister of the Porbander state. His mother Putlibai was also a Hindu and was Karamchand's fourth wife. His first three wives had died childbirth. Growing up with a devout mother the young Mohandas would be imprinted with many of the qualities and trait that would lead him as an older adult - including compassion for less fortunate caste members, vegetarianism, fasting for self-purification and mutual tolerance between individuals of different creeds. He was in a nation of arranged marriages and would be married when just thirteen. He would father three children but was not a good father as was the case with virtually every warrior in this work, including Catherine the Great, George Patton and Moshe Dayan. He was very strict in a paternalistic nation where the man was in power and the women did what they were told. An example was Gandhi refusing to permit his young wife leave their home without asking his permission. Such an authoritarian environment was quite surprising as his fight with the British took an opposite tack of pure egalitarian tolerance. Quite the paradox and it would transfer into his change from a trained lawyer in 1900 to a cult leader and guru for a nation that had not known independence for many millenniums who would preach, *"Non-violence requires much more courage than violence."*

It would be in 1915 when Gandhi would leave his turmoil in South Africa and return to a life in his homeland India. He had gained much media attention while fighting for Indian rights in Africa and that lead to his first speech in India at the convention of the Indian National Congress. His appeal had been to just leave Indians to be treated as normal, hard-working people, but it would soon come to the legal constraints to such a mission. In April 1918, during the latter part of World War I, the Viceroy invited Gandhi to a War Conference in Delhi. Gandhi agreed to actively recruit Indians for the war effort, interesting work for a devout pacifist. In the Zulu War of 1906 he had recruited volunteers for the Ambulance Corps. In a June 1918 leaflet entitled Appeal for Enlistment Gandhi wrote "To bring about such a state of things we should have the ability to defend ourselves, that is, the ability to bear arms and to use them. If we want to learn the use of arms with the greatest possible dispatch, it is our duty to enlist ourselves in the army." Gandhi's first major achievement would come in 1918 when the power elite of Britain told Indian farmers what crops they could grow – indigo and high cash crops instead of the food crops necessary for their survival. Suppressed by the militias of the landlords the Indians lost this battle and became mired in extreme poverty. The villages were dirty and alcoholism would become rampant. Now in the throes of a devastating famine, the British levied a tax which they insisted on increasing and with the situation desperate Gandhi established an ashram and organized scores of his veteran supporters and fresh volunteers from the region. It would be the first major emergence of Gandhi as an Indian martyr to be reckoned with. He showed a willingness to be beaten, incarcerated and starved in order to make his message heard by the aristocrats in charge. But his main impact came when he was arrested by police on the charge of creating unrest and was ordered to leave the province. Hundreds of thousands of Indians protested and rallied outside the police station demanding the courts to release their new patriarch. Their demands were reluctantly granted and that would prove to be the genesis of Gandhi as an Indian warrior on a mission for freedom. His first move was to lead organized strikes against the British landlords. They suddenly became alarmed over this mass movement and signed an agreement granting the poor farmers more compensation and control over farming until the famine ended. It was during this agitation, that Gandhi was addressed by the people as Bapu –

Father - and Mahatma - Great Soul, as he was now fifty years old and a hero father type sent from above to lead the Indians to a better life.

Charismatic Powers Proved Prophetic

One of Gandhi's rallying calls came from deep within. This well-read martyr would say, "I have strived to reach *Moksha – Self-Realization.*" This was an ability to go within to better understand and deal with externalities. "*What you think,*" he would always say to his disciples, "*is what you become.*" That is a takeoff from the Oracle of Delphi where Alexander had visited so many years before and saw the signs for success, **Know Thyself**. While still in South Africa in 1912, this warrior fought long and hard just to be permitted to be a normal businessman. Every single day his freedom was denied and the Indian National Leader Gokhale would describe this diminutive freedom fighter saying, "*Gandhi has in him the marvelous spiritual power to turn ordinary men into heroes and martyrs.*" How did he achieve such charismatic power? It was his communications power that would turn friends into disciples and forced enemies to listen. At mass meetings he would sit in a lotus position, smile and sway and touch his palms together in a Hindu greeting and the masses in attendance would kneel and weep in adoration of his incredible dedication and zealous leadership.

By 1930, Gandhi and seventy rugged volunteers marched from Ahmadabad to the Gulf of Cambay to protest a British tax on salt that was highly detrimental to every household in India. Several of his disciples were arrested during this march and it gave the dissidents wide publicity and made Gandhi the untitled leader of the movement for Indian freedom. This was a warrior with an imperious style and self-confidence that followers were unable to resist and his adversaries began to fear. Louis Fischer would write, "*Self-confidence filled him with exuberant energy and a radiance that no critic or follower could resist.*" This would lead the masses to crown their leader with the name *Mahatma – Great Soul*. It was given to him by a Nobel winner poet Tagore in 1915 as Gandhi landed in India to take up his cause for Indian independence. During his many battles with the British hierarchy and aristocracy he was put in jail, threatened with death and it would cause him to tell Governor Smuts quietly, "*You can't put 20,000 of us in jail,*" upon which the Indian governor would capitulate as he knew Gandhi was correct.

Shaman Fantasies as Motivational Mantras

The Indian concept of *Brahmachyra* would be the mantra used by Gandhi in his personal quest for self-realization within in order to realize his dreams. The word 'shaman' means complete control of the senses in thought, word and deed. Gandhi lived by this mantra most of his adult life and offered testimony to his dedication to it saying, *"So long as I was a slave to lust my faithfully to my wife was worth nothing. Procreation and the consequent care of children are inconsistent with public service."* And it would be public service for a cause that would catapult this warrior to the very top. As our greatest strength can become our greatest weakness and vice versa, it was true of the Mahatma. Like virtually every warrior in this work, Gandhi's early life and upbringing was wrought with many problems that could have kept him from doing anything worthwhile in life. Escaping into mythical books and hero-mentors, Gandhi would build a strong introspective ability and strength. Words from his reading and thinking would cause the British great anguish. When he told the media how he could deal with imprisonment and threats he said, *"The amount of the denial is a function of the intensity of the desire."* Such powerful words from a philosophical maven would give him that inner power of a warrior wizard. He truly believed that, *"The material things in life must be sacrificed for the spiritual possibilities of life."* When one is willing to die for their cause, they have a far better chance of realizing their cause. At thirty-seven, he took the Hindu vow of *bramacharya – celibacy* and never again had sex with his wife. He already had five sons and would have a long line of secretary/nurses who would massage his body, bathe him and sleep with this man who said, *"Remaining sexually pure is like walking on the sword's edge."* He would admit to sleeping with attractive young naked girls to test his resolve and did so well into his sixties. That is inner power of self-restraint.

Gandhi fit the model of what Swiss psychotherapist Carl Jung labeled "Syzygy" – an ability for a machismo man to tap into their feminine side and for a highly feminine woman to tap into her repressed masculine nature. Gandhi proved highly capable in this arena. Biographers told of his ability to came across to the media as both masculine and feminine with author Fischer saying, *"There was in him something feminine. He looked very male and had a male's steel strength of body and will yet he was also uncomplicated and gentle and softy tender."* In Gandhi's first book, *Indian Home Rule* (1908), he told of writing it using both hands, not unlike other visionary men such as like Leonardo da Vinci who painted the Last Supper using one hand until fatigue set in and then using the other. Another visionary Michelangelo did the same while painting the Sistine Chapel. Gandhi was a bit odd in that he adamantly refused to take medicines, drank no alcohol, took no stimulants but indulged in mud baths and the right foods in what he considered was the path to longevity. The mind for him was the most important element in life's successes and he seemed to have a flair for programming his mind to deal with his enemies and would write, *"When thinking right and living right there is no room for worry or impatience. A person must be smaller in success than defeat."*

Epiphany that Proved Transformational

Books often become the guns for some warriors and Gandhi is the poster boy for this attribute. At twelve he was inspired by both books and plays and delved into them voraciously. His favorites were *Harishchandra* and another titled *Shravan* and he would say, *"At age 79 these books are still living realities for me"* and adding, *"I regard the Ramayan of Talisdes as the greatest book in all devotional literature."* Later he would tell the media that John Rushkin's *Unto this Last* would be the one book that transformed him. One of his lines on learning was, *"I think that the true textbook for the pupil was the teacher, not the book."* Schools should come to grips with this simple insight which is without doubt axiomatic. Gandhi's work in South Africa dramatically changed him. Discrimination was rampant with white Europeans in charge of the nation with Indians like Gandhi with a law degree from Oxford put into the same category of the black Africans. When in court defending a man as an attorney, a magistrate in Durban told Gandhi to remove his turban. It was bothersome but he still felt he could alter such behavior with time. Then the ultimate outrage occurred when in June 1893 he was thrown off a train at Pietermaritzburg when he refused to move from first class to a third class coach despite the fact he had a first class ticket. He then left the train and too a stagecoach for the rest of his journey. These incidents proved to be a turning point in his life as he was transformed from a young man wanting to fit in and alter discrimination, to a man on a mission via social activism. It was ironic that he was being discriminated with in South African courts, an arena in which he had been trained. He then requested the Natal Legislative Assembly to change their old-fashioned laws against racism. They refused and it would lead to many appeals including circulating petitions to both the Natal Legislature and the British Government. It was all for naught. It was in Durban that he would found the Natal Indian Congress in 1894, with himself as Secretary. Through this organization the Indian rebel would mold the Indian community of South Africa into a homogeneous political force. They published leaflets detailing their Indian grievances against the British discrimination taking place in South Africa and a great deal of the press would hit the Indian news media making him a hero back home.

Gandhi returned briefly to India in 1896 to bring his wife and children to live with him. On his return in January 1897 a white mob attacked he and his family and tried to lynch him. That was the turning point for Gandhi who now knew that he would have to take more drastic measures but decided to adopt non-violent forms of protest and reform known in India as _satyagraha_ - devotion to the truth of non-violent resistance. He recruited his fellow South African Indians to defy the laws and be prepared to suffer the consequences. They followed Gandhi's lead but paid a price in a cruel seven-year struggle in which thousands of Indians were jailed along with Gandhi. Several of his disciples were flogged and many shot for daring to burn their registration cards or when they engaged in other forms of resistance. Writing on the subject of immigration in 1903 Gandhi spoke of more immigration in an attempt to appear objective on this highly fueled subject: "*We believe as much in the purity of race as we think they do. We believe also that the white race in South Africa should be the predominating race.*" Then on March 7, 1908 Gandhi wrote in the *Indian Opinion* of his time in a South African prison saying, "*Kaffirs are as a rule uncivilized—the convicts even more so. They are troublesome, very dirty and live almost like animals.*"

Eccentric Wizardry and Empowerment

Was Gandhi different? Sure he was! It was not just due to his being left-handed in a right-handed world, although he was ambidextrous in both his physical abilities and also in his mental ability to flip-flop adroitly between the right and left hemisphere of his mind. His unique to sublimate all earthly passions and needs is what made him an eccentric warrior as he was proving to be a renegade for the white-majority. The paradox of Gandhi was that he was a very spiritual man but adamantly refused to use dogma as a right. Such open-minded ideologies were not limited to religion since by this time, although married and monogamous, he no longer had sex with his wife. The couple spent hours together but would not say a word. Here was a physically frail man who was powerful and resilient. And the quiet asceticism was in contrast to his violent temper. He said little but thought a lot and this mysterious combination led to his becoming one of history's first Servant Leaders. It would be his rare eccentricities that would bring down a world-power through the power of words despite him being pathologically shy. This introvert admitted to his weakness saying, *"I could not bear to talk to anybody in school."* But the truth about introverted warriors is that they are delving into books for power. This was true for Alexander, Catherine, Napoleon, Mao Zedong, Patton and Norman Schwarzkopf. It was their minds that they were controlling their destiny. It is a fact that extreme extroverts are often talking so much they seldom learn what transpiring while introverts are internalizing things and when they speak they are well-equipped with authentic information. Introverts like Gandhi do not have to be pontificating all the time as it takes away from valuable thinking time.

Gandhi, like many visionary warriors, kept a diary in which he recorded important happenings and where he could be totally candid without having it come back to haunt him. From those diaries biographers have been able to grasp the thinking of a driven man on a mission for freedom. It was from the diary that we learn of his only sleeping but three to four hours each night. By this time in mind 1944 he was released from prison as the British were more concerned with Hitler than Gandhi. He was now 75 years old and they felt the bad press was worse than keeping this aged man behind bars. Gandhi had spent 2089 days in prison or six years of his life. While in South Africa he had spent 249 days in prison for his activism. Gandhi had finally concluded that his life was life's work should have a wider purpose of discovering truth in context with the Indian lore known as _Satya_. He tried to achieve this by learning from his own mistakes and conducting experiments on himself as shown in the title of his autobiography The Story of My Experiments with Truth. In this work Gandhi would say that the most important battle to fight was overcoming his own demons, fears, and insecurities, summarizing his mantras with *"God is Truth,"* and then modifying his words with *"Truth is God."*

Influence on the World

Gandhi was forty-five, when in 1915 he returned home to India a hero, but now committed to spend the balance of his life fighting for freedom of all men. By this time he had become a gentle ascetic, now seen as a savant in loin cloth He had arrived in South Africa at twenty-three with high expectations as a young lawyer. He soon became disenchanted with the laws of men on a mission of power and would leave Africa as a missionary for peace and freedom. He spent much of his life on Indian freedom from the yoke of Britain but it was a frustrating task due to the misogyny of power brokers. Gandhi's work with the untouchables would be seen as one of his legacies as he was determined to show that despite physical, intellectual and moral differences, all men were equal and deserved to be treated as such. India is noted for its caste system and Mahatma was notorious for entering a temple where he was open for assassination and thus infuriate the holy man in charge when he said, "there is no such thing as an untouchable." Even though he fought for the equality of the untouchables he tried to keep the caste system intact due to its impact on societal growth and fought long and hard for the right to keep just the four main castes but did not want any one of them to be higher or lower than another. He was fearless in his resolve and would make more headway than most had expected. Because of his work two reform movements in India abolished the caste system and the idols of the Gods. They are the Bramo-Samaj and the Arya-Samaj. Indian biographer Lavanam would write:

> **"Mahatma Gandhi is the most famous person of this century and he may also be the most misunderstood person of modern history. Gandhi had so many facets: the traditionalist, the religious innovator, the leader of Indian national liberation, the social reformer, the visionary, the revolutionary, the international human being and then, toward the end of his life, the secularist."**

Pretty strong stuff considering other men and women like Winston Churchill, Golda Meir, and Nelson Mandela left their marks on their nations. Because of Gandhi, freedom was achieved in India. However, his leadership of the freedom movement was a thing of the past due to similar attributes. Gandhi would surely have become ever more important had he not been assassinated. From the outset of his public life in South Africa, Gandhi relied to a great extent on a religious approach to reach the people for social remedies – turning to religious rhetoric since he felt that religion and a belief in an almighty god was the catalyst for brotherhood. This warrior often used the word Rama to mean Purushothama, the personification of all good human qualities. When he began to talk about the god Rama, he did not mean anything like the mythological Rama, but the rule of good human beings. How many of his followers understood this? Few! Years later he would see that would not work due to the problems between such sects as Hindu and Muslim and Buddhism in India. That led him to a servant leadership style. He then began to separate truth from god. Gandhi's life was a study in contrast and paradox as he saw himself as doing God's work yet recognized only the individual's conscience would prevail in the long run. This charismatic leader of millions was able to mystify the mighty and confound intellectuals. By taking a vow of abstinence he left many disciples bewildered and when it was discovered that he took many young women into his bed, others were shocked. Such behaviors were in contrast to his words for being reasonable and sensible. But no one denies that he did take a whole nation on his shoulders and changed the world. Trace his rise to power and fearless campaigns of non-violence and non-cooperation with injustice that defeated the British Empire. His grandson, Arun Gandhi, in a rare interview said that Dalai Lama was highly influenced by his grandfather.

Chapter Eleven

Patton – A Perilous Potentate

"Lead me, follow me or get out of my way."

At a very young age Patton told his family, "I want to grow up to be a hero," and most of his behaviors were to that end. He read voraciously about the lives and heroic deeds of Alexander the Great, Joan of Arc, and Napoleon, among more recent military mavens. As a young man, he was enthralled by the battles that took place in military history. It would lead to his participating competitively in the very first Pentathlon Olympic Games that were held in 1912. Patton had just graduated from West Point and took third place in the Steeplechase and in the 400 meter run and not so well in the other three. When he finished the last race the pure passion that he had expended took its toll and he collapsed and many thought he was dead. Such zealous behavior would show its face for the rest of his tumultuous life. Few men have been as driven as George S. Patton. From his youth in the Los Angeles area he was a driven with a mercurial temperament that would frighten his adversaries. Patton wrote daily in a journal like Gandhi and would say, *"Compared to war all other forms of human endeavor are insignificant."* These are the words of a man on a warrior mission to win at any cost. Such people are prone live on the very edge but have a unique way of not falling into life's crevices. Warriors like Patton are the personification of men with great courage born of worshipping heroes out of books and he, like other winners, are victims of their greatest weaknesses. When passionately driven we tend to go where mere mortals fear but also becomes victims of our vicissitudes. Such drive would define this man who would be labeled one America's warrior wunderkinds but his men called him *"Old Blood & Guts."* It came from his maniacal drives that were always beyond the pale of ordinary men. Winning for Patton trumped all else as can be seen in his speech to his men, *"Never, ever say, we must succeed, we will Succeed!"* Losing was not in his lexicon of possibilities. Risk-taking was the fuel that drove him in private life and in combat.

Testimony to the Patton way comes from his being told in 1942 that he would lead the assault on Northern Africa. This consummate strategist and tactician went out and bought an airplane having never flown a plane. Why? He wanted to get up in the air to learn how a fighter pilot though when over a new territory. Then he signed up take flying lessons. How many people buy a plane first and then learn to fly? This is what entrepreneurial genius Sam Walton, founder of Wal-Mart did. But such behavior is not found in traditionalists. Ironically, both these visionaries were in their 50's when they pulled off the stunt. What does Patton then do after he learns to fly it? He takes the plane to the west coast where there are deserts similar to what he would encounter in North Africa and flies over the Nevada, Arizona and California desert areas to see what they looked like from the air. His combatant would be the mighty German General Rommel and he wanted to be better prepared than him and takes his assigned men to the deserts in Indio where the temperature was 130 degrees that summer in 1940. He would label it Little Libya. In his training, he made his men run a mile in under ten minutes and walk eight miles in the scorching desert sun, carrying heavy backpacks and had to finish in two hours. They had no hot water and he pushed them with his many aphorisms like, *"Do not steamroller men, attack their weaknesses."* Patton left for Africa with 24,000 men in one-hundred ships and would try to motivate them while on their way with words like, *"Sitting on a tank watching the show is fatuous, killing wins wars."*

Helen Keller told her associates, *"Life is either a daily adventure or nothing."* Such was the ideology of Patton and others who are driven to win at all costs. Another prescient example comes from American entrepreneur Ted Turner who bet his whole fortune when launching *CNN*. Ted was willing to bet every single dime he had - a cool $100 million - on his idea for 24-hour news. Had *CNN* tanked he would have been a pauper. At the time his lifelong CFO quit saying that Ted took far too many risks.

Others called him mad with the Wall Street Journal editorial saying, "*The industry doubts Ted Turner knows his ass from a hole in the ground. The networks say CNN just can't be done.*" Ted ignored their sage advice and bet all $100 million on his dream and later would be worth $10 billion. This risk-taking nature was found in Patton who was willing to bet what he had to make his mark in the world. Both he and Turner had been diagnosed with bipolar illness – where they could be way up or way down at any given time. In this work those so inclined were Hernan Cortes, Catherine the Great, Napoleon, and Mao Zedong. When the media spoke with Ted Turner, a man who used his temerity to win the America's Cup in sailing, he told them, "I have a lot of flags on my boats, but I don't have any white ones." Wow!

Big time thrill-seekers like Turner and Patton have been labeled by psychologists as "Big T" personalities. American psychologist Frank Farley coined the term Big T for people who are thrill-seekers with a very high dosage of testosterone flowing through their veins. Farley told the media, "*Big T's tend to be more creative and extroverted, take on more risks and have more experimental artistic preferences and prefer more variety in their sex lives.*" Patton was a poster boy for those words and would classify him as the typical Big T personality. Patton was an extrovert with a creative bent and had the propensity for extramarital flings. But the most telling of his nature was his motivational messages to his troops such as, "*We're gonna keep fighting. Is that CLEAR? We're gonna attack all night, we're gonna attack tomorrow morning. If we are not VICTORIOUS, let no man come back alive!*" The textbook description of someone who thinks like this has been classified as shown below from Farley's work. Keep in mind this is a continuum that everyone fits differently so see where you fit on such dimensions such as risk-taking, sex drive, creativity and aggression:

Table 7

BIG T'S	**LITTLE t's**
High Arousal Types	Low Arousal Types
SEEK NOVELTY	SEEK FAMILIARITY
HIGH INTENSITY	LOW INTENSITY
LOVE AMBIGUITY	REQUIRE CLARITY
RISK-TAKER	RISK-AVERSE
THRIVE ON CONFLICT	RESIST CONFLICT
NEED VARIETY	NEED SIMPLICITY
LIBIDINALLY DRIVEN	LOW SEXUALITY

George Patton was a Big T in spades. He grew up in California that many studies show to be very high in the above qualities. Why is that true? Think about how America was settled. It was Big T's from Europe that landed on the Eastern shores of the United States. Why did they come? They refused to tolerate subjugation and power hungry autocratic leaders in Europe. Was it risky? Very! But for Big T's the risk was worth the potential for a life where they were in control of their destiny. Their ships landed in barren and unknown territories like Plymouth Rock, Virginia and New York. The less adventurous remained and founded those cities but the Big T's kept moving west until they could no longer move on and that is why many label California as the land of fruits and nuts as a double-entendre The high-testosterone types have left an indelible mark on a nation that has ranked in the top three in risk-taking propensity for many years. These Sensation Seekers have been shown by medical research to have more dopamine rushing through their systems and through neuro-transmitters push their adrenalin buttons. It is interesting that California types like Patton are vigilantes on impossible missions. It was in Hollywood and Silicon Valley that these vagabond warriors would come to roost as they could no longer move further west. Data shows that the state of California has led the nation in innovation and new product launches. A few years ago there were more Nobel Prize Science winners in this one state than all of the other states put together. History will someday show the parallel of Silicon Valley and that of Athens and the Enlightenment. The West has been way ahead of other parts of America in originality and entertainment, science and computers. California is the 25th largest economy in the world ahead of Austria, Taiwan, Greece and Denmark. In this Big T land of zealot's creativity is permitted more than in less thrill-seeking arenas. Big T's flourish in Silicon Valley since it is okay to think outside the proverbial box. Big T's hover everywhere and they know they are permitted to push the envelopes of conventional wisdom. The California success story is told best by what it has produced in terms of paradigm shifts and other economic breakthroughs. Examples of some of the products originating on the West Coast and then migrating East in a reversal of that initial Big T migration is shown below:

- First Animated Films @ Disney
- First Integrated Circuit @ Fairchild Camera – Bob Noyce
- First Stereo System@ Ampex in Sunnyvale
- First transcendental function calculator at HP in Palo Alto
- First MPU @ Intel – Noyce Sunnyvale
- First Video Game @ Atari Los Gatos – Nolan Bushnell
- First programmable PC at Apple Cupertino
- First Family Entertainment Restaurant -Chuck E. Cheese, Cupertino
- First Internet Browser – Netscape Mountain View
- First Routers – CISCO & Tesla Electric Car in Silicon Valley
- Revolutionary Search Engines – Yahoo & Google, Mt View
- iPOD's, iPHONES, iPAD's at Apple
- Social Networking firms: Facebook, eBay, Twitter, Craig's List all in Silicon Valley

Patton's Path to Glory

The path to the top is never easy, but especially for those afflicted with dyslexia like George Patton who struggle mightily with his affliction when young. Patton had to be tutored and thus didn't enter a traditional school until age eleven. Not being like other students bedeviled him for many years and would contribute him failing his first year at West Point. For such warriors tenacity is important. And those so afflicted must work harder to fix their problem. In their quest to be very special they must work much harder and not internalize their ineptitude. With Patton being both dyslexic and bipolar, he was a truly special case. His turmoil was never said better than poet T. S. Eliot who wrote, "Only those who will risk going too far can possibly find out how far they can go." Seneca told us that ignorance is the cause of fear and the scientist who cured polio, Jonas Salk wrote in his memoir, "Risk always pay off. No matter how they work out. They either teach you what to do or what not to do." George Patton must have been listening to these aphorisms. His high dose of testosterone would take him to new vistas that most men would never see. He lived life with more flair than most. Studies show that fearful skateboarders judge a hill to be steeper than do braver souls who are not worrying as much. The proof comes from master motivational psychologist Abraham Maslow who told us, "What is necessary to change a person is to change his awareness of himself."

George Patton's charge through a military career was enhanced by being a Big T but it almost buried him numerous times. This passionate warrior was born in San Gabriel, California on November 11, 1885. This was some three decades after the California Gold Rush that brought many thrill-seekers to this magic land. Although he was technically the third George Smith Patton, he was given the name Junior. The Patton's of Scottish heritage and highly steeped in military history. Patton's father was an acquaintance of John Singleton Mosby, a noted cavalry leader of the Confederate Army in the American Civil War. Young George grew up hearing Mosby's stories of military lore from an early age. It would motivate him to become a general and hero in his own right. Young George Patton would later lecture on the nature of a warrior saying, "There's only one proper way for a professional soldier to die: the last bullet of the last battle of the last war." Early in life Patton decided that his goal in life was to become a hero since his ancestors had fought in the Revolutionary War, the Mexican War and the Civil War. He grew up hearing wondrous tales on the brave warriors would grow up fighting for man's rights. After a year spent at Virginia Military, due to being passed over by West Point, he would finally get accepted due to family pressures and would finally gradate on June 11, 1909. That led to his first commission as Second Lieutenant in the 15th cavalry Regiment. A year later he would marry Beatrice Ayer, an heiress he had met on Catalina Island. But in the interim he had competed in the Pentathlon based on his West Point time, since in those times the military had preference for competing. In the Olympic Games he had to push his limits by using a .22 caliber revolver when the army used what he considered a more appropriate weapon the .38 caliber. Patton was docked for missing the target, though he contended the lost bullet had simply passed through a large opening created by previous rounds from the .38 what would leave much larger holes.

Early Years and Trek to Eminence

In the summer of 1913, Patton received orders to report to the commandant of the Mounted Service School in Fort Riley, Kansas, where he would be an instructor in swordsmanship. He became the school's first Master of the Sword. Patton's first exposure to battle took place when he was to serve the legendary General John J. Pershing's staff during the expedition to Mexico. Then in 1915 Patton was sent to Fort Bliss along the Mexican border where he led routine cavalry patrols to insure safety at the border. Then he became an aide to General Pershing as they took an exposition into Mexico to fight the infamous Pancho Villa. It would be career-altering time as he would have a special rapport with Pershing and his sister visiting would start dating the General whose wife had just passed. Patton gained recognition from the press for his attacks on several of Villa's men as he was proving to be a valiant warrior of the first mettle. Pershing was highly impressed with Patton's determination and promoted him to Captain and gave him command of the Headquarters Troop. During his time in Mexico he showed a willingness to be out in front of his men, like his hero Napoleon, and it would become one of his signature moves in World War II. In Mexico Pershing would put this young tiger in charge of the newly established United States Tank Corps. Later he would have him train new soldiers in the art of this new motorized warfare. He was given the task of directing ideas, procedures and even the design of the uniforms to be worn by those in assigned to the tanks. He and his men achieved victory at Cambrai, France during the world's first major tank battle in 1917. After this battle he would gain respect and commendations. His temerity would cost him at St. Michael, France when he would was wounded by a German shell that entered his thigh and executed near his rectum. On the way to the hospital he commanded the ambulance to stop by staff headquarters, as only an over-zealous warrior would do, and he could file his report on the battle prior to going to the hospital for treatment.

Using his first-hand knowledge of tanks, Patton would be put in charge of organizing the American tank school in Bourg, France where he would train the first 500 American tankers. Under his command were 345 tanks that he led into a battle at Meuse-Argonne in September 1918. Patton had worked out a plan where he could be in the front lines maintaining communications with his rear command post by means of pigeons and a group of runners to offer sage advice on communications. Patton's bravery led to the Distinguished Service Cross for Heroism which would be just one of many such medals for valor. Even at this early stage Patton would be outspoken and said what he thought. He would become an ardent advocate of tanks as a military force to assist the cavalry. Patton was more the visionary and saw them as the future of modern warfare and would initiate experiments on radio communications between tanks, cavalry troops and the command, and assisted in the invention of co-axial tank mount for cannons and machine guns.

When the German Blitzkrieg began in Europe, Patton convinced Congress to give armored warfare a place in the deployment of troops and engagement and it would lead to the formation of the Armored Force in 1940. Patton was transferred to the Second Armored Division at Fort Benning where he was named Commanding General on April 11, 1941. Two months later this warrior would appear on the cover of Life magazine as a man on a mission. It was at this time that Patton's warrior nature was coming to the fore and he was given the nickname *Old Blood and Guts*. His men saw in him a true warrior who was always ready to do battle on the front lines. When America entered the war after the Japanese attack on Pearl Harbor on December 7, 1941 Patton was ecstatic and on November 8, 1942 Patton would be put in command of Operation Torch for the invasion of North Africa. Much of his success there and later was due to his insights into the minds of the enemy as he would say with such emotion on his landing on the coast of North Africa, *"Rommel, you magnificent bastard, I read your book! We're not just going to shoot the bastards, we're going to cut out their living guts and use them to grease the treads on our tanks. The bilious bastards who wrote that stuff about individuality for the Saturday Evening Post don't know anything more about real battle than they do about fornicating."*

Following the Allies' disastrous loss to Rommel's forces in North Africa, in February 1943, Patton was given command of the army to replace Lt. General Lloyd Frendenall as head of the 2nd U.S. Corps. Upon taking command, the force was quite down and demoralized due to the huge losses in men, material and momentum. At this time Patton was a two-star general and came in firing issuing a simple war directive, *"Use steamroller strategy; that is, make up your mind on course and direction of action, and stick to it."* But he understood that strategic inflexibility depends upon tactical flexibility and he them to attack the enemy where they were weak and *"Hold them by the nose and kick them in the pants."* Few leaders in any discipline would be as blatantly aggressive as Patton. He would be the driving force that would be respected by the higher command but it would be what they feared in him. After succeeding in North Africa, Patton was given command of the Seventh Army for the invasion of Sicily. It was here that Patton would show his stripes both good and bad. When under pressure Patton would come face to face with his inner demons, a trait quite common in bipolar personalities. His landing was in concert with the British Eighth Army and together they would free Sicily from the enemy. It would be in Sicily that the egregious slapping incidents would take place. After much controversy, Patton would be given command of the Seventh Army by Eisenhower and then the Third Army in France. In October 1945 this warrior was given command of the Fifteenth Army in American-occupied Germany, but on December 9th he suffered injuries as the result of an automobile accident and died 12 days later. This warrior went to his maker on December 21, 1945 and his wife would insist that he be buried where he would have wanted with his troops.

Charismatic Powers Proved Prophetic

When the movie *Patton* was being made, they hired a young movie maven named Francis Ford Coppola who studied the life and motives of this military hero who many lived and many hated. Coppola saw that Patton was a unique man with the power of poetic metaphor that he wanted to capture in that opening scene with Patton on a stage with a giant American flag behind him and spouting euphemisms on heroic behavior and saying, *"I don't ever want any messages from you saying that we are holding our positions. We aren't holding anything. We are attacking and moving forward. You SOB's got that?"* The Hollywood moguls fired Coppola, telling him his work was just too audaciously different for American movies. Coppola got the essence of General Patton and would be redeemed a few years later when the film won the 1970 Best Film Oscar for the accurate appraisal of an American motivator. The film was accurate in the sense it portrayed a hard ass that was adored by his soldiers who would give him the nickname of Old Blood & Guts. They respected his temerity and need to win at all cost. On his passing they offered incredible words about their leader. The military would erect a statue of him that still stands in front of the West Point library. He was lionized as a true warrior of the first order. An example is a letter home from one of his men on his death:

> **"We lost one of the greatest men that ever lived. The rest of the world thinks of him as just another guy with stars on his shoulder, but he was a soldier's leader. I am proud to say that I served under him in the Third Army. Others saw him as a swaggering big mouth, a Fascist-minded aristocrat, but not me."**

Every day of his life Patton trained his mind and body for the role he had always wanted to play in his own Greek Tragedy. His nephew, Fred Ayer, Jr. would say in a book, *Before the Colors Fade: Portrait of a Soldier*, "*General Patton was a man who believed in the aristocracy of achievement and in the sanctity of his country's course. He was conceited, sometimes ruthless, often inconsiderate and outwardly very, very tough. He was often too much the impetuous showman and yet a deep and careful thinker. But he was also magnificently well-read, deeply religious, softhearted, emotional and easily moved to tears.*" His nephew would say that Patton possessed the finest military mind America ever produced and credited this with his diligent study of military history. Patton would write of this saying that his father had motivated him, "*Papa always told me that the thing was to be a good soldier and next to be a good scholar.*" In *War as I Knew It*, Patton would offer his ideas on being a warrior, "*To be a successful soldier you must know history, dates and even the minute details of tactics. What you must know is how man reacts. Weapons change, but man who uses them change not at all so to win battles you do not beat weapons, you beat the soul of man.*" Not only was Patton a voracious, he had a kind of photographic mind for past history. Friends were shocked when he quoted from Napoleon and Shakespeare, the bible and even from the Koran for his mission in North Africa. Patton liked to offer words of motivation to his men saying, *"The object of war is not to die for your country, but to make the other bastard die for his. We're not just going to shoot the bastards, we're going to cut out their living guts and use them to grease the treads on our tanks."* After his infamous slapping incident in 1943 General Dwight Eisenhower wrote a distraught mother, *"The easy thing for me would be to send General Patton home, but his boldness, his drive, his speed and his mesmerizing manner has minimized tragedy in American homes."*

Shaman Fantasies as Motivational Mantras

Patton was very spiritual to the point he was considered to be fueled by a Shaman mystique since he believed he had been reincarnated from a great warrior from the past. He told friends that god had destined him for military greatness. When a British general told him, *"You know George, you would have made a great Marshall for Napoleon,"* and George said, "I did" and meant it. His nephew would write that he was a diligent student of the past, *"He could accurately foretell much of the future."* Patton had a will of granite to destroy the enemy and also a capacity for melancholy on the pure ugliness of combat. When he arrived in Normandy he wrote in his journal that he attended a Field Mass *"where all of us were armed. As we knelt in the mud in the slight drizzle, we could distinctly hear the roar of the guns, and the whole sky was filled with airplanes on their missions of destruction ... quite at variance with the teachings of the religion we were practicing."*

George Gosselin, a much-decorated veteran of Patton's army would tell the media about his tough demeanor saying, "This man, who was so hard on himself and others, was totally soft on God and would tell his men, 'There are three ways that men get what they want: by planning, by working, and by praying. Any great military operation takes careful planning. Then you must have well trained troops to carry it out. But between the plan and the operation there is always the unknown. That unknown spells success or failure. Some people call that getting the breaks; I call it God and God has His part or margin in everything." While stationed in Hawaii as a colonel he maintained a personal library containing hundreds of books — histories, biographies, memoirs, and political works — nearly all of which had been read and annotated with margin notes. This warrior's unique gifts of retention would prove indispensable during the Third Army's mad dash across Europe. This taskmaster would collect relics like maps and works of art. Colonel Allen said, "He knew the entire road net of France and Germany by memory, and the details of every major battlefield."

Epiphanies Proved Providential

When Patton was ten, he was called "Georgie." He had already decided that he wanted to grow up to be a famous general and would spend endless hours in his youth learning the things that he felt a general must know in order to become an icon. This drive stayed with him into adulthood. His love of war bordered on the arcane. But his blatant outbursts led to big time anxieties. Earlier in 1916 when he was getting started as a warrior he was assigned to capture or kill Poncho Villa. It would leave him with many of the qualities that would make him a true leader. In this skirmish with Mexican outlaws he would survive and when leaving would carve two notches in his pearl handled Colt .45 that he would carry with him to his time in Europe in World War I. In that war, he would experience a kind of metamorphoses that would lead to his later success. It was in the St. Michael offensive that one afternoon Lt. Colonel Patton led a tank attack against the enemy and would be shot. On that day, Brigadier General Douglas MacArthur was in command and according to the U.S. Army Historical Foundation: *"Lieutenant-colonel Patton sported a Colt .45 pistol with an ivory grip and his engraved initials. A pipe was clenched in his teeth. The brigadier MacArthur wore a barracks cap and a muffler his mother knitted for him. As they spoke to each other, a German artillery barrage opened up and began marching towards their position. Infantrymen scattered and dove for cover, but the two officers remained standing, coolly talking with each other."*

In that battle, Patton was seriously wounded at Meuse Argonne and a brave underling Joe Angelo brought him to safety. He had suffered a leg injury from a German machine-gun bullet and was evacuated to a military hospital where he would recover. On his return home to America he was given the Distinguished Service Cross and the Purple Heart. Two decades later General Patton would play a leading role in World War II that history would cast him as one of the most famous although controversial military figures in U.S. history. Later that year in World War I while in France Patton was taken to visit an amphitheater where Caesar had pitched his tent. On that day he would feel a deep sensation within that would motivate him to be feared and not experience fear himself. *"Lead me, follow me or get out of the way"* would become his mantra. He would tell his men, *"Now if you are going to win any battle you have to do one thing. You have to make the mind run the body. Never let the body tell the mind what to do. The body will always give up. It is always tired in the morning, noon, and night. But the body is never tired if the mind is not tired."* This is the epiphany from within that Patton knew well that one must have or they will not prevail.

Eccentric Wizardry and Empowerment

When Patton took Palermo he would receive a number of grand praises for his incomparable leadership from British Field Marshal Montgomery. Eisenhower issued him the Distinguished Service Cross and is men were exuberant. While basking in his success he decided to visit a hospital where many of his injured men were recovering from war wounds. Patton was a tough guy but was horrified when he saw soldiers without legs or arms and with faces blown away by shrapnel. As he kept stopping to see the men he there he saw Charles Kuhl who had no apparent injuries and asked, *"What's wrong?"* Kuhl responded, *"I guess I can't take it."* Patton was taken aback at such a comment from a soldier of his and slaps Kuhl in the face and walks out quite upset. He would give orders to have this pansy removed from the hospital and asked why told the orderly, *"He is a cowardly cop out."* The next day he returned to the hospital and ran into another man, Private Bennett and seeing no injuries asked Bennett about his injuries and Bennett responded, *"It's my nerves. I can't stand the shelling."* Patton went berserk and screamed, *"Your nerves? Hell, you are just a goddamned coward,"* and slapped him like he had Kuhl. Before leaving he looked at Bennett and yelled, *"You're going back to the front lines and you may get shot and killed, but you're going to fight. If you don't, I'll stand you up against a wall and have a firing squad kill you,"* and with that pulls his ivory handled pistol from its holster and shouts, *"You goddamned whimpering bastard."*

The hospital medical officer heard it all and would send a report to both Omar Bradley and Eisenhower. This warrior had hit the wall and his angst had taken him over the edge. Talk about an eccentric warrior. This all had come after he had landed in Sicily and told his men, "When in doubt, ATTACK." They had but some men are not emotionally prepared for what transpires in such a world where life is in the balance. Kuhl would be asked about what had happened while working for the Bendix

Corporation in Indiana and told the journalist, *"Patton was a great general. At the time it happened, I think he was pretty well worn out himself."* Patton was worn out and would pay dearly for his outburst. His need to inspire men with strong rhetoric came from a man who was a zealot. He would say later, *"All men are afraid in battle. The coward is the one who lets his fear overcome his sense of duty. Duty is the essence of manhood."* The one thing about Patton is that there was never a middle ground. His men loved him or feared him and some hated him but none were indifferent to him. The Sicilian incident led to a rebuff from both Bradley and Eisenhower, but both Generals respected him while fearing his potential for bizarre acts. Recognizing his bombastic nature they reprimanded him but sent him north to use his wrath to beat the Germans in the Battle of the Bulge. Those in his command may have chafed under his severe discipline but they totally respected him as a true warrior. Patton's legacy is certainly distinctive, being a warrior with a flamboyant flair and a colorful personality.

Influence and Legacy

Patton's devoted study and intuitive insights permitted him to anticipate what the enemy might do in an engagement and that kind of intuitive insight would be his legacy for future military men around the world.. He was a true visionary when it came to anticipating the moves of his adversaries, a similar talent of men like Napoleon. In his tome, *War as I Know It* he would write a prophetic description of the mind of a magnificent warrior:

> **"I have studied the German all my life. I have read the memoirs of Hitler's generals and political leaders. I have even read his philosophers and listened to his music. I have studied in detail the accounts of every damn one of his battles. I know exactly how he will react under any given set of circumstances. He hasn't the slightest idea what I am going to do. Therefore, when the time comes, I'm going to whip the hell out of him."**

Just prior to his engagement in the Battle of the Bulge, where he was a key to the allied victory he spoke to his men like only Patton could saying, *"Now there's another thing I want you to remember. I don't want to get any messages saying we are holding our position. We're not holding anything. Let the Hun do that. We are advancing constantly and we're not interested in holding onto anything except the enemy. We're going to hold onto him by the nose and we're going to kick him in the ass. We're going to kick the hell out of him all the time and we're going to go through him like crap through a goose!"* Patton was portrayed in the 1970 Academy Award winning movie Patton and it is a must-read for wannabe warriors as it shows the pure zeal and determination of a man among men. He was played by George C. Scott who shocked the audience with his now-famous opening monologue on that stage in front of the American flag, an actor that had captured the flamboyance of this warrior.

During his command of the Third Army in World War II, Patton was put in charge of winning the Battle of the Bulge and would kill or 1.4 million Nazi soldiers. And his unit would suffer the lowest casualty rate of any Allied army in the European Theater. A later assessment of Allied generals that was compiled by the German *Oberkommando* described Patton as, "*The most modern, and the only, master of the offensive among Allied commanders. Patton is the most dangerous general on all fronts. The tactics of other generals are known and countermeasures can be affected against them. Patton's tactics are daring and unpredictable. He fights not only the troops opposing him, but the Reich*." Biographer Axelrod would add to his eulogy writing, "*Patton bequeathed to the army the ideal of the warrior leaders, a commander who could be the greatest leader.*" In the Gulf War, a half a century later, Schwarzkopf admitted to having mimicked the strategies of Patton by attacking the weakness of the enemy. He would label it a *Hail Mary* when attacking Iraqi forces of Saddam Hussein in 1991. When German Field Marshall von Ronstadt was asked who was the best allied military man he told the press, "*Patton was your best as he had outfoxed and outfought the Nazi's at the Battle of the Bulge.*" Dwight Eisenhower would say in his memoir, "*He is the most outstanding soldier our country has ever produced*" describing him as a Titan in a Greek Tragedy. After the Sicilian slapping incident Eisenhower wrote, "*Patton's emotional tirades and impulsiveness made him instable in many ways but the more he drove his men, the more he would save their lives.*"

The incredible success of Patton has been attributed to his optimistic attitude and the tactical maneuvers of attacking an adversary's weakness. During his 13 months in combat in Europe, WW II military historian Colonel Paul D. Hawkins wrote, "*Patton never issued a defensive order.*"

Chapter Eleven – Patton – A Perilous Potentate

His mantra was attack, attack, attack and if in doubt, attack again. Never, ever give the adversary a chance to regroup or reorganize. This egomaniac walked his talk and showed up with his ivory handled pistol and was always in an impeccable wardrobe. As discussed he believed he was mystically empowered saying, "*We have never retreated; we have suffered no defeats, no famine, no epidemics. This is because a lot of people back home have been praying for us.*" By September 1944 Patton was in command of the Third Army and would blitz across France and crush any German in his way to glory. Once he was in sight of the German border he wanted to go for the kill but was told to stop. Allied Commander Dwight Eisenhower diverted the crucial supplies from Patton's Army to British Commander Bernard Montgomery to the chagrin of Patton who was now immobilized and could only watch and would say, "*It was my opinion that this was the momentous error of the war.*" In his memoir he would say, "*Stopping Patton's army from a thrust into Germany prolonged the war and cost greater Allied casualties.*" Those in the know were outraged as was Patton who sensed that the Russians under Stalin would be the new enemy. Eisenhower's decision is what gave the Soviets the chance to take over Berlin and create the Eastern Bloc for Communism. Eisenhower said it was about saving lives but Patton never bought it. In any case Patton's army was stalled in April 1945 and it would cost America billions for decades as this warrior was within 50 miles of Berlin. Once again Patton's superiors issued a nearly inexplicable order that told him to withdraw 100 miles west. The vacuum was quickly filled by the Red Army, which swarmed over Czechoslovakia and eastern Germany and historians would find this to be the anomalies of life as a warrior. Unfortunately, Patton's voice was stilled before it could be raised to protest the perfidy of the political leaders making the big decisions.

Chapter Twelve

Moshe Dayan – Predictably & Inextricably Powerful

"It is not in our hands to prevent the murder of workers… and families… but it is in our hands to fix a high price for our blood, so high that the Arab community and the Arab military forces will not be willing to pay it."

The story of Moshe Dayan can be likened to the story of Israel itself. He was a man who was born on a remote kibbutz that had been purchased from an absent Arab sheik and grew up learning that he was an outcast as a Jew in an Arab dominated territory. He would become an unconventional warrior with zany ideas of how to remain in the region of his birth where life was tough. He learned early in life that when your neighbors want you dead there is no compromise. If you do not believe like those in power then you are likely to be killed or ignored. The Israelis in early 19th century Palestine grew up knowing life was difficult and you fought or you would perish. Dayan almost died of pneumonia at three and at four watched as his father burned down a wooden building to stave off aggressive Arabs trying to take their land or their lives. Finally when fifteen, Dayan took life into his hands and joined the militant group for Zionism known as Hagannah – a secret organization formed to protect the Jews living in Palestine from the Arabs who not only hated them but surrounded them. And eight years later in 1937 he joined Wingate's 'night patrols' and two years later finds himself in a British prison. Such is the life of a person growing up in a fire bed of discontent.

As he grew up in the early part of the 20th century, he witnessed constant attacks and deaths of friends and family and would learn the art of survival. In June 1941 he came close to ending it all when he was shot in the head by a French militant and lost his eye. The irony of this is that fifteen years later the French would give him one of the highest honors of war – the *Legion d' Honneur*. When help arrived, he looked at them and said, *"I've lost the eye, but if I can reach a hospital in time, I'll live."* Such is the pragmatism of a man reared in a world where life and death were cheap. From the age of 26 when he was injured he would wear an eye patch and it would become a badge of honor. Dayan would become one of Israel's most famous fighters for sovereignty and fame fortune would be his. Why? He had been weaned on the art of war in a place where daily hostility was a way of life. When you do the impossible you become a superman to those watching from afar. Most people in their living rooms are unable to relate to facing death each day. Daring would become this warrior's destiny and his heroics would spawn many disciples from a man who eked courage and a certain kind of surreal splendor.

Dayan was born in Arab country in a Jewish kibbutz, only the second to ever have formed in this desert arena. He would grow up in a kibbutz in Degania just south of the Sea of Galilee and would study science at the Hebrew University in Jerusalem. The British at the time was the imperial power that controlled Palestine and administrated the rules and lifestyle. They looked at the Zionist organization Hagannah as little more than a renegade terrorist organization with a mission to undermine their Palestinian rule. Members of this band of warriors were regularly arrested – a fate that befell Dayan when he was in his thirties. Ironically on his release he would fight for the British as the Second World War was beginning and his enemy was fighting to maintain their control in the Middle East. The Nazi hatred of the Jews was probably behind his actions since they were a far greater threat to Israeli's than the British. The Brits were imperialists but the Nazi's admittedly hated the Jews and wanted them wiped off the face of the earth. During the war he would be assigned to an auxiliary force and the Free French Army to rid Syria of Axis forces comprised of Germans and Italians. During this skirmish he would suffer a very bad injury and would lose his left eye – thus the patch. At this time he would become friends with Ben-Gurion who would become the nation's future Prime Minister. During the war Ben-Gurion was the leading voice for the Jews in Palestine along with Golda Meir. An indication of his high risk-taking propensity was his comment, *"When I see shells exploding around me, I am able to remain calm. When I hear bullets whistling, I have no reaction."* Wow!

After World War II the Haganah militants had grown to a powerful force of 30,000 men and would wage a guerilla war against the British for independence. And in 1948 The British withdrew from their Middle-East colony and the state of Israel was born in the Jewish War of Independence in 1949. By 1953, Moshe was promoted to Chief of Staff of the Israeli Defense Force. The Jews had come from America and Russia and other places and bought farms, but the Arabs never accepted them as neighbors. Dayan was dedicated to defending his birthright and won many battles against the Arabs surround this small nation. On June 1, 1967 he sent the Israeli Air Force to strike the Egyptians and would destroy 200 of their aircraft on the ground. That got their attention. In a series of battles against the Syrians, Jordanians and Egyptians his troops won battles they were not expected to win. But when the Yom Kippur War erupted he would be criticized for not being prepared despite having won against superior forces in the air and on the ground. In this legendary skirmish 350,000 Jews were surrounded by four million Arabs and they would win this historic battle in two weeks. At the time Golda Meir was the Prime Minister. *The New York Times* asked her how such a small nation could defeat one that outnumbered them by so much and in her succinct style responded, *"We had a secret weapon, No Choice."* But one of her weapons was a tiger named Moshe Dayan. Just prior to leaving for their Jewish holiday - Golda had sensed a problem due to a strong intuitive sense of movements taking place in Egypt, Jordan, Syria, Iraq and Saudi Arabia. This resilient Prime Minister was worried and sent Moshe to the front to reorganize a strategy to win this potential engagement.

Yom Kippur is the holiest day in Judaism. As Egyptian and Syrian forces crossed ceasefire lines to enter the Israeli-held Sinai Peninsula and Golan Heights. This was territory that had been captured by Israel and had been occupied since the 1967 Six-Day War. The conflict led to a near-confrontation between the two nuclear superpowers – Russia and America. After the initial skirmishes it became obvious Israel was without the tanks and firepower needed to stave off defeat on the Sinai desert and placed a call to her friend Henry Kissinger, the American Secretary of

State in Washington, DC. The lady answering the phone in the middle of the night was not sympathetic and told her to call back in the morning as Mr. Kissinger was still fast asleep. The indomitable woman warrior was as determined as any male about to be annihilated and screamed through the phone, *"And I'm surrounded by 4 million Arabs and will be dead by morning and the Israeli State will be history. Wake up the asshole. I need tanks."* They woke Kissinger who arranged to send tanks and other armaments from Europe. Dayan, who was leading the fight, was given the weaponry he needed to fight the battle of his life.

The Path to Glory

After the 1948 skirmishes when Israel was to gain independence was the time that Dayan would begin his rise to power. By 1950 he was in charge of the GOC Southern Command. That was when he would be quoted by the media and came up with aphorisms like, *"When in charge, take charge."* During this period he ordered the destruction of a number of Muslim holy sites that would infuriate religious zealots and make him their mortal enemy. During this time he had mixed emotions about his role in the nation's survival and somewhat ambivalent about remaining a militant warrior or living the good life and it led to his poem, *The Owl and the Fox*, the most famous of his verse. He was now the fox, lean and hungry and the owl being the IDF, Training Division, with him the fox teaching new recruits on what it means to be a Zionist warrior. He begins this diatribe with the words, *"So, suitable armed with pencil and paper, Take down the relevant exercise data"* and he ends his poem with, *"Knock out the enemy with the famous one-two."* With this he spent six months in London attending a Senior Officer School of Devices with an emphasis on the use of armor to fight. Returning as a master he would return and become Chief of Staff of the Israel Defense Force. After his successful invasion of the Sinai in 1957 the French honored him with the *Legion d'Honneur* for his having commanded the Israeli forces in the 1956 Suez Canal crisis. In this battle he led a small band of men and pulverized the Egyptian forces in just six days. One-quarter of the Egyptian army had been defeated, two infantry divisions lost and one armored brigade captured. Moshe's troops had killed 3000 Egyptian solders and captured another 7000 and his planes had shot down twelve Egyptian jet fighters. They had lost 180 soldiers and another 700 were wounded. This would begin the adulation as a hero since the terror attacks ceased for almost ten years and Dayan would emerge as an international celebrity with the papers calling him a superman and the commander of the American Marine Corps saying, "He is an amazing tactician."

In 1957 he turned forty-two and a time when he felt a man should no longer be in the trenches and decided to retire from his role as Chief of Staff of military operations. He admitted to despising armies that consisted of elderly generals, smoking pipes and no longer able to fight. Moshe never saw himself in such a role and told the Prime Minister that January 1958 was the end for him. He and female companion Shimon Peres toured Asia and Western Europe for three weeks. This arrogant man acted with a similar gusto as one Howard Hughes around the same time. Hughes was the richest man in the world and when the famed Las Vegas hotel, the Desert Inn, they told him he could not have his suite since Arnold Palmer and Jack Nicklaus were in it. Hughes bought the hotel and canceled the Golf Tournament of Champions. Moshe had a similar moment on arriving at a posh Indian hotel and was told that the British Prime Minister Harold Macmillan had arrived and his entourage would be taking all the rooms. Dayan says to the clerk, "You go tell Macmillan that Moshe Dayan, the man who made him Prime Minister is here and requests that one of his people vacate a room for one night." The clerk checked this imperious man's passport and runs upstairs and returns to say a room had been vacated. In addition to his arrogance, strength of purpose and awesome insight into military strategies, Dayan was a man of strong introspective insights. He would be introspective on his successes and failures and he told the press, "*I made a mistake in allowing the Israel conquest of the Golan Heights. As defense minister I should have stopped it because the Syrians were not threatening us at the time.*" During the Golan Heights initiative he became a bit more reticent and it would lead to much dissension among Israeli's political leaders. Muky Tsur was a leader of the United Kibbutz Movement and argued against one of his ideas on the Golan Heights. But Dayan was intransigent and would move to his own plan and refused to capitulate to naysayers or political pundits. His attitude changed dramatically once he became defense minister and in 1967 he bypassed both the Prime Minister and the Chief of Staff in ordering the Israeli army to attack and capture the Golan territories.

Early Years and Trek to Eminence

Dayan was born in a rural kibbutz in a Palestine area known as Degania near the Sea of Galilee. It was less than a mile from where history has Jesus being baptized. At the time this was a remote province of the Ottoman Empire with little water or other redeeming qualities. Life was tough and survival even tougher when the majority of those around you hated your guts as an intruder. His dad Shmuel had bought the land from an absentee Arab, Sheik Majid a Din. The common language was Yiddish. It was near the shores of Lake Kinneret that is part of the Sea of Galilee. His mother Devorah considered herself to be a revolutionary woman who loved literature and learning. She would be the primary influence on his early life and the reason he would excel in painting, music and poetry. His parents had been immigrants from the Ukraine in Russia, coming to Palestine to find the freedom to be a Jew without discrimination or the horrid pogroms they had faced in Russia. Ironically, it was Golda Meir's parents who had immigrated to America from the Ukraine and she too would be involved with Dayan to preserve a free nation where they could live and love without fear of retributions due to their belief system. The Dayan's had arrived in Palestine just prior to the Russian Revolution. Dayan was the second born on the kibbutz in which they had settled and he would have a younger sister and brother.

He had been named Moshe after Moshe Barsky the first member of the kibbutz to be killed by an Arab attack. Talk about being imprinted early. Moshe attended the Agricultural School and had written his first poem – The Song of the Harp - published in a school paper at age ten and at twelve wrote The Hangman, a very sophisticate poetic verse. But by fourteen, he had become interested in freedom fighting. He became a member of the Jewish militia known as the "_Hagannah_." It was obvious that life in this land was about survival with the Arabs hating him and the British imperialists in control. Zionism was the reason his parents had emigrated into Palestine and the freedom to be Jewish without being persecuted. It would become his life's work. IQ tests were not part of the educational process in his era but since many studies show that Russian Jews are smarter than the normal. Moshe fit the profile. But he was recalcitrant from an early age, loving to write and kept a journal and wrote a number of memoirs and loved to write poetry. In many senses he was a poetic patron of iconoclasm not unlike Napoleon. In 1934 Moshe was a student at the agricultural college when Ruth Shwarz, a Jewish girl from London, was a schoolmate. They soon became fast friends, then lovers, and were married On July 12, 1935 when Moshe was nineteen. His new wife gave Moshe lessons in English as that was her primal language and they would honeymoon in London where Moshe was to attend Cambridge and study agriculture. It was not to be when the Hagannah summoned Moshe back to Palestine to quell the Arab hostilities.

In 1938, at age twenty-three, Moshe joined the Palestine Supernumerary Police and became a motorized patrol commander. Dayan was assigned to a small Australian-Arab reconnaissance task force that had been formed in preparation for an Allied invasion of Syria and Lebanon. Using his home kibbutz of Hanita as a forward base, the unit frequently infiltrated Vichy French Lebanon by dressing in Arab clothing and made covert surveillance missions. It was this insidious subterfuge that charged his batteries and made him a warrior with a mission that he would maintain for the balance of his life. The night prior to his first major engagement his unit crossed the border and secured two bridges. When they were not supported by other forces they didn't retreat back to safety, but took the initiative and attacked a nearby Vichy police station and captured it in a firefight. A few hours later, as Dayan was using binoculars they were attacked and he would take a French bullet in the head and it would push metal and glass fragments into his left eye causing severe damage. It would be six hours before he was found and rescued but Dayan had already lost his left eye. The eye damage was too severe to fit a glass eye as most would have done so he was forced to adapt and use an eye patch that would become his trademark as a man's man and warrior ready to do battle. In his memoirs he would write, "*I reflected with considerable misgivings on my future as a cripple without a skill, trade, or profession to provide for my family.*" And adding, "*I was ready to make any effort and stand any suffering, if only I could get rid of my black eye patch. The attention it drew was intolerable to me. I preferred to shut myself up at home, doing anything, rather than encounter the reactions of people wherever I went.*"

Charismatic Powers Proved Prophetic

Moshe Dayan was a maverick on a mission of redemption for his people and himself. His legacy was never more elegantly articulated than by Shimon Peres who wrote, "*Dayan was a great realist but also a man who had a poetic soul. He had a vision that saw things nobody else saw (right-*

brain ability) and he enchanted other people in a way nobody quite understood." When the Anwar Sadat, the President of Egypt came to Palestine to try and come to an agreement and to stop the fighting, the ever-poetic Dayan composed a limerick as he was about to leave:

**A great wind came suddenly
And the bells of peace chimed
Courageously,
President Sadat
In Israel landed
Did it happen or was it a dream**

Dayan was a majestic and fascinating warrior with a mystifying effect on many in and out of Israel. Historian Dr. Moredechai Bar-On, Dayan's bureau chief, had never been a fan of Dayan's but would write, "*I speak as a man who was very much against Dayan's policies after he became defense minister, but I can't ignore his personal strength of purpose. He was no man's dupe and was very independent. He feared no man, and said whatever he felt like saying. That is power, the kind which you don't usually find among leaders. Dayan never sought public approbation. Any support he received he earned through the power he welded and not through political maneuvering.*" These are pretty strong words from a man who didn't even agree with your strategic moves or ideas. During Israel's combative history there would not be a man with more adulation who was elevated as a military hero. Historian Yossi Argaman wrote a eulogy on this Middle East warrior:

"Moshe Dayan symbolized the national and military rebirth and the revitalization of Jewish strength, the myth of the Jewish fighter. He climbed so high, that he became a kind of god. His clerks at the Ministry of Defense even dressed like him. He would walk around in a brown suede coat, and everyone followed suit. He had a magical influence. I don't remember anyone, not even military heroes, who had such an influence and who were elevated to such heights on a national level."

Shaman Fantasies as Motivational Mantras

Dayan was a demigod with a surreal-like personality. For him life was a mythical adventure and due to this he was a leader who people loved and a questionable husband and father as he was seldom home and was a roustabout on a mission to be loved and to love. The media in Tel Aviv said of him, *"Dayan put the arrogance in army,"* and spoke of the ardent Zionist as being too smug and having far too much ego and lack of modesty, a loner who was like a Black Knight on a mission of glory. This warrior was a man with divergent loves. He had always had a love affair with archeology. Shortly after the Six-Day War he was told of a new archaeological dig near Holon, south of Tel Aviv. Not wanting to arouse suspicion he entered the dig alone and began looking for artifacts. Without warning the entire dig caved in on him and almost buried him alive as the only thing out of the mud and dirt was his hand. He was lucky as a band of children were walking by and saw his hand protruding from the caved-in hole. They dug him out and he was still breathing as he crawled from the archeological dig. It did leave him with speech impairment due to a loss of oxygen to his brain and one hand would remain partially paralyzed. When he passed, his extensive archaeological collection was sold to the state and left a legacy of this warrior who had a mythical nature for chasing both history and the future.

This Russian-Jew learned early how to survive in the bush and in the deserts. This was his strength in fighting against city-born Palestinian's who wanted him and his people to leave. As a very young man he would learn to fight as a guerrilla combatant against Arab raiders during the period of the British rule. This warrior was jailed briefly as a very young man for his daring to be a member of the hated Hagana organization. It would leave an imprint and make he look above and beyond what was transpiring. Then when he lost his eye when still in his mid-twenties he would go through a surreal time when he saw life as short and to go and do what mere mortals feared. In each of the many wars and conflicts he was out front due to a global sense of destiny rather than getting caught up in the little stuff that becomes an Achilles heel for most political men and women. Not so for Dayan who listened to his right-mind – an artistic trait for right-brain dominant types – and went beyond what traditionalists deemed correct. When was a commander in the Israeli army during the first Arab-Israel war (1948–49) he was chasing destiny more than mere mortals. He became the Army Chief of Staff during the

Suez Crisis (1956) and later agriculture minister (1959–64) due to his being seen as a man operating above the norm. When he was appointed defense minister just before the Six-Day War (1967) he had the same shaman ideology. Then his victory brought him widespread adulation and he was able to be different and still maintain power.

Epiphany that Proved Transformational

Biographer, Robert Slater, wrote that the eye injury for this warrior "was the turning point of Moshe Dayan's life. He believed he was going to die. He did not. Nor did he become a helpless cripple." We all know those individuals who are dealt such a bad hand and then crawl into a welfare state and never, ever amount to anything. It all happened due to his participation in the Haganna organization to help preserve the rights and freedoms of a people to live peacefully on land they had bought from the Arabs. Due to his membership he was arrested by the British in 1939 as such memberships were outlawed at the time. Ironically, his release coincided with the beginnings of WW-II. He then joined the British forces in February 1941 and be sent to North Africa where he was shot and almost killed and lost his left eye. His disability caused him some psychological pain but it made him far more potent than the personal pain leading him to write in his autobiography: *"I reflected with considerable misgivings on my future as a cripple without a skill, trade, or profession to provide for my family."* He added that he was "*ready to make any effort and stand any suffering, if only I could get rid of my black eye patch. The attention it drew was intolerable to me. I preferred to shut myself up at home, doing anything, rather than encounter the reactions of people wherever I went.*" A professor at Haifa University would offer insight into this warrior:

> **"Dayan was a very artistic character. When I look at him in pictures and movies there is something in his demeanor, something in his face that is almost inhuman. He looks bionic with an unmoving look, even his voice lacked intonation, very mechanical.** *This is a man with a remarkable personality.* **There is something very private about him. I fail to see his sex appeal, although he was quite successful with the ladies, a Yiddish pirate. His myth was constructed on the foundations of his biography and from some magical**

aura he carried with him. Something in his speech, his sparkling smile, his look."

Eccentric Wizardry and Empowerment

Convention was not in this man's lexicon. He held many laws in contempt. Early in life this warrior had been programmed to fight for his rights and sovereignty. It would make the military the centerpiece of his life's work. When he was in charge of the Israel Defense Forces he would tell his soldiers, *"Always be different, unconventional and challenge the rules. Never go by the book and retain the element of surpri*se." Biographer Slater would write, *"Living on the edge of death stimulated him, made him feel that he was living life to the fullest."* He went on to describe this warrior as unorthodox yet imaginative but creative in his quest to live life where he wanted and how he wanted. Ariel Sharon said, *"He would wake up with a hundred ideas and of them ninety-five were dangerous; three more were bad; the remaining two, however, were brilliant*." This was a very mysterious man of many contrasts that confounded both foes and friends. Dayan's mysterious power seemed to come from his complex personality. This was a man of many contrasts that would border on paradox. He was an army man who loved being in the field, a true intellectual who enjoyed reading and writing and extremely interested in the bible but got off on killing and maiming. He was well known for a long line of passionate and scandalous romantic liaisons. While married to Ruth he left unceremoniously to live with his true love Rahel Rabinovitch. His was sitting on a plane reading a book when this young, vivacious and beautiful girl sits next to him. His wife Ruth was home waiting for his return from the Suez Canal crisis. Rahel would say of first meeting Moshe on the plane, *"By the time I reached Israel, I knew my life had changed completely...I knew I was a different person....He had a very attractive appearance and actually you never thought of how he looked, you just saw a head. I found in him a kindred spirit."*

Moshe was very indolent as a father and family man. In his memoir he wrote, *"If I had to do it over I would prefer to not have a family."* Talk about pissing off your kids. His son Assi got his own revenge by writing his own book in which he said, *"I remember you as an SOB, the worst person and full of yourself, full of shit. You are the one who invented screwing as a national item who sends his bodyguard to give my kids chocolate on their birthdays. Anyhow, I want you to know that I simply hate your guts."*

On the positive side Dayan was an archeology enthusiast. He often took his hobby far beyond the pale of the ordinary and never would apologize for anything he did or said. The public was so appreciative of his warrior deeds they pardoned him and didn't care. Moshe was arrogant, over confident and a zealot on a mission. He epitomizes the bright and arrogant warrior as he would buy into the adulation and could be found waltzing around radiating the flame burning from his Six Day War victory. But ironically it would be his complacency that led to many fiascos that led to the Yom Kippur War. "Dayan put the arrogance in army" said one of his countrymen. *"The over-familiarity, the smugness, the lack of modesty, it wasn't there before his time. Nevertheless he was always a loner."* Dayan was an introverted Black Knight or Superman, ready to jump in and save the nation. Many would call him a demigod, as he would show up with his legendary eye-patch and would come across as Mr. Invincible. Such fearlessness is what makes a warrior function and makes them special. In a book, his daughter detailed his perpetual need for womanizing and greed that would include using the country's military resources to satisfy his legendary passion for archaeological artifacts. An internal hunger for the nation's roots was never far away from his lifelong campaign to maintain the Israeli state. In 1980, Moshe Dayan described the only two things he could do, *"reap the wheat, and fight back the guns."* Moshe was quite adept at public relations and military strategy.

Influence on the World

The legacy of Dayan is that he fully understood that if assaulted by a bully, hit back, rather than be a victim. Bully's want to pick on easy queries, and don't want to get bloody themselves. During the mid-20th century there were many moderates who wanted to just negotiate and talk and not hit back when hit. Not Moshe who adopted a hard-fisted stance against those that attacked and killed his people. Dayan saw negotiating with the Arabs who wanted the Jews gone was never going to work and called it, "unrealistic, irrelevant and dangerous." It would be his aggressive nature that would protect the nation from those that would destroy it. Moshe knew that being surrounded by 100 million hostile Arabs that compromise was a no-win game and like a bully, one had to show resilience and let them know they were going to fight to the very death. It worked for a long time. Henry Kissinger, the Jewish American Secretary of State watched this bizarre puzzle and told the press, *"I always thought he would be the one who would make peace, because he was the one who understood the Arabs."* The ultimate savvy of a true warrior is to understand your adversaries. It is why he had prevailed in two major confrontations, the 1956 Sinai campaign, the 1967 Six Days War in which he came away with many new territories captured from the retreating Arabs and then the surprise attack that became the Yom Kippur War. The nation was surprised and not ready when the Syrians and Egyptians attacked and almost destroyed the nation in October 1973. But his tenacity returned and he won this war in days as he took charge as if he was totally in charge creating his own policies and power moves.

For most of his career, Dayan could do little wrong however during the turbulent arena in the 1970's there were those who saw this man as too hawkish. For man he let his ego get in the way of what was right for the long run in Israel but he saw the larger picture and would tell the press, *"Our only objective is to thwart the attempts of the Arab armies to conquer our country."* In 1974, Dayan moved from his warrior posture and became a politician but in 1977 when the Labor Party was defeated in a general election and Menachem Begin took over control of Israel Dayan became the nation's Foreign Minister. He was only there a short time when he resigned from this position in October 1979 and would die two years later of a fatal heart attack, having lived too hard with too much drinking, too much loving and too much fighting. Military historian Yossi Argaman wrote:

> **"Moshe Dayan symbolized the national and military rebirth and the revitalization of Jewish strength, the myth of the Jewish fighter. He climbed so high, that he became a kind of god. His clerks at the Ministry of Defense even dressed like him. He would walk around in a brown suede coat, and everyone followed suit. He had a magical influence. I don't remember anyone, not even military heroes, who had such an influence and who were elevated to such heights on a national level."**

Dayan's career is probably unequalled in Israel's short history. One testimony of doing well in life is that he came from nothing and died a multi-millionaire. This warrior was a very successful military leader who developed a legendary status. He successfully crossed over to politics after having been a battler for most of his life, much of which was of the guerilla warfare kind. He held a number of highly influential government posts before he left politics. Senior military figures have tried to do the same – move from the military to politics - but many have failed in this endeavor. *"You can't ignore the fact that he was one of the most fascinating figures in the history of the State of Israel"* wrote historian Dr. Moredechai Bar-On who was Dayan's bureau chief. He was insightful in his sense of the Jewish state and what that entailed and in 1973 wrote, from the peaks of Massada, *"During the last 100 years our people have been in a process of building up the country and the nation, of expansion, of getting additional Jews and additional settlements in order to expand the borders here. Let no Jew say that the process has ended. Let no Jew say that we are near the end of the road."* In addition to his military prowess, Dayan had been a farmer, poet, amateur archaeologist, a politician, a statesman and a man who said what he thought with honest integrity from his perspective and went right to the point.

Chapter Thirteen

Norman Schwarzkopf – Perfectionism Prevails

"Leadership is a potent combination of strategy and character. But if you must be without one, be without the strategy."

Norman's father was a U.S. Army Brigadier General, thus it was not a surprise when he would follow his childhood dream and end up at West Point and a military warrior of the first order. This would lead to him fighting for his country with two trips to Vietnam and one to the Middle East. He had spent time as a teenager in Iran with his father and that experience in a far different culture would imprint him with many nuances of how the different culture thought and acted. As a teenager Norman would spend four years living and learning in Tehran, Iran, Geneva, Switzerland, Frankfort, Germany and Rome, Italy. These were assignments that his father had taken as a General in the U.S. Army. He had taken his son along for the experience and to escape from an alcoholic mother. The kid from New Jersey would learn new languages like German, French and some Italian. He would date European girls and attended school with students who were European, African, Asian and fellow Americans. It would lead to a learned boy who came to understand the vast cultural divide between his homeland and the Middle East. It groomed him for a life in the military and would offer precious insights into his autobiography, *"It Doesn't Take a Hero."* Learning to cope and interface with diverse cultures were eye-opening experiences. He was with his dad at a political dinner in Tehran and was pressured into eating the eye of a sheep while with his dad and the Iranians watched in amusement. Such events are learning experiences beyond the pale growing up in Trenton, New Jersey and attending the Friday night football games with a pizza. But the most important modeling that would take place was the worship of his hero-mentor mentality father. It led to his wanting to go for the gold and leaving a legacy that included:

- Two Distinguished Service Medals
- Three Silver Stars
- The Distinguished Flying Cross
- Three Bronze Star Medals
- Two Purple Hearts
- And three Meritorious Service Medals

When the mind is molded early it programs a boy to find his way through tough terrain later. This happened to Norman when he was sent off to a military academy in the 6th grade and was suddenly forced to show up on time for dinner, make his bed, sort out his clothes, and learn to fight his own battles. Such experiences forces one to learn to cope with a whole new environment, new kids, new ideas and how to be your own boss. Even more difficult for Norman was being the only boy in a home with an alcoholic mother. Those who find themselves in the midst of battles early in life grow up with a stronger sense of independence under pressure. They become more hardened and when deciding on a career they often take the tough road to test their mettle.

Norman became an exponent of competing in tough terrains and is why he would later sign up for two tours of duty in Viet Nam – 1965-1966 and then in 1969-1970. It would be in his role as the top man in Desert Storm that he would earn the accolade "Stormin' Norman." How? For daring to go where the weak only dream and developing an innovative strategy that Iraq never quite understood. By the time he ended up in Desert Storm he had already led American troops in the Gulf War. Later he would tell the media about his take on such a mission, "It doesn't take a hero to order men into battle. It takes a hero to be one of those men who goes into battle." This warrior of many talents was noted for his candor with aphorisms like, "Anybody who says they're not afraid of war is either a liar or they're crazy" and then said, "When placed in command, take charge." These were the words of a left-hander in a right-handed world who would have a right-mind mentality. It permitted him to use metaphors like, "Any general who is worth his salt knows that war is not a Nintendo game, war is not something that's fought by robots." Norman grew up worshipping heroes out of books, radio shows and his dad who had hosted a 1930's radio show Gangbusters. In his autobiography he spoke of his mental impressions on those early years of WW-II. After Pearl Harbor his dad left for the Middle East and he would write, "Tojo and Hitler and Mussolini and Santa Claus got all jumbled up in my mind."

The early hero-mentors that each of us have early in life can become motivational tools for us to follow later in life when the roads we travel are not always smooth. In his memoir he wrote of the enormous influence hid military dad had on his life and especially when he left for the Middle East after Pearl Harbor and brought the family together and walked out with his West Point saber and handing it to the seven year old, "As the only man in this house, I'm leaving you in charge. Son I'm depending on you. The responsibility is yours. I'm placing this saber in your keeping until I come back." Norman wrote:

> **"My father's saber was a sacred thing in our family. We called it his West Point sword, because he had gotten it the year he graduated in 1917 – Duty, Honor Country. The West Point Creed was his motto, and it became mine."**

It left an indelible imprint as when he became a general in the Army he would be known as a tough but caring officer. His rise to General was unique in that it was a slow but upward progression. After he had attended the U.S. Army War College at Carlisle Barracks, Pennsylvania his trek began. It wasn't long before he was asked to serve on the Army General Staff at The Pentagon as deputy commander for the U.S. Forces in Alaska. It was at this time that he was promoted to Brigadier General and put in charge of the U.S. Pacific Command. When that tour was completed successfully he served as Assistant Division Commander for the 8th Mechanized Division in Mainz, West Germany. It was in Europe that he was promoted to Major General. A short time later he was given command of the 24th Mechanized Infantry Division in Fort Stewart, Georgia, but when the coup in Grenada took place under the sponsorship of the Castro Cuban government, he was asked to go there and fix the problem. There were many American students on the island and the operation to insure their safety it was put under the command of a U.S. Navy Admiral, since it was an island nation, but with Schwarzkopf an advisor to make sure the Army units attached were effective. Norman won the confidence of his superior and named Deputy Commander of the Joint Task Force. While the Grenada operation proved more difficult than had been anticipated the coup was quickly thwarted and order restored. In 1988 Schwarzkopf was at the Pentagon when he was promoted to Lieutenant General and it wasn't long before he was put in charge of the Gulf War effort along with Colin Powell. From there he was once again promoted to the Commander-in-Chief of the U.S. Central Command at MacDill Air Force Base, in Northern California. From here he was given responsibility for all operations in Northern Africa, the Middle East and South Asia. In this capacity he began preparing for an engagement in Persian Gulf.

It wasn't long before Iraq invaded Kuwait which would become the problem for Schwarzkopf and be labeled Operation Desert Shield - the defense of Saudi Arabia. As commander Schwarzkopf was concerned that operational forces in the theater were inadequately supplied and equipped for large-scale combat in a desert environment. During preparations for Desert Storm he would come up with an innovative uniform for his men to fight in the desert conditions. It was a camouflage combat uniform that would be made of 100% cotton poplin without reinforcement panels in order to improve comfort for U.S. troops operating in the hot, dry desert conditions. A total of 500,000 of his uniform were produced for his troops in the desert. His operational plan would be named Operation Desert Storm after Iraqi forces had occupied Kuwait. That is when Norman had his troops attack from the rear rather than head-on. He would be commended for his innovative strategy and credited with bringing the ground war to a close in just four days. The media became a fan of his and he was soon dubbed "Stormin' Norman."

Testimony to his role-modeling demeanor he had during this whole time kept a quote from General Sherman on his desk to help him deal with the major responsibility at hand. It read, *"War is the remedy our enemies have chosen. And I say, let us give them all they want."* The day before he attacked the Iraqi forces, Newsweek had printed a map on the American strategy. Schwarzkopf was appalled and called Colin Powell in a panic and said, *"Newsweek has just printed our entire battle plan for the world to see."* From this point on he would know that what makes you can often break you. This inveterate planner had others trying to mimic his tactical strategies and when some would guess his thinking, others did not. Such are the vagaries of life in the fast lane. It is often defined as 'accidental sagacity,' something that Norman had in spades. After Desert Storm, Norman was given an honorary rank of *Legionnaire 1'ere Classe* by the French Foreign Legion - the only American so honored. During a formal ceremony in Aubagne, France, the plaque was presented to him with accolades on his personal heroics beyond the call of duty and an unrelenting mental strength and resolve. It was a gesture of "you are one of us" by the French government as a sentiment as a fellow Legionnaire and it was then that the epithet Stormin' Norman hit the mass media. Schwarzkopf said in a document about the French Foreign Legion: They also gave me a card saying: "*If you are anywhere in the world and you get in trouble, call this number and we will come to your aid!*"

The Path to Glory

When at West Point, Norman would meet and marry a TWA flight attendant, Brenda Holsinger. They met appropriately at an Army football game in 1967 where the tactics were attack and win at all cost. Brenda was twenty-six at the time and they would have three children but he was not always there at their births. When he finally finished his tour in Vietnam he was quite vocal about the way Washington had handled its war effort and told *Insight*, "*The United States military did not lose the war in Vietnam period. In the two years I was in Vietnam, I was in many battles. I was never in a defeat, but came pretty close a couple times. The outcome of the Vietnam War was a political defeat, but it was not a military defeat.*" He was vocal about his life and military acumen and told Barbara Walters on a 20/20 TV interview in the early 1990's, "*I've been scared in every war I've been in. Any man who doesn't cry scares me a little.*" Then being interviewed by the *New York Times* he said:

> "**Maybe I would describe myself as owlish – wise enough to understand that you want to do everything possible to avoid war then be ferocious enough to do whatever is necessary to get it over with as quickly as possible in victory.**"

He would be asked to talk about his war experiences in 1992 after returning from an engagement in the Middle East and offered some insightful personal strategies when in such a tough task:

- **You must have clear goals.** And you must be able to articulate them clearly. One of the advantages we had in Kuwait was the clarity of the mission - - Kick Saddam Hussein's butt out of Kuwait. The goal was clear and simple, and something that every one of our troops understood.

- **Give yourself a clear agenda.** Every morning write down the five most important things for you to accomplish that day. Whatever else you do, get those five things done. Insist that the people who report to you operate the same way.

- **Let people know where they stand.** Everyone knows you do a disservice to a B student when you give them an A. That applies not just to schools, as the grades you give the people who report to you must reflect reality and their performance.

- **What's broken, fix now.** Don't put it off. Problems not dealt with lead to other problems. Besides, something else will break and need fixing tomorrow.

- **No repainting the flagpole.** Make sure all the work your people are doing is essential to the organization.

- **Set high standards.** Too often we don't ask enough from people. In my duty on helicopter maintenance I asked them how much of the fleet was able to fly on any given day. The answer was 75%. People didn't come in at 74 or 76, but always at 75, because that was the standard that had been set for them. I said, 'I don't know anything about helicopter maintenance, but I'm establishing a new standard: 85%.' Sure enough, within a short time 85% of the fleet was available on any given day. The moral: people generally won't perform above your expectations, so it's important to expect a lot.

- **Lay the concept out, but let your people execute it.** Yes, you must have the right people in place. But then step back. Allow them to own their work.

- **People come to work to succeed.** Nobody comes to work to fail. It seems obvious. So why do so many organizations operate on the principle that if people aren't watched and supervised, they'll bungle the job?

- **Never lie. Ever.** Schwarzkopf said there had been a big debate about whether to use disinformation to mislead the Iraqis during the Gulf War. "We knew they were watching <u>CNN</u>. Some people argued that we could save American lives by feeding incorrect information to our own media." Schwarzkopf vetoed the idea because he felt it would undermine the military leadership's credibility with the American public.

- **When in charge, take command.** Leaders are often called on to make decisions without adequate information. As a result, they may put off deciding to do anything at all. That's a big mistake, said Schwarzkopf. Decisions themselves elicit new information. The best policy is to decide, monitor the results, and change course if necessary.

- **Do what's right.** The truth is that you *always* know the right thing to do. The hard part is doing it.

Many of this comes from his autobiography, *It Doesn't Take a Hero*, published in 1992 in which he related his experiences in a first person dialogue on some of the trials and tribulations in his trek to the top. When he landed in Saigon in his first tour of duty in Vietnam he was having dinner with a friend in a hotel and the Vietcong stuck with bombs and killed thirty-one, including nine Americans. He and his buddy finished dinner under the table. And he describes the next morning as being even more of a disaster when he was told by the personnel officer that due to his education and expertise he would be assigned to developing computer models for the rest of his tour. He almost collapsed as he was there to fight and not sit behind a desk and made strong appeals for reassignment. It worked so they sent him the next week into the jungles to fight. Such is the price of glory from being a former football player and being used to being hit and hitting back.

Early Years and Trek to Eminence

Schwarzkopf was born in Trenton, New Jersey. His mother was Ruth Alice and his dad Herbert Norman Schwarzkopf. He was a junior but never called same by his family or friends. Norman's dad had served in the US Army prior to becoming the Superintendent of the New Jersey State Police after retiring from active military service between the two wars. Herbert would work on the infamous Lindbergh kidnapping case and it made him highly popular with those looking for someone to halt unrest which is why he was sent to the Persian Gulf when fighting broke out. After the war when Norman was 12 he joined his father in Tehran, Iran in the time when Operation Ajax was happening. Norman attended school in Iran and soon saw the dramatic cultural divide between the Middle East and New Jersey. It would leave a lasting imprint on him as he attended Community High School in Tehran, followed by school in Switzerland at the International School of Geneva at La Châtaigneraie and then one semester in Frankfort, Germany. In these schools he befriended Arabs, Asians, Africans and learned the nuances of culture. His father sent him back to New Jersey to get prepped for West Point and he would graduate from Valley Forge Military Academy near Philadelphia as valedictorian of his class. Testimony to his sharp wit and savvy, Norman is a member of Mensa, the high IQ'rs with an IQ in excess of 140. After high school Norman attended the Valley Forge Military Academy as he was and always had been what has been called an "army brat." That led to his acceptance at the United States Military Academy at West Point where he would graduate 43rd in his class in 1956 with a Bachelor of Science degree.

The military helped with his Master's Degree from the University of Southern California where he received a Master of Science in mechanical engineering in 1964 – with a specialty in guided missile engineering. This USC program had steeped him in aeronautical and mechanical engineering. Later he would attend the U.S. Army War College and he was on his way to becoming a warrior icon. After graduating from West Point he was given advanced infantry and airborne training at Fort Benning, Georgia and then as a platoon leader of the 2nd Airborne Battle Group at Fort Campbell, Kentucky. After finishing his Master's Degree at USC, he would serve at West Point as an instructor in the mechanical engineering department. This was a time when many of his former classmates were heading to Vietnam and the chance to go fight was too much for him to resist and asked for a tour of duty over there where men were fighting. Initially he would serve as a task force adviser to a Vietnamese Airborne Division and while there he would be promoted from Captain to Major. When his tour of duty in Vietnam was over he returned to serve his remaining two years teaching service at West Point. It was then that he made Lieutenant Colonel and married Brenda Holsinger.

Charismatic Powers Proved Prophetic

One of the most remarkable incidents in a very distinguished career happened on his second tour in Vietnam in March 1970. It was in this wild guerilla war that his charisma emerged. Schwarzkopf received word one day that his men had encountered a minefield on the notorious Batang Peninsula. He used his rank as battalion commander to get a helicopter to take him to the scene of the action. On arrival he found many of his men trapped in the minefield. Norman decided to try and talk them through to safety. Then one of the soldiers tripped, was severely injured by the explosion, but was still conscious. As the wounded man flailed in agony, those around him feared he would set off other mines and kill them all. Schwarzkopf had been injured by the initial explosion, but still crawled across the minefield to the wounded man. He held him down while another man put a splint on his shattered leg. When another soldier stepped away to find a tree branch for a splint, he set off another landmine and was killed him along with the two soldiers near him. In this chaos his artillery liaison office lost and arm and leg due to mine explosions. Then the warrior took control. He led the surviving men to safety and ordered division engineers to mark the locations of the mines with shaving cream so to prevent further deaths. For his bravery under duress, Norman would be awarded a third Silver Star. It was in Nam that he would show his valor and leadership and earn a reputation as an officer who would risk his life for the soldiers under his command. This warrior had a strong sense of being a man for his men and would later write, "*Let people know where they stand. Everyone knows you do a disservice to a B student when you give them an A+. That applies not just to schools. The grades you give the people who report to you must reflect their delivery.*"

Shaman Fantasies as Motivational Mantras

In *It Doesn't Take a Hero*, he offered much insight into the mental magic of a warrior who could escape what "is" to go where you "might want to be" when he wrote, "*I had a crush on Snow White.*" This is the thinking of a hero-worshipper early in life escaping into the head and heart of a animated film character. This was told of when he was just seven years old and his dad was leaving for duty in war torn Europe. That was the time his dad had given him his valued West Point saber as a weapon of warfare just in case the family was in jeopardy. After leaving full-time service, Schwarzkopf admitted to the media, "*Alexander the Great was one of my heroes because he had conquered all the known world by the time he was twenty-eight.*" This kind of hero-mentoring leaves its mark on future superstars. They learn early how to win and what it means to lose.

One of the most mythical imprints would take place in the mind and heart of young Norman when his dad was the founding commander of the New Jersey state police. In that role he would track down and arrest Bruno Richard Hauptmann, the convicted killer of aviator Charles Lindberg's baby. During this time he continually heard his dad being interviewed on the nightly news. It would leave its mark on a boy looking at his dad as a media hero. Then his dad became a narrator on the popular radio program Gangbusters and Norman later admitted that he would stay up very late just to hear his dad on the popular radio show. It was then that his father ingrained in him that great warriors are 'selfless servants' committed to a sense of duty with honor. It was quite the disparity for a boy being reared in a home with mostly women - mother and two older sisters. Later he would admit the upbringing had an impact on his personality saying, "*I wasn't your normal, tough, macho young boy,*" this from a tall, over two-hundred pound guy with big muscles. After the war, his dad was then sent off to Iran to establish a police force for the Shah he took Norman with him. Prior to the rest of the family coming over it was just he and his dad in a foreign country with strange foods and people dressed in long capes and burkes. Many children who never travel to such a place at such a young age are not so savvy on cultural divides. Norman learned early and never suffered from xenophobia. For the next five years Norman travelled around Europe with his dad, living in Italy, Germany, Switzerland and Italy prior to returning to New Jersey for high school. He attended school with Arabs, Germans, Italians, Yugoslavians and many other ethnic groups who were so different from his former New Jersey friends and told *Insight*:

> "I came to understand that you judge a person as an individual. I also learned that the American way is great, but it's not the only way. There are a lot of other ways things are done that are just as good, and some of them are better."

Epiphany that Proved Transformational

Schwarzkopf experienced life-changes when young but was still undergoing life-changes, especially as Commander in Chief of U.S. Forces in Operation Desert Shield. Between August and January 1990 he assembled 765,000 troops from twenty-eight countries of which 541,000 were American. There were hundreds of ships, thousands of planes and tanks under his command. When prolonged negotiations failed to dislodge Iraqi forces from Kuwait, Desert Shield became Desert Storm and success or failure would rest squarely on his broad shoulders. In January of 1991 he came face to face with the Herculean task that was his alone to master and wrote in his autobiography about the night prior to his going in:

> "At midnight I went back to my office. I felt as if I were standing at a craps table in some kind of dream. I'd bet my fortune, thrown the dice, and now watched as they tumbled through the air in slow motion onto the green felt. Nothing I could do would change the way they landed. I sat down and did what soldiers going to war do. I wrote my family saying how much I loved them."

Never again would this general just be another guy from New Jersey. From this moment on, he would be known as *Stormin Norman* - a man who dared to go where others feared and not prone to get lost in old-fashioned ideas or procedures. From that time he would be a warrior on a mission to do what was right and he won quickly and decisively. An example is when that desert camouflage combat uniform was produced in 100% cotton poplin and the bureaucrats in Washington told him, "It's not in the budget." Not a good thing to tell a commander trying to win a war and with his men facing death in a desert. When the cost concerns about providing the right uniforms for his men became an issue he attacked and won the paper battle. And this offensive operational plan named Operation Desert Storm that would be what separated him from the pack. When he sent troops into Iraq behind the Iraqi forces he shocked them and won the war in weeks, not months or years.

Eccentric Wizardry and Empowerment

Yes, you can be straight and be left-handed and also be a man who can be counted on in the face of imminent danger. But the left-handed perspective often has a right-brained outlook and vision that befuddles adversaries. Even more important is a man who is willing to take a different tact can win battles he or she shouldn't win. When a tennis player hits a down-the-line backhand when the opponent is expecting a cross-court shot, the iconoclast has a significant edge. No matter the battle traditionalists expect a by-the-book approach. Warriors like Napoleon, Patton, Geronimo and Schwarzkopf take an out-of-the box approach they win wars they shouldn't have won. When you take such a tack the opponent stops and wonders what is going on and that is when you are the master in charge. That is why a Martial Arts Master never attacks an opponent until they stop. Why! Because they think and when most men think they are doomed. Thinking takes most warriors to a surety land and that is not a winners land. This was never the style of Norman who had been a high school and college football player, used to fighting battles in the trenches. In Desert Storm engagement - an imperial power from the Middle East and an American warrior was soon over due to his ability to take a different path to the win. But the Iraqi's should have taken a look at Norman's early life. They would have found that this General had spent his teen years in Iran where he attended the Presbyterian Mission School in Tehran. This man had eaten their food, dated their girls and had many Arab friends and was not doing battle with them so he knew them well. There was a time when he was there that his dad insisted that he swallow a raw sheep's eye at dinner so he knew the cultural nuances way better than any man the U.S. could have sent.

This warrior was cocky and aggressive. In the tradition of most warriors he was never afraid to go where the pack feared. As Dr. Gene's adage goes, *"If you don't know where you are going, any road will take you. Buy why go?"* Going behind the lines of the Iraqi's in the Desert Storm initiative is what made him seen as a true visionary commander.

Schwarzkopf considered leaving the military after Nam in the early 1980's as he felt the Army was on a downward spiral. But this man was a warrior who didn't give up easily. During a period of the Doves and the Hawks he would tell the *New York Times*:

> **"I don't consider myself dovish and I certainly don't consider myself hawkish. Maybe I consider myself as owlish – wise enough to understand that you want to do everything possible to avoid war then be ferocious enough to do whatever is necessary to get it over with as quickly as possible."**

Influence on the World

People magazine summed up the image of the man the media had dubbed, Stormin' Norman saying, *"Martial mastery and human sensitivity,"* not something said of many warriors. That momentous period in the Middle East when he commanded 500,000 troops in a quick take down of the Iraqi troops under the command of Saddam Hussein he would leave a legacy not soon forgotten. Norman is America's hero," screamed 20/20 on ABC back in the early 1990's. Newsweek at the time called him a "fatherly meatpacker," and quoted him saying, *"A soldier doesn't fight very hard for a leader who is going to shoot him on a whim."* Another paper would describe this warrior as a "230 pound pussy cat." "Norman is America's hero," screamed 20/20 on ABC back in the early 1990's. One of the things he has shown is that from those years spent in the Middle East he was savvier than most American politicians who speak a lot about the American way when they don't understand there are other ways. When Schwarzkopf retired from active military duty he told the media, *"Early on I learned that the America way is great, but it's not the only way. There are a lot of other ways things are done that are just as good and some of them are better."*

When in charge Norman told his soldiers, "You must have clear goal, and you must be able to articulate them clearly. Give yourself a clear agenda. Every morning write down the five most important things for you to accomplish that day. Whatever else you do, get those five things done. Insist that the people who report to you operate the same way." Such was the way of a man in charge of many who were not as educated or as smart or as driven. One of his greatest legacies was that here was a

Chapter Thirteen – General Schwarzkopf–Perfectionism Prevails

warrior who looked closely at his adversary's strengths and weakness and attacked their weaknesses and avoided their strengths. When a warrior is not in tune with what is right he or she fails. When lost in their own self-serving wins they also lose. Schwarzkopf was never guilty of such thinking. He knew the importance of following rules, but only up to the point that they didn't interfere with winning life's battles. If they do then they must be subjugated to what is right, not what is written in some policy manual. Such insight is what makes a warrior win more than those lost in their own reverie. He wrote of this saying, "Leadership is a potent combination of strategy and character. But if you must be without one, be without the strategy." He was a master at doing what was right no matter what the book said or some individual at the top said to do. He did what was right and won.

Chapter Fourteen

Warriors have Messianic & Charismatic Powers

"The only way of discovering the limits of the possible is to venture a little way past them into the impossible." - Arthur C. Clarke

Eccentricity reigns supreme in the lives and wins of the world's great warriors. Alexander believed he was a messianic and came to believe he was not normal and thus didn't have to behavior normally. Olympia told her son he had been conceived by the Greek god Zeus. Is that wild or what? Napoleon believed he was possessed of supernatural power telling his associates, *"I can divine everything in the future."* Such grandiosity is beyond the pale of normal but in his case it fueled his trek to the top and almost led him to conquer all of Europe. General George Patton actually believed he was reincarnated from past military leaders and as a renegade warrior told his men, *"I don't want you to love me. I want you to fight for me."* An author with a psychiatric degree wrote on the behavior of Napoleon and said, *"There was a fire in his veins to such a point that he came to believe he was a supernatural man."* And the Little Corsican pursued different paths that only a supernatural being would dare. He was a zealot on a mission of power and didn't behave like the establishment, rising each morning at one o'clock and staying active throughout the day with few men or women able to stay with him. When questioned on his decision to attack Egypt he countered, *"I am not a man like other men; the laws of morality do not apply to me."* Another bipolar warrior with a death-wish kind of behavior was Adolph Hitler who proclaimed, *"I shall become the greatest man in history. I never make a mistake."* When first coming to power he was asked his mission and told the crowd, *"Do I intend to eradicate whole races? Of course I do."* German youth had to belong to the Hitler movement and forced to pledge, *"I consecrate my life to Hitler. I am ready to die for Hitler, my savior."* Mao Zedung was not much different in his messianic drive and his physician and biographer Zhisui wrote, *"Mao was devoid of human feeling, incapable of love, friendships or warmth."* This was a man who stopped bathing since, *"it is a needless waste of time that I cannot afford."* Biographers say he didn't take a bath for the last ten years of his life and never brushed his teeth that were rotted, but due to his power still slept with thousands of women. That is being different way beyond what is considered reasonable or logical.

What Makes Us *Strong* Makes Us *Weak*

Aeschylus in his work on Prometheus spoke of the Greek God Zeus's trying to keep his two sons in line and being so-called normal. This treatise was written some 2,500 years ago, but offers prescient insight into the differences of traditionalists, sometimes called bureaucrats such as Zeus's son Epimetheus. This Greek god was a son that never violated rules or questioned his master's orders and would never do what his leader told him to do. But his twin brother Prometheus was not so inclined and was his brother's direct opposite. It is why history has labeled Prometheus the poster boy for entrepreneur eminence and a metaphor when speaking of creative genius. In Greek lore Prometheus was the titan that brought light to mankind as the maestro of innovation. Prometheus was defiant and ignored the preachments of his father Zeus. Today's psychologists label "change masters," those with what Jungians call 'intuitive-thinkers' as the ones who make things happen and become the ones leading paradigm shifts. The warriors in this work were Prometheans and got to the pinnacle of power by ignoring the sage advice of others. They had a much larger view of the world than those who followed them. Were they conventional? Never! Were they harried and tortured? Sure were! In the case of Prometheus, Zeus had him chained to a rock and had a vulture eat his liver. In the case of Joan of Arc, she was burned at the stake for daring to be different and violating Christian dogma. George Patton dared to be different and lost many top commands. Geronimo was so inclined and would end up on a white-eye reservation. Others like these warriors had the same temperament – intuitive-thinking visionaries – and paid dearly for their daring. Nikola Tesla died a pauper despite having created alternate current of energy and conquistador Cortes never became Spain's head man in Mexico for daring to be different.

Leonardo da Vinci and Michelangelo were also men with a divergent personality and defiant enough to ignore the herd mentality. It is why they have left a legacy of work that traditionalists treasure but they had to die to become a legend. Such warriors represent a tiny portion of any given cohort – typically only about two percent. Writers have labeled Prometheus the *"Forethought God – wisest of all the Titans."* They have labeled Epimetheus has been labeled the *after-thought God where Surety reigns supreme.* Promethean personalities tend to dominate in fields where vision and opportunity reign and is why they are often labeled *"architects of change."* Such individuals thrive because of what has been shown as their qualities:

- ✗ They are highly inquisitive;
- ✗ Analytical visionaries of the first order;
- ✗ Always chase life's possibilities no matter the risk;
- ✗ Have a global vision and don't suffer the little stuff or details;
- ✗ Try new things to sate some raging inner passion to the chagrin of mates;
- ✗ Master Builder Types who love to build new castles in the sky but seldom move in

Prometheans who are so inclined are very different from normal. They have the temerity to ignore old dogmas. They are ardently inquisitive and love to seek knowledge in all venues. That is why this works warriors kept breaking new ground and attacking new places such as Cortez in playing Conquistador and defeating Montezuma. They are imaginative and prone to be frivolously wild as was Geronimo and General Patton. It is interesting that the Promethean female tends to refuse liaisons with inferior males while their male counterparts are prone to seek highly promiscuous behaviors in their mates. There are a myriad of lurid examples of this from Catherine the Great to Mao Zedung and the love lives of many American presidents. When bad stuff happens, Prometheans tend to deal with it philosophically. Most understand that business is like war or a game with the spoils going to the victor. For them winning and losing is part of the game being played. They recognize when you go into a battle you win some and you lose some. But in the case of warrior superstars they win far more than they lose. Prometheans are indoctrinated early to become masters of their fate. They are prone to see problems as temporary roadblocks that must be dealt with on the trek to the top. They have a very philosophical bent - change-masters building new castles in the sky but often don't want to move in once finished as they are inclined to chasing imaginary dreams. Michelangelo was such a personality saying, *"The greatest danger for most of us is not that our aim is too high and we miss it, but that it is too low and we reach it."* Sun Tsu wrote of this in The Art of War saying, *"Invincibility is in oneself, vulnerability is in the opponent."*

Such a mindset was rampant in Japan when the kamikaze pilots were willing to die to win and when attacking an opponent they would scream *Tora Tora.* They were on a mission from the emperor and willing to go where most men fear. And that included their infamous bombing attack on Pearl Harbor. Such a gutsy move caught the American politicians in Washington off guard and almost wiped out the American navy. *Tora Tora* means a tiger attacking and opponent. In World War II, American paratroopers picked up on a similar motivation screaming *Geronimo* as they jumped behind enemy lines. To Ernest Hauser--a Western journalist--writing about the Japanese attack on the American stronghold is a dichotomy. The typical Japanese is a "*nervous, emotionally high-pitched, sensitive person,*" but it was this inscrutable kindred spirit was a split-personality. The Japanese have another word for internal motivation - *kaizen –meaning a* continuous improvement in all aspects of one's life. It is there way of saying you must become aggressive to become powerful. It is a fundamental philosophy of life in that little island nation. American psychologist Frank Farley once wrote about the concept of such types and labeled them Big T's for high thrill-seeking and abnormally high testosterone. Farley wrote, *"Men who are high in stimulation-seeking also have rather high testosterone levels. The Big T person will become either a creator or a destroyer. They are often unhappy and tend to very strong sex drives."* Do those words define the lives and lore of the warrior wunderkinds?

Warriors leave a legacy of power and blood in their wake. It takes a different person to do this and they tend to chase different targets than the norm. They don't need as much sleep. Why? Such people are super-charged for some dream that turns them on and wires them with more energy. Think about those you know who sleep a lot or are depressed. They have no reason to get up and sleep away their life in order not to deal with a life of mediocrity. The fuel driving the warrior is high psychic energy. Such people have a strong chance of being manic-depressive that has been seen here in Alexander, Catherine the Great, Cortes, Mao Zedung and George Patton. It is ironic that these people sleep little and eating is but a reason to keep going but seldom get ill as often as so-called more normal people. Examples of this can be seen in the lives of Alexander, Catherine, Napoleon, Cortes, Mao, Geronimo and Dayan – all of whom had many wives and many more lovers. Despite such a libidinal drive they used those passions on the battlefield as if it was a bedroom blitz. Despite such a frenetic lifestyle they achieved more in less time than most people could comprehend. The vitality released massive doses of neurotransmitters from an over-charged libido and they were maniacs on a mission for most of their lives.

Table 8

Warriors are Manically Driven Zealots

Cyrus the Great – He dreamt of marrying the East & West in Constantinople. He did!

Genghis Kahn – A Mongol on a Mission Impossible and in seven years conquered the world.

Alexander the Great – Lived life in fast lane and conquered the world by thirty but dead by thirty-three.

Attila the Hun – *Kill or be killed,* the motto of one who killed his brother for power.

Joan of Arc – Vigor to realize her dream and vision led her on a manic ride through France.

Catherine the Great – Hypo-manic woman who slept sparingly and worked diligently.

Hernan Cortez – "I love to travel but hate to arrive" vagabond warrior on heroic trek.

Napoleon Bonaparte – Grandiosity of a bipolar madman – *"Sleep is a waste of my time."*

Geronimo (Goyathlay) – Freedom to be on a horse and riding to nowhere was his life.

Mao Zedong – Slept sparingly, saying, "For me there is only 200 days in a year."

Mahatma Gandhi – Slept but three hours a night even into his 60's and 70's.

George Patton – "Compared to war all other forms of human endeavor are insignificant."

Moshe Dayan - Showed up with an eye-patch and unmitigated arrogance.

General Schwarzkopf – "When in charge, take charge. War is not a game for sissies."

An example of such mania was universal in these warriors as shown below in Table 9 with Attila the Hun operating by the mantra, "Kill or be killed" and Catherine the Great spending $.5 billion in 2000 dollars on paramours and admitted to being hyper-kinetic. Napoleon told his staff, "Sleep is a waste of my time." Gandhi was similarly driven and admitted to sleeping but three hours each night and told his constituency, "Non-violence requires much more courage than violence." The Indian messiah was quite the renegade and biographer Fischer said of him, "No ism held Gandhi in its grip. He never hewed to a line. He was independent and unpredictable." Mao Zedong was a similar rebel and wrote, "For me sleep is a waste." General George Patton in one of his typical tirades told his men, "The object of war is not to die for your country, but to make the other bastard die for his. We're not just going to shoot the bastards, we're going to cut out their living guts and use them to grease the treads on our tanks." When Francis Ford Coppola was in his twenties he was given the task of writing a movie on Patton. This young artisan delved deeply into the driving force that was Patton and decided to start the movie with his pontificating in a torrid talk to his men. In his research Coppola characterized Patton as a warrior with a passion for poetic expression. The moguls in charge of the picture fired Coppola for daring to tell the truth that they believed would befuddle American movie goers. When the movie Patton was released they would leave the Coppola scene in and it would win the Best Picture Oscar in 1970 at the Academy Awards. Coppola would say, "Patton was a gentleman with a poetic sense of metaphor on life and it is what made him special." In that opening scene Patton told his men, "I don't want any messages that you are holding your positions. We ain't holding anything. Now you SOB's know just how I feel so go out there and let me lead you into battle." Table 8 offers insight into the nefarious ideas and ways of the warriors who win.

Mania and Its Impact on Behavior

The textbook definition of mania is the need to get more and more done in less and less time that would be eulogized by the inventor of the Geodesic Domes, Buckminster Fuller, who concocted a system labeled Dymaxion-Sleep in which he taught himself to put himself into a 6-hour trance-like sleep and then awake and work for six hours and then back to sleep and on and on. He did this for years and it was when he was in his 50's and 60's. Other warriors were of a similar bent. Fuller was also into speed and the consummate Type A work-a-holic who coined a mantra for ultimate success that he labeled *Ephemeralization – Achieving more in less time or fewer resources*. Catherine the Great, Napoleon, Mao and Dayan would have had a great rapport with Fuller. Once on a cruise when Fuller was in his sixties he was spotted in the audience and asked to stand up and say a few words. Bucky took the mike and didn't sit back down for 2.5 hours. Mao had gone days at a time during the Long March without going to bed and Gandhi admitted to sleeping only sparingly. Such maniacal work ethics is but one of the factors found in those with a driven need to reach the pinnacle of power. In psychology the factors found in such people are:

Table 9

Bipolar Propensities of Warrior Wizards

✓ They have rushing sickness; need to get more and more done in less and less time

✓ Most all have an elevated and often distorted sense of optimism with happy mood

✓ Most have a higher than normal activity and energy level

✓ They tend to be frenetic, sleep less than the norm and are non-stop addicts

✓ These types are fast in their habits, eating, walking, talking and thinking

✓ They are always ending the sentences of others before the other is finished

✓ The manic has ambitious and grandiose plans far beyond the norm

✓ They have a habit of taking on more and more responsibility

✓ Most have a huge interest in sexual conquests and activity

✓ They all sleep far less than the norm but when they hit the wall they drop

✓ They are afflicted with impulsive moves and are impatient to a fault

✓ Much data shows that many are prone to suicidal tendencies

The above traits and characteristics have been found in all disciplines, but the warriors seem to have excelled in them. Napoleon considered suicide when quite young and always took on far more than he should have and it led to many of his problems. When he entered Moscow he expected a fight, maybe to the death, but when he found a burned out city with no animals to slaughter and eat and no food he went into a state of depression. This pompous titan was used to being eulogized by a beaten foe as had been the case in Egypt and Italy and when that didn't happen he went to his tent and never left for weeks. He lost a half million men due mostly to his depressed state and egoistic ideas of being the conquering hero. Mao Zedung worshipped Napoleon and had a similar manic manner with some of the same results and admitted that he had considered suicide as a teenager. For him political power of a warrior 'grew out of the barrel of a gun.' In a speech in Moscow after taking command in China he told the audience, *"I am prepared to lose 300 million men if necessary to win."* In The Little Red Book he wrote, *"We, the Chinese nation, have the spirit to fight the enemy to the last drop of our blood, the determination to recover our lost territory by our efforts, and the ability to stand on our own feet in the family of nations."* History shows that Cyrus the Great, Attila the Hun and Genghis Kahn were equally driven to win no matter the cost and Gandhi, like Mao had considered committing suicide as a teenager.

Type A Personalities - Polyphasic & Melodramatic

Kay Jamison, in her book, *Touched with Fire* (1993) described the manic personality as those with, "increased energy, intensified sexuality, increased risk-taking, persuasiveness, self-confidence and heightened productivity all linked with increased achievement and accomplishment." Who wouldn't want to have such a behavior advantage? Such inexhaustible energy was found in the lives and loves of these warriors. They were hyper and very multi-tasking oriented. All had many ideas and projects in their minds at any given time, no matter how engrossed in some existing battle. Such people are highly skilled at juggling many balls at once and think nothing of it as was the case when both Catherine the Great and Napoleon would dictate to four to six staff members at one time and kept this juggling act in tact without losing a beat. Thomas Edison always had 15-20 projects in development at the same time and was not happy if he didn't. Today such people are found watching a movie with a kid on their lap and holding a conversation or texting on their cell phone. Such individuals are not content with doing just one thing and feel inadequate if they are not taking on many tasks simultaneously. They tend to be afflicted with very short-attention spans and take on unreasonable tasks that push them to the limits. What makes them is what breaks them. This was never truer than in the bipolar Napoleon who said prophetically, "I will lose a man but never a moment." One biographer of Napoleon said he was in perpetual motion and concluded, "The very mania that gave him such advantages in battle doomed him to waste the victories and destroy his empire."

The message in all of this is 'get crazy to get creative and to get command.' Why? When crazy most normal people don't mess with you since they have no idea what you might do. But even more important, you can go where logic or inhibition prevents most people from going. The secret of super success is finding the pack and going elsewhere. The map is not the territory but most traditionalists don't get this simple metaphor. The great wizard in the Wizard of Oz was not giving out brains, hearts, courage or a trip back home. He was giving out pedigrees that altered the thinking of those not so inclined. Catherine the Great was guilty of all kinds of over-the-top obsessions but history would be most intrigued by what one of her ambassadors called her *'uterine frenzies.'* This woman with an indomitable spirit would say, "*I have the most reckless audacity.*" Catherine was adored by the elite and those that benefited by her incredible vision but some conservatives were outraged. Prince Mikhail Shcherbatov wrote, "*She is the most egregious illustration of the monstrous regiment of women that had engineered the ruination of the morals of Russia.*" By nine in the evening the Russian Empress would collapse from exhaustion from a day that leaders of either gender could have tolerated. She was infamous for firing off drafts at a speed that vexed the copyists. Both she and Napoleon dictated with a machine gun kind of rhetoric and if their secretaries didn't get it down they would be off on some other tangent. But this whole passionate energy thing is shown best by those that worked with these warriors. Napoleon's General de Segur wrote, "*In moments of sublime power, he no longer commands like a man, but seduces like a woman.*" What he was saying is that Napoleon's passion for what he wanted came across with boundless sexual energy. Napoleon wrote in his memoirs, "*Imagination rules the world,*" in noting that he eminence was not as rational as emotional.

Chapter Fourteen – Warriors have Messianic & Charismatic Power

Contemporary research offers a great deal of insight into a warrior's lifestyle and behavior. "When rats press a button and directly stimulate a pleasure center in the limbic system of their brain, the rats press the button endlessly, as often as 500 times an hour to the exclusion of everything including eating." And of course this was the case of Catherine the Great, Napoleon, Mao Zedong and others like Cortes who were afflicted with ADD. Today we know that one-third of ADHD children score in the 90th percentile for creativity. The warriors in this work qualified and that is precisely why most were highly innovative. It has been noted that these subjects were passionate to a fault and expected others around them to be so inclined. General George Patton was most guilty in this area and it came out when he slapped the anxiety-driven soldiers in Italy. The vitality flowing through their minds and hearts made them great and often caused them great grief. Siddhartha, the Buddha said it quite well many centuries ago, "All that we are is a result of what we have thought." Shakespeare was also steeped in this saying, "There is nothing either good or bad but thinking makes it so." The new data on brain plasticity is now verifying this to be absolutely true. If we don't like what we do or think, new research on brain plasticity shows us how to change it. We all have mind-infections and if we want to program them out we can, but it is not easy. Many old-times still believe if we are an introvert and want to be more extroverted it is not possible, that is not true! But it took a long time to get how we are and takes a like time to stop being what we are. We must go through what once was labeled 'brainwashing' – the remaking of our thinking through sensory deprivation or shock. We do become what we think so be very careful what you are thinking. It can make you or break you. The warriors in this work were so inclined and brimming with infectious energy, irrational confidence, and really big ideas and those ideas were instrumental in making them icons. One writer on the psychology of the myths with us all wrote:

"Whether the hero happens to gain a princess, a kingdom, a healing medicine, a talisman, or some other reward appears immaterial. He actually earns self-integration, balance, wisdom, and spiritual health. In every case, phantasmagorical adventures of the hero symbolize inner development."" - Alexander Eliot, The Universal Myths

Passionate Power Prevails

Those warriors willing to go where the weak fear typically have passion to burn. See Table 10 below on High Psychic Energy and Low Psychic Energy. It offers insight into how passion can fuel the trek to the very top. There is a middle ground that must be taken as below it are the world's Underachievers – about 40 percent or more than a normal population and another 40 percent or more that are Overachieving. Notice that only a small percentage of about ten percent are able to control their inner drives be passionate warriors who do well. Those without sufficient Psychic Energy end up underachieving and those with too much can self-destruct as we have seen with some in this work. Most people do not have sufficient go-go psychic energy to hit the pinnacle of power and others go too far and die. The underachievers are not sufficiently aroused to hit the very top. Some over-achievers are just too wired and hit the wall. Most of the warriors in this work were overachieving and they did pay dearly at times for having lived to far in life's fast lane, but most, even when they saw the downside they were unable to change. They lived fast and would go to places mere mortals fear. Such inner drive is what fuels the passionate and it was draining for many but they were unable to stop doing what they were doing. The need for speed of the bipolar General Patton is what fueled him and it also what led to him being relieved from command on New Years Day in 1943. Speed and audacity had helped him defeat the Nazi juggernaut but when he tried to use the same techniques on his own men it backfired. One soldier altered his Old Blood & Guts nickname saying, "Sure. It's our blood due to his guts." We all pay a price for what makes us and it will often break us if we are not aware of what makes us tick.

Table 10

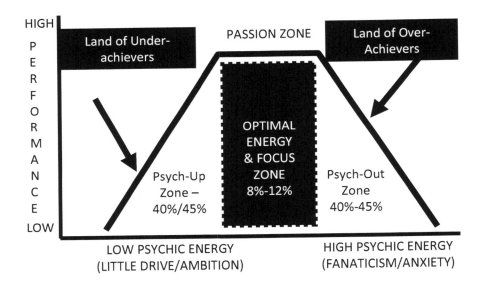

Passion Propensity Curve
Heightened Arousal Enhances Achievement

Chapter Fifteen

Wunderkind Warriors Tend to Be Transcendent

"Transcendence from mediocrity to eminence often occurs at a point just beyond the apparent limit of one's ability" - David Hawkins Power vs. Force

Empowerment results from positive energy fields as shown in the previous table. Whether we know it or not our extrinsic behaviors are nothing other than the external manifestation of internal feelings. Shakespeare offered prescient insight into this when he told us that the eyes are the windows to the soul. General George S. Patton saw this truth and told his troops, *"Now if you are going to win any battle you have to do one thing. You have to make the mind run the body. Never let the body tell the mind what to do. The body will always give up. It is always tired in the morning, noon, and night. But the body is never tired if the mind is not tired."* He was saying that it is impossible to act like we are strong and unafraid but it is difficult to fool the mind. It is not what a person says but what they did and that was so true in the life and success of Alexander the Great who defeated an adversary and then permitted them to live and govern and many times he adopted their culture as his. We can fool other people but we can't fool ourselves as was shown so well by the greatest psychological novelist of all time, Theodor Dostoevsky in his immortal work *Crime & Punishment.* His protagonist Raskolnikov killed dispassionately and got away with it but in the end walked into the police and confessed. Dostoevsky described this as *"ideological self-intoxication."* At 3:00 o'clock in the morning you know the real truth and if unable to deal with it you will pay a big price for your ineptitude. Raskolnikov had fooled everyone including the police but not himself.

"Pessimism is rampant in cultures on their way out," wrote existentialist philosopher Frederick Nietzsche. It is still so true today as when some economist talks of an impending recession, people stop buying capital assets and things get worse and they people spend less on gifts and sure enough the words become a self-fulfilling prophecy. Eminent psychiatrist and writer David Hawkins drew a matrix depicting the positive mindsets that he labeled a hierarchy of Energy and Enlightenment. In his book *Eye of the Needle* (2001) Hawkins shows the correlation between positive energy and the trek to enlightenment. At the bottom of his hierarchy are many people with negative energy, anger and shame. At the top are the consummate positive energy types like Alexander the Great and Catherine and Napoleon. They represent a very small percentage of any given cohort. In Hawkins system 85 percent of the world is below the demarcation point of success. They walk around with negative ideas and thoughts and are the world's pessimists. Studies have shown that about 6 percent of the population finds fault with all things including baseball, babies and holidays. Negative energy permeates their life and work just as positive energy is crucial for reaching the pinnacle of power. Hawkins claims to have tested thousands before coming up with his hypothesis on what it takes to become empowered. In his system about 15 percent are able to reach success such as was the case of these warriors. Only one-hundredth of 1% have a chance at enlightenment- that fabled land tread by the likes of Genghis Kahn, Joan of Arc, Gandhi and Mother Theresa. They envisioned what others did not see and did so with a smile on their face and optimism in their hearts.

A paradox exists in reaching the pinnacle of power. If a warrior thinks too much and too long about what could destroy them it will. Being prudent therefore is contra to being eminent. When going for a big win you must be willing to bet all to win all. Joan of Arc said it best, "*I am not afraid. I was born to do this. One life is all we have and we live it as we believe in living it. But to sacrifice what you are and to live without belief, that is a fate more terrible than dying.*" Abraham Lincoln offered the consummate insight into this when he said, "*You can't strengthen the weak by weakening the strong.*" Joan offered further insight at her trial when she told the inquisitors, "*People are hung sometimes for speaking the truth.*" George Patton was labeled "Old Blood & Guts by his men but he offered them sage advice saying, "*Lead me, follow me or get out of my way.*" Chaos, calamity, trauma and near-fatal experiences were part of the trek each of these warriors took Few were as devastating as in the life of Geronimo who had two wives, his mother and four children killed. Why? For no other reason than they were Apaches seeking freedom to live life on their own land. What does all this tell us? One must be willing to taste the bottom if they want to make it to the very top. Followers are not so inclined to live with the downside in order to win big. Breakdown in the warrior world precedes breakthroughs. The *Law of Increasing Entropy* says that the order of life takes place amid great chaos.

Nobel Prize winning scientist Dr. Illya Prigogine documented the reason for this in his monumental work titled Dissipative Structures. In this pivotal work he told us, *"Psychological suffering, anxiety and collapse lead to new emotional, intellectual, and spiritual strengths. Confusion and death can lead to new scientific ideas."* Studying these warrior wizards offers validation for these words. Prigogine knew that when we break a bone it will never break in that place again once it heals correctly. Why? It heals stronger where it was broken. His work was oriented around showing that the emotional system had a similar propensity as a bone and wrote, *"Many systems of breakdown are actually harbingers of breakthrough."* When the enemy killed Genghis Kahn's dad when he was nine they programmed in the mind of this young boy how to be stronger when he grew up.

Moderation in all this is not the path to eminence. True warriors are driven zealots who when hurt emerge stronger from the problem. They have become reprogrammed to face the bifurcation point that Prigogine said we meet disaster and will either crawl into a bottle and self-destruct or reemerge stronger than before the calamity. In his Nobel work he wrote, *"All dissipative structures are teetering perpetually between self-destruction and reorganization."* Nietzsche was an advocate of overachieving and wrote, *"The sedentary life is the very sin against the Holy Spirit."* For those that have associated with a true warrior know they are unique and will trample those in their path. That is why these warriors were without friends. Attila the Hun, Napoleon, Gandhi, Mao Zedong, Geronimo and George Patton admitted to being friendless as was true for gurus Hitler, Jim Jones or David Koresh. What we can learn from this is that energy attracts and negativity repels. Wax enthusiastic and people will be drawn into your sphere of influence. And it isn't possible if you don't have a fantasy dream to chase. Those that do are not easily dissuaded or brought back to normality. The message here is that energy emanates from inner dreams and influences on everything we do and think. A parable in Corinthians 12:10 says, *"When I am weak, then I am strong."* This merely validates what we all know that weakness for the wannabes programs them to try harder to overcome the adversity.

The Anomaly of Power v Force

For the wannabe warrior it is true that no matter how hard you try or how much you want power the less chance you have of getting it. Why?

Chapter Fifteen – Wunderkind Warriors Tend to be Transcendent

You will permit the wrong things to be important in your quest. Back off and chase an elegant dream and it comes with time. No matter how many guns one nation has some other nation can build bigger and more powerful weapons. Those who become deluded by their power through force are setting themselves up for a fall. Becoming content is always dangerous since those with less capability are always working to offset your edge. Those that become too satisfied are already on a downward slide to mediocrity. In the inimitable words of psychiatrist David Hawkins in *Power & Force (2002)*, *"Power makes you strong. Force makes you weak."* Omnipotence is about finding an internal power and using it to grow and expand. Hawkins told us, *"Power is needed to transcend limitations and dethrone the mind from its tyranny as a sole arbiter of reality."* Nietzsche labeled this as an ascendance to the will-to-power. When the will is in control, the body follows faithfully. That is the true path to power for anyone in any profession.

When looking closely at the rise to power of these warriors it soon becomes obvious that most had a real challenge to move past to reach their goals. Joan of Arc was an illiterate farm girl and would tell a king how be become crowned. Is that a bit audacious? Out of her belief in the supernatural came Sainthood. Napoleon had been sent to Italy to bring this young arrogant upstart down and he returned a victor and within four years would be crowned emperor. Had Catherine not been threatened with death she would never have ascended to the throne as the Empress of Russia. Had Mahatma Gandhi been able to cross examine he would have become a good lawyer but never the patron saint of Indian freedom. Adversity is a catalyst for eminence and crucial in the rise to the very top. Few people are aware that the bottom is good, not bad, as it conditions you for greatness. Without pain we cannot know pleasure, and without the stupid we would never know that we are smart. That is the paradox of life in the fast lane. If we were never sick we would never feel so good when healthy. So when things are really bad just remember that the ache is part of the process of finding happiness. In this author's research over 90 percent of the eminent people studied experienced some major life-threatening or traumatic experience that altered their life and led them to the top. It was true in every single case of these Warrior Wunderkinds. What almost destroyed them turned out to be a transformational event in their empowerment. If you're not dying, you're not growing, since you are probably not worried enough to be better. Don the warrior robes of steel and go for it.

Be Different, Break Rules and Opt for Change

This is the secret of becoming a Warrior Wunderkind. Do you think Alexander or Catherine ever listened to traditionalists in their rise to power? No chance! Did Joan of Arc listen to what the church wanted her to do in the battle of Orleans? Never! Did Napoleon listen to the French aristocracy? It would never have happened and didn't and if he had succumbed he would never have achieved what he did. Napoleon wrote in his memoirs, *"I reign only through the fear I inspire."* George Patton was the poster boy for military arrogance and insolence. When he slapped the private and was brought to bear by the media and Dwight Eisenhower he smiled and apologized but never acquiesced saying, *"I won't have cowards in my army."* Those that conform to the wishes of others become mediocre due to not telling the power elite to get lost. Psychology now knows that between 95% - 98% of all decisions are self-serving. The top dogs are unaware they are doing what they are doing for personal aggrandizement. It is a snare of mediocrity. Thus, those that conform to societal or traditional pressures never alter paradigms. For them safe becomes the mantra to chase and it destroys any chance for success. True warriors never, ever listen to the herd. Followers trying to be safe are destroyed by their need for surety. They frustrate innovative warriors by interfering with their drive to the top. The pack calls them eccentric because they dare to be different. Since the Stone Age the power elite have created dogmatic rules in order to maintain control. To gain control they try to frighten the masses with hell or death and tell them they know the way. Those refusing to comply are punished or extinguished. Socrates was poisoned as is the case with all those who dare challenge the prevailing authority. Those in power purposely program the pack for mediocrity in order to maintain control. Thus true warriors never listen to the advice of so-called experts.

Warriors are change-makers. They live and love in a fantasy world I have labeled **Newville**. Their opposites are *Change Resistors* who live in a place called **Sameville**. *Yes* and *Let's do it* are the mantras of choice in *Newville* with *No* and *Can't* the mantra of choice in *Sameville*. If a modern physicist or doctor was transported back 100 years they would be considered insane for the way they practice their professions. Today, what a freshman science student learns is obsolete by the time they graduate, thus lifelong learning is not only good, but mandatory. Think about the fact that it took 268 years for scurvy to be eradicated in the British Navy. The navy knew the secret but refused to change. When a heart-bypass patient is told to change or they will die, only 10 percent changes. Everett Rogers did pioneering research on this field on idea adoption and found that in any social system a new idea is rejected. Bruno was burned at the stake for saying the earth moved. It only took a few decades for the British health system to agree that washing hands by doctor's surgery would reduce infections in their patients. So change is never easy but warriors do it well.

Surprisingly, half of the warriors in this work were left-handed and most were manic. Being weird and unconventional was often their most redeeming quality. Fear is the asset the true warrior takes advantage of and never was this more apparent than when Cortes landed on the shores of Mexico and burned his eleven ships, telling his men, "*There is no turning back. Win or die.*" Such behavior is not good for the afternoon tea set. Studies reveal that Napoleon so feared losing at cards he cheated. Did anyone say anything about it? Don't think so if they wanted to keep their position or life. Edgar Allan Poe offered an elegant aphorism on this principle. "*Men have called me mad but the question is not yet settled whether madness is or is not the loftiest intelligence.*" To quote a manic-depressive Kay Jamison of Johns Hopkins University:

"Who would not want an illness that has among its symptoms elevated and expansive mood, inflated self-esteem, abundance of energy, less need for sleep, sharpened and unusually creative thinking, and increased productivity."- *Touched with Fire*

True warriors on a passionate mission are not messed with and are given a lot of space. Friends and family will see you as a ticking time bomb especially when a man like Attila the Hun killed his own brother to take power and others would no longer question him. Napoleon admitted in exile, "*I loved no one, including my brothers.*" Validation of this premise comes from one of the brightest philosophers to ever live, John Stuart Mill who wrote, "*That so few dare to be eccentric marks the chief danger of our time.*" David Thoreau was even more profound saying, "*If a man cannot keep pace with his companions, perhaps it is because he hears a different drummer. Let him step to the music he hears however measured or faraway.*" Further validation comes from Anthony Storr, a man who spent his life looking at the underlying factors in gurus like Alexander, Joan of Arc and others like Freud and Carl Jung. Storr wrote in *Feet of Clay*, *"The majority of gurus are madmen. Without being radical they would be destroyed by the establishment."* Since it was eccentricity under control that fueled the warriors trek to the top what role, if any, did it play in their undoing? It was paramount for some and not so much for others. An ascetic like Mahatma Gandhi was a mystery as he was ambidextrous writing his diary with either hand and androgynous in the sense that most he spoke of his femininity as well as his masculinity. That is quite bizarre for a warrior, worshipped by millions, for his indomitable spirit and refusal to bow to the power of the British Empire. The following table offers some insight on eccentricities as a source of power.

Table 11

Eccentric Power of Warrior Wunderkinds

Left-Handed: <u>Alexander the Great</u> – Julius Caesar – Charlemagne – <u>Attila</u> <u>the Hun</u> - <u>Joan of Arc</u> – <u>Napoleon</u> – Churchill – Hitler - <u>Gandhi</u> – Fidel Castro - <u>Schwarzkopf</u> - Colin Powell

<u>Sun Tsu</u> - "Give out rewards that are not in the rules, give out directives that are not in the code"

<u>Cyrus the Great</u> - "Soft countries breed soft men"

<u>Alexander the Great</u> – Believed he was Achilles on a messianic mission

<u>Attila the Hun</u> – *"When you're right, you're right"* from a driven lefty

<u>Joan of Arc</u> – Burned as heretic and androgynous dress to beat the Brits and was also left-handed

<u>Catherine the Great</u> – Femme Fatale wrote, *"I have the most ruthless audacity"* and meant every word of it

<u>Hernan Cortez</u> – Radical Conquistador with a High Testosterone mania for battle and beating new foes all the time

<u>Napoleon Bonaparte</u> – Egomaniac said, "I can divine everything in the future" as he had gone over the edge and believed he was a god

<u>Geronimo</u> (Goyathlay) – A Renegade Rebel wanting to be free and defied US troops and was never captured

<u>Mao Zedong</u> – "Dogma (Rules) are less useful than shit" from bipolar ruffian who was far more different than most warriors

<u>Mahatma Gandhi</u> – *SATYAGRAHA* = Non-Violent opposition to Authority

<u>George Patton</u> – *"Rules are made to break"* – Generals can slap cowardly privates

<u>Moshe Dayan</u> –Danced to a different drummer than any normal person

<u>General Norman Schwarzkopf</u> – "Do what's right, not what the rules say"

Beyond the eccentricities and other variables found to be important in the lives and success of warriors there is always a legacy that is different depending on their primal personality trait. It differs with each one but there are so many similarities such as their optimism, daring, passion, intuition, charismatic power, tenacity and eccentricities and a hero-mentoring beyond the pale of logic. Attitude trumped skill in the warriors who won. Most were willing to push the windows of opportunity and did something quite telling in their trek to eminence. Alexander the Great modeled the behavior in war of his hero Achilles while his protégé Napoleon utilized his unique Right-Hemisphere advantage – being left-handed as a strategic and tactical force. Joan of Arc was androgynous and Gandhi a servant leader. George Patton worshipped past heroes like Napoleon as did Schwarzkopf. Geronimo had an Indian spirit named Ushen that spirited him beyond the norm. Catherine the Great was willing to permit her passions to win the day. Mao Zedung was a modern Robin Hood in China. Table 12 offers a simplistic outline of the innovative qualities that were adopted by warriors in this work and it seems to be pertinent no matter your discipline whether in war, business, sports or relationships.

Table 12

Legacies of Warriors Who Win

Alexander the Great – Hero-Mentoring – Modeling Excellence ala NLP

Joan of Arc – Androgyny works–Tap into opposite gender to find optimum life in synch

Catherine the Great – Be Passionate & You Too can find happiness at the end of the day

Hernan Cortez – Burn your past like he did and then the only way is forward

Napoleon Bonaparte – Envision Globally and Operate Locally like this left-handed visionary

Geronimo (Goyathlay) – Chase your god-given rights and you won't ever be caught either

Mao Zedong – Tenacity of life's Long Marches prevails against all odds – never, ever give up

Mahatma Gandhi – Servant Leaders start at the bottom to get to the very top

George Patton –*Competitive Charismatic's* is the weapon of winners & less-inclined to capitulate

Moshe Dayan – Image is everything so don an eye-patch to show your valor to the world

Norman Schwarzkopf – Attack weakness and tap into strengths and you'll win most battles

Gene N. Landrum, PhD
Professor Emeritus–Hodges University

E-mail: genelandrum@earthlink.net
Website: genelandrum.com

"When it comes to geniuses, Gene Landrum wrote the book." - Scripps-Howard May 5, 1996

Dr. Gene is a high-tech start-up executive turned educator and writer who teaches in graduate school and once started five firms and took three to over $100 million in two years. Gene's doctoral dissertation was on the Jungian Psychology of Success titled *The Innovative Personality*. His many books are on the art of success and what makes the great tick. Dr. Gene's most sought after titles are:

Sex in Pelican Place – The Wild Side in the Sun, Sand & Surf (2011)
Cover Your <u>Ass</u>ets & Become Your Own Liability (2010)
The Innovative Mind: Stop Thinking, Start Being (2008)
Paranoia & Power: Fear & Fame of Entertainment Icons - (2007)
Empowerment: in Business, Life & Sport (2006)
The Superman Syndrome – You are what you believe (2005)
Entrepreneurial Genius – The Power of Passion (2004)
Eight Keys to Greatness – How to Unlock Your Hidden Potential (1999)

Warrior References

Alexander, John. T. (1989). *Catherine the Great – Life & Legend*, Oxford University Press, NY, NY. NLP – modeling other icons

Amdur, Richard. (1989). *Moshe Dayan*. Chelsea House, New York, NY

Axelrod, Alan. (2006). Patton – Lessons in Leadership, Palgrave Press, NY, NY

Barrett, S. M. (1996). Geronimo – His Own Story, Meridian Books, NY, NY.

Cawthorne, Nigel. (2003). *Victory – 100 Great Military Commanders*, Capella, London

Creveld, Martin Van. *Moshe Dayan*. Weidenfeld & Nicolson, New York, NY

Fischer, Louis. (1954). *Gandhi*, New American Library, NY, NY.

Fuller, J.F.C. (1960). *Alexander the Great,* Da Capo Press, NY, NY.

Debo, Angie. (1976). *Geronimo*, University of Oklahoma Press, Norman, OK

D'Este, Carlos. (1996). *Patton, A Genius for War*, Harper-Collins, NY, NY.

Geyl, Pieter. (1949). *Napoleon – For & Against*, Yale University Press, New Haven

Greene, Robert. (2001). *The Art of Seduction*, Viking Press, N.Y., N. Y.

Hart, Michael. (1978). The 100: A Ranking of the Most Influential Persons in *History*, Citadel Press, NY, NY

Herold, J. Christoper. (1963). *The Age of Napoleon*. American Heritage, NY, NY.

Hershman, D. & Lieb, Julian. (1994). *Brotherhood of Tyrants*. Prometheus, Buffalo, NY.

Kelly, Christopher. (2009). The End of Empire & Attila the Hun, W.W. Norton, NY, NY.

Lister, R. P. (1960). *Genghis Kahn*. Barnes & Noble, NY, NY.

Longford, Elizabeth. (1969). Wellington – *The Years of the Sword*, Harper & Row, NY, NY

Mandela, Nelson. (1993). *Mandela Speaks*, Pathfinder Press, NY, NY.

Markam, Felix. (1966). *Napoleon*, A Mentor Book, NY, NY.

Persico, Joseph E. (1995). *Colin Powell*, Random House, NY, NY.

Petrova, Ada & Watson, Peter. (1995). *The Death of Hitler*, W.W. Norton, NY, NY.

Petre, Peter. (1992). General h. Norman Schwarzkopf – It doesn't take a hero, Bantam Books, NY, NY

Renault, Mary. (1975). *The Nature of Alexander*, Pantheon Books, NY, NY.

Scwarzkopf, Norman. (1994). *It Doesn't Take a Hero* : The Autobiography of General H. Norman Schwarzkopf, Bantam Books, NY, NY.

Seward, Desmond. (1989). *Napoleon & Hitler,* Viking Press, NY, NY.

Slater, Robert. (1991). *The Life of Moshe Dayan*. St. Martin's Press, New York, NY

Terrill, Ross. (1981). *Mao*, Harper, NY, NY.

Troyat, Henri. (1984). *Ivan the Terrible*. Dorset Press, NY, NY.

Twain (Clemens), Mark. (1995). *Joan of Arc*, Gramercy Books, NY, NY.

Wallace, Irving. (1981). *The Secret Sex Lives of Famous People*, Dorset Press, NY.

Zhhisui, Li Dr. (1994). *The Private Life of Chairman Mao*. Random House, NY, NY.

General References

Ariely, Dan. (2008). Predictably Irrational – The Hidden Forces that Shape our Decisions, Harper-Collins, NY, NY.

Baumeister, Roy & Smart, Laura. (1996) American Psychological Association, Psychological Review Vol. 103 The Dark Side of High Self-Esteem.

Begley, Sharon. (2007). Train Your Mind, Change Your Brain, Ballantine Books, NY, N. Y.

Boorstin, Daniel. (1992). The Creators. Random House, N.Y., N.Y.

Branden, Nathaniel. (1994). Six Pillars of Self Esteem. Bantam, NY

Buckingham, Marcus & Coffman, Curt. (1999). First, Break All the Rules, Simon Schuster, N. Y., N. Y.

Byrne, Rhonda. (2006). The Secret, Atria Books, New York, N. Y.

Campbell, Joseph. (1971). The Portable Jung. Pneguin Books, N. Y.

Christensen & Raynor. (2003). The Innovator's Solution. Harvard Press, Boston, MA

Collins, Jim. (2001). Good to Great. Harper Business, New York, N. Y.

Conger, Jay. (1989). The Charismatic Leader, Jossey-Bass San Francisco, CA.

Csikszentmihalyi, Mihaly. (1996). Creativity – Flow and the Psychology of Discovery. Harper-Collins, N.Y.

Diamond, John. (1979). Your Body Doesn't Lie – Unlocking the Power of Your Natural Energy, Warner Books, NY, NY

Diamond, John, MD (1990). Life Energy, Paragon House, St. Paul, MN

Doidge, Norman. (2007). The Brain that Changes Itself, Viking Press, New York, N.Y.

Dweck, Carol. (2006). Mindsets. Balantine Books, NY, NY.

Farley, Frank. (May 1986). Psychology Today, "Type T Personality" pg. 46-52

Franzini, Louis & Grossberg, John. (1995). Eccentric & Bizarre Behaviors John Wiley & Sons, N.Y.,N.Y.

Frankl, Victor. (1959). In Search of Meaning. Pockey Books, N.Y.

Gardner, Howard. (1997). Extraordinary Minds. Basic Books, N.Y.

Gardner, Howard. (1993) <u>Creating MInds</u>. Basic Books - Harper, N.Y.

Garfield, Charles (1986). <u>Peak Performance</u>, Avon Books, NY, NY

Gelb, Michael. (2002). <u>Discover Your Genius</u>, Harper-Collins, N.Y., N.Y.

Gladwell, Malcolm. (2005). <u>Blink</u>. Little, Brown & Co. N.Y., N. Y.

Goleman, Daniel. (1995). <u>Emotional Intelligence,</u> Bantam, N.Y., N.Y.

Gordon, Jon. (2003). <u>Become an Energy Addict</u>. Lonstreet Press, Atlanta, GA

Grabhorn, Lynn (2000). <u>Excuse me, Your Life is waiting</u>, Hampton Roads Publishing , Charlottsville, VA

Gross, Ronald. (2002). <u>Socrates Way</u>, Penguin Books, New York, N.Y.

Hawkins, David (1999). <u>Power & Force</u>, Veritas Publishing, Sedona, AZ

Hawkins, David (2001). <u>The Eye of The I</u>, Veritas Publishing, Sedona, AZ

Hunt, Valerie. (1996). <u>Unfinite Mind</u> – Science of the Human Vibrations of Consciousness, Malibu Publishing Co, Malibu, CA

Jung, Carl. (1976). <u>The Portable Jung</u>. "The Stages of Life" Penguin, N.Y.

Kanter, Rosabeth. (2004). Confidence – How Winning Streaks & Losing Streaks Begin <u>and end</u>, Crown Business Publishing, NY, NY

Keirsey, David. (1987). <u>Portraits of Temperament</u>. Prometheus, Del Mar, Ca.

Keirsey, D. & Bates, M. (1984). <u>Please Understand Me</u>. Prometheus, Del Mar, Ca.

Hill, Napoleon. (1960). <u>Think & Grow Rich</u>. Fawcett Crest, N. Y.

Homer-Dixon, Thomas. (2000). <u>The Ingenuity Gap</u>, Knopf, N.Y.

Hutchison, Michael. (1990). <u>The Anatomy of Sex & Power</u>. Morrow, N.Y.

Jamison, Kay. (1994). <u>Touched with Fire</u>. The Free Press, N.Y., N.Y.

Kurzweil, Ray. (2005). <u>The Singularity is Near</u>, Viking, New York, N. Y.

Kurzweil, Ray. (1999). <u>The Age of Spiritual Machines,</u> Penguin, N.Y., N. Y.

Landrum, Gene. (2010). <u>Cover Your Assets & Become Your Liability</u>, Morgan-James, NY, NY

Landrum, Gene. (2008). <u>The Innovative Mind</u>, Morgan-James, NY, NY

Landrum, Gene (2007). Paranoia & Power, Morgan-James, N.Y. N. Y.

Landrum, Gene N. (2006) Empowerment, Brendan Kelly Publishing, CA

Landrum, Gene N. (2005). The Superman Syndrome, iUniverse, Nebraska

Landrum, Gene (2004). Entrepreneurial Genius, Brendan Kelly Publishing, Canada

Landrum, Gene. (1999). Eight Keys to Greatness, Prometheus Books, Buffalo

Landrum, Gene. (1997). Profiles of Black Success. Prometheus Books,

Landrum, Gene. (1996). Profiles of Power & Success. Prometheus, Buffalo, NY

Landrum, Gene. (1994). Profiles of Female Genius. Prometheus Books, Buffalo

Millman, Dan. (1980). Way of the Peaceful Warrior. New World Library, Novato, CA

Millman, Dan (2006). Wisdom of the Peaceful Warrior. New World Library, Novato, CA

Murphy, Michael & White , Rhea. (1995). In the Zone – Transcendent Experience in Sports Penguin Books, Middlesex, England

Orloff, Judith. (2004). Positive Energy. Harmony Books, New York, N. Y.

Ornstein, Robert. (1972). The Psychology of Consciousness. Penguin. N.Y.

Ornstein, Robert. (1997). The Right Mind. Harcourt/Brace, New York. N. Y.

Pickover, Clifford (1998). Strange Brains and Genius, William Morrow, N.Y.

Prigogine, Ilya. (1984). Order Out of Chaos, Bantam Books, N.Y.

Rogers, Everett. (1995). Diffusion of Innovations. The Free Press, N.Y., N. Y.

Rosenzweig, Mark. (1971). Biopsychology of Development, Academic Press, NY

Senge, Peter. (1990). The Fifth Discipline. Doubleday, New York, N. Y.

Simonton, Dean Keith. (1994). Greatness. The Guilford Press, N. Y.

Storr, Anthony. (1996). Feet of Clay – A Study of Gurus. Free Press, N. Y.,

Storr, Anthony. (1993). The Dynamics of Creation. Ballantine, N.Y.

Time: (1998). Great People of the 20th Century, Editors of Time, NY, NY.

Valentine, Tom & Carol. (1987). Applied Kinesiology, Healing Arts Press, Rochester, Vermont

Walker, Harris. (2000). <u>The Physics of Consciousness</u>. Perseus Books, NY

Weeks, David & James, Jamie. (1995). <u>Eccentrics: A Study of Sanity & Strangeness</u>, Villards, N. Y., N. Y.

Wolinsky, Stephen. (1994). <u>The Tao of Chaos</u>, Bramble Books, CN

Index

10856825R0

Made in the USA
Lexington, KY
29 August 2011